NB BY J.C.

BY THE SAME AUTHOR

Just Go Down to the Road: A Memoir of Trouble and Travel
Syncopations: New Yorkers, Beats and Writers in the Dark
This Is the Beat Generation
Exiled in Paris: Richard Wright, James Baldwin, Samuel Beckett, and Others on the Left Bank
Talking at the Gates: A Life of James Baldwin
Gate Fever: Voices From a Prison
Invisible Country: A Journey through Scotland

Thom Gunn in Conversation
The Picador Book of Blues and Jazz (editor)
The New Edinburgh Review Anthology (editor)

JAMES CAMPBELL

NB BY J.C.

A WALK THROUGH
The Times Literary Supplement

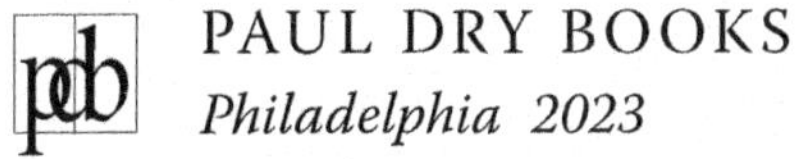
PAUL DRY BOOKS
Philadelphia 2023

First Paul Dry Books Edition, 2023

Paul Dry Books, Inc.
Philadelphia, Pennsylvania
www.pauldrybooks.com

The introduction was first published in the Winter 2023 issue of the *Hudson Review* as "A Walk Through the Times Literary Supplement."

Printed in the United States of America

ISBN 978-1-58988-175-4

Library of Congress Control Number: 2023932514

to

Maren Meinhardt

and

Peter Stothard

I make haste to agree once more with Mr. Eliot that for the normal critic, the purpose of literature is to amuse. If that word feels too light, then substitute another: entertain . . . Entertainment is a tremendous as well as a delightful thing, and there are plenty of writers, God knows, who do not succeed at it.

—Mark Van Doren, *The Happy Critic*

I am ashamed of my century
for being so entertaining
but I have to smile

—Frank O'Hara, "Naphtha"

Contents

NB BY **J.C.**

Introduction

THE LITERARY SUPPLEMENT of *The Times* came into being on January 17, 1902, a few days before the first anniversary of the death of Queen Victoria. It was conceived as a convenience, a bearer of excess baggage from the overloaded *Times*—"a makeshift." The idea was to find a place for the increasing numbers of book reviews, with their accompanying column-length advertisements, now clogging up the pages of the newspaper. With a busy parliamentary session in prospect, the management wished to keep space free for debates about the conduct of the war in South Africa and related matters, such as the construction of the original concentration camps—an innovation of which *The Times* disapproved. Casting back in 1930, the editor of the *TLS*, Bruce Richmond, found it "almost a shock to look at the first number with its hesitating announcement that 'During the ensuing session of Parliament' a supplement dealing with books will be published"—during that session but not beyond. It is easy to assume now that continuation was certain from the start but, in fact, the *Lit Supp*, child of 1902, hadn't a license to survive into 1903.

When the parliamentary session closed, it was expected that the makeshift *Supplement* would close with it. Thanks to the manager of *The Times*, Charles Moberly Bell, however, it was discreetly steered into a second year. In his letter of 1930 to Mrs. Moberly Bell, Richmond remembered how it staggered past the final week of parliament, "when your husband . . . immersed in graver troubles, seemed to have forgotten to stop it."

Only seemed to have. During those busy days, Bell was present in the editorial office with another member of the management, "coasting round and round the room jingling his keys and discussing high matters," while Richmond busied himself with the new books. "Without any apparent interruption of his talk [he said] in a sort of stage whisper as he passed me—'If I were you, I shouldn't remind anybody.'" So, Richmond concluded, "I reminded nobody—and here the thing is to this day."

Richmond guided the thing through one world war, on to the brink of another, navigating two further premonitions of closure, before stepping down in 1938. Having spent thirty-six years in the chair, he is the longest-serving editor of the *TLS*, possibly the most enduring in British weekly journalism—neither Robert Rintoul, founder of the *Spectator* and its editor between 1828 and 1858, nor Kingsley Martin of the *New Statesman* (1930–1960), outdo him. The first of these threats, in 1914, was followed by another eight years later. The proprietor of *The Times* by then was Lord Northcliffe, crudely characterized by some as the Rupert Murdoch of his day. "Send for Richmond," Northcliffe instructed one of his lieutenants in telegraphese on March 27, 1922. "Tell him Lit Supp deprives Times 20,000 readers. Literary side of Times very weak since Supp started." He threatened to do away with the *Literary Supplement*, not because it was failing but because it was thriving. "Shall merge Supplement in Times beginning with Friday week's number."

How close Northcliffe came to killing off the *Supplement* was recorded in an article by one of Richmond's editorial assistants, Harold Child:

> The number of March 30 was almost ready for press when a sudden order came from Lord Northcliffe: the next number but two was to be the last, and this death-sentence was to be published. . . . Into the leading article on the front page

> a "box" was introduced, announcing in italic type that No. 1056 (April 13, 1922) would be the last number of the *Literary Supplement*. . . . But once more the journal was to owe its continued existence to something like an oversight. The order had not penetrated into every department concerned. In one quarter there was some doubt about its validity. Twenty minutes before the paper went to press, the box was removed from the front page and the number of April 13 showed no sign of its narrow escape. That summer Lord Northcliffe became too ill to take an active part in his business. In August he died (*TLS*, January 18, 1952).

In common with two long-serving editors of a more modern era, William Shawn of the *New Yorker* and Robert Silvers of the *New York Review of Books*, Richmond rarely, if ever, wrote anything for publication himself. His talent was to enable the writing of others: to take a good piece and make it better. In a fond tribute published in the *TLS* in 1961, T. S. Eliot recalled that Richmond "did not hesitate to object or delete, and I had always to admit that he was right." Like other victims of the blue pencil through the ages, Eliot might have felt on occasion that those deletions were wounding, if not plain wrong. But, again like those others, once obliged to see his work from a different viewpoint, he was inclined to come round.

Virginia Woolf on the whole shared Eliot's esteem for the exacting editor, though at times she flinched at the pencil's sharpness. Her first review was turned down. The book was *Catherine de' Medici and the French Reformation* by Edith Sichel. Richmond told the twenty-two-year-old hopeful that his preferred style for pieces in the *Literary Supplement* was more "academic" than this effort (he later found someone else to write about the book; Sichel herself was a regular reviewer). Given a second try, Virginia Stephen, as she then was, received two guide books, one to "Thackeray Country," the other to "Dickens Country," This time it was a success. The piece appeared under the heading "Literary Geography" on March 10, 1905, and the

Lit Supp had a new, bright, young writer. The relationship occasionally dipped, with the editor's readiness "to object or delete." Years later, Woolf protested to her Diary that there would be "no more reviewing for me, now that Richmond re-writes my sentences to suit the mealy-mouths of Belgravia." She persisted, however, and was to become one of the paper's best and most prodigious reviewers.

Editors of literary journals are forever in search of new voices and bright ideas with which, when combined, they hope to attract young readers. This in itself is not new. Writing to the books editor of *The Times* on Christmas Eve 1901, three weeks before the appearance of the first *Literary Supplement*, Moberly Bell lamented: "I find *The Times* patronised mainly by older men and alas they die. . . . I don't want to abandon the traditions of *The Times* but I want to move with the times."

Thus do things continue from one era to the next—the thing in this case being the one referred to by Richmond in 1930. In the second half of the century it became familiarly known as the *TLS*.

THE NB BANNER was an attempt to introduce something new and bright into the *TLS* in the autumn of 1987. It was not at first the portal to the free-standing column it would later become, but sat at the top of a page as a section heading, sheltering a miscellany of non-review articles. The reader turning the page on to this version of NB, near the middle of the paper, would be aware of a modulation from the plainsong of *TLS* book reviews to something sparkier—a scherzo or a minuet—intended to create a more journalistic mood, occasionally light-hearted, though no less serious for that. The introductory acts on that first NB page of September 11, overseen by Isabel Fonseca, were a discussion by Anthony Glees of Peter Wright's book *Spycatcher* ("probably the most important publishing event of the decade") and a report on the Nicaraguan Book Fair, a gathering that was mixed in with "celebrations of the Eighth anniversary of the Sandinista Revolution." The author, Amanda

Hopkinson, told readers that Alice Walker refused to sign copies of *The Color Purple* at the official United States stand.

Over the following weeks, K. K. Ruthven wrote about Ezra Pound's happy habit of treating other writers' verses as the raw material for his own, Jane O'Grady discussed the phenomenon of mushrooming literary prizes, and Timothy Garton Ash and others wrote retrospective evaluations of literary magazines and specialist periodicals. A hint of NB to come can be traced to Christopher Hitchens's full-page American Notes, by then a regular feature of the paper. In December, however, Hitchens announced at the foot of his monthly column that, as he had been writing American Notes for five years, "I should prefer to stop while there is still a chance that people will ask why instead of why not. Godspeed to the NB page, on which I still hope to appear from time to time."

The NB page was also the progenitor and original guardian of Hugo Williams's Freelance column, one of the most popular features ever to appear in the *TLS*. It took a hesitant step out of his Islington living room on January 8, 1988, with the observation, "Coffee is the drug of the chronic freelance."

In time, Freelance would be overseen by me, and Hugo would come to be identified with the column. He would carry on writing it for over twenty-five years, irregularly at first, then fortnightly, going down to monthly in the new century. The burden was shared by other writers, notably P. J. Kavanagh in Gloucestershire and Michael Greenberg in New York—each acting as Hugo's foil on the alternate week, the intention being to offer a different tonality. The routine changed again when I assembled a team of writers that included A. E. Stallings in Greece, Adam Thorpe in the Cévennes, Zinovy Zinik dreaming of Moscow in Chalk Farm, Lydia Davis in and out of her garden in upstate New York, Alan Taylor roaming Edinburgh and its environs. It was my hope to have each of them give the reader a sense of reporting from his or her own patch.

In addition, I made regular columns ready for the page by William Boyd, Barton Swaim, Michael Dirda, D. J. Taylor, Caryl

Phillips, Will Self, Sean O'Brien, Nicholas Murray, Katherine Ashenburg, and others. Dealing with them was almost always a pleasure: querying an obscurity here, requesting smoother continuity there, cutting an excess sentence at the top, suggesting a concluding one near the bottom. These working partnerships are, ideally, instructive to both writer and editor. I conceived of the page as Isabel Fonseca—and no doubt the paper's editor at the time, Jeremy Treglown—had thought of Hitchens's American Notes: as an invitation to the reader to take a lighter step in the weekly tread over the firm ground of the *TLS*.

When it emerged as a separate entity, the NB column had a similar purpose. It arrived as part of a new design on February 8, 1991. Both the feature and the design—"we hope that readers will find the lay-out clearer and more attractive"—were introduced by the paper's incoming editor, Ferdinand Mount, who had lately taken over from Treglown. Occupying at first about a third of a page, the column was the work of David Sexton, already a respected critic and the first staff appointment made by Mount.

Sexton wrote a waspish, cheeky NB with a *Private Eye* touch (he was also a contributor to that magazine). He had a predilection for taking on, and taking down, the establishment: prize-giving committees; literary festivals that were barely literary, more like celebrity parades; Arts Council bureaucracy; the well-publicized daytime and nighttime doings of a band of successful male writers who were then around the age of forty-five. His first column addressed the row in progress between Salman Rushdie and John le Carré, over a harsh review by Rushdie of le Carré's latest novel, *The Russia House*.

For Rushdie, it was cuttingly personal: he alleged that le Carré had accused him of having brought the Iranian fatwa down on his own head on purpose, "to profit from the notoriety that would result." Put like that, it was an absurd notion; more likely, le Carré meant to raise an objection, in response to a sour review, to what he and some others saw as a characteristic arrogance in aspects of Rushdie's behavior—"almost colonialist arrogance," le Carré called it. As to the criticism of his own latest work, he suggested that the author of *The Satanic Verses* disliked books that offered readers "accessibility." Rushdie rejoined that, in the role of critic, he had a responsibility not to let an exalted reputation stand in the way of "calling a turkey a turkey."

It was rapid-fire stuff, relayed by Sexton with a feeling of being written off the top of the head. At the foot of each dispatch were fixed the initials "D.S." As it grew familiar to *TLS* readers, the column began to lay claim to a regular half-page. A colophon was devised, depicting two cherubs, one grappling with a massive fountain pen, the other holding an open notebook, on the pages of which the pen was inscribing something or other—possibly that week's NB. A well-stuffed hobby horse for the contentious columnist was the growth of political correctness. Some of D.S.'s comments from the early 1990s would seem topical if printed for the first time thirty years on:

> Alison Prince was asked to change the opening phrase of her book, *A Job for Merv*: "Things were looking black" was objected to in favour of "things were looking bad". . . . Another author had a list of racial pejoratives removed from a book even though they were "roundly condemned in the text". A publisher, Heinemann, actually sent a contributor a list of suggested names for ethnic characters. An illustrator, Val Biro, reported being required to fill a racial quota.

When David went on holiday, or had pressing business to attend (a stint of jury service, for example), he asked me to house-sit. So it was that I began an apprenticeship as the NB scribe. The first stage in the process happened in July 1993.

The lead item for the week tackled Susan Sontag, who was the object of worldwide admiration at the time for her audacious plan to mount a production of *Waiting for Godot* during the siege of Sarajevo, at the heart of the war in Bosnia. Sontag ignored many of Beckett's strict stage directions, while at the same time taking liberties with the text. A large section of the play was cut. Beckett was no longer alive to extend or withhold his blessing, and the director and her team, hunkered down in Sarajevo, did not wait for permission from his famously obstinate estate. Possibly they did not even ask. "Sontag plans to enlarge her troupe to include actresses in her production of the all-male play," I wrote. "She wants 'three Vladimir-Estragon couples. . . . One woman-woman, one woman-man, one man-man.'"

Who could object? It's not clear that the Beckett estate ever did. Yes, but I had a column to fill, and bland gestures of solidarity in the direction of the entrenched theatricals were not likely to be of much interest. I happened to know through a friend that Beckett had refused to endorse an all-female production of *Waiting for Godot* by a troupe from Holland. After his death, they took it to court, as a matter of freedom of expression, and a Dutch judge ruled in their favor. They went ahead, with an announcement stating the objections of the playwright's estate made from the stage each evening before the house lights went down.

From a skeptical point of view, it could appear that the play that had made Beckett's name was no longer his by right. "Sontag seems similarly disposed to disregard an author's prerogative," I wrote, after making reference to the Dutch actors, following up with a quote from Sontag: "Beckett was still thinking in that old way of thinking; that if these characters are to be representative then they should be men."

This was an example of sheer cant, a sort that was to become more common as the 1990s progressed and the new century began. It wasn't an "old way of thinking" to suggest that performance rights in theatrical works, and conditions attached to granting them, rested with the authors of those works (or with their estates), just as publication rights in Sontag's books should lawfully remain with her. Asked at that feverish time if she would have commended a pirate publication of one of her books by a Sarajevan publishing house, she might well have uttered a spontaneous "certainly," but few would encourage the precedent.

A remark made by an exasperated Vladimir Nabokov regarding *Lolita* came to mind and added a little ballast to the argument. He was addressing the wily but invaluable French publisher Maurice Girodias, of the Olympia Press, who had dared to issue Nabokov's once untouchable novel, then had shamelessly assumed ownership of it. "Dear Mr Girodias, *I* wrote *Lolita*." And, said J.C., "Beckett wrote *Waiting for Godot*."

One commentator had suggested that Sontag on the stage was fiddling while Rome burned. With more justice, we could have been accused of fiddling in a comfortable London office while she took her chances in war-torn Sarajevo. You are conscious of these things at the time. But you have a story to write. The path for going-against-the-grain was laid then. It is not all there is, but it has its uses.

I WORKED FOR six editors of the *TLS*. One of them started me off, as a reviewer, in 1980. One hired me as a part-time editorial assistant in 1983. One installed me in the NB chair. One offered space to expand NB, giving it the back page, the first article subscribers would see when unwrapping the latest issue. One tolerated the column's campaign against the increasing, and increasingly reflexive, warnings of "you can't say that" which began the work of deadening literary production in the second decade of the present century. The sixth had barely started on the job when management obliged him to instruct several editors, including myself, to put down their blue pencils once and for all.

I encountered John Gross, my first editor, at the *Times* building on Gray's Inn Road in the spring of 1980. He was standing at the entrance to the *TLS* offices on the second floor as if guarding his cultural project, arms folded, with a characteristic half-smile on his lips. Through the poetry and fiction editor, Blake Morrison, John gave me my first reviewing assignments for the paper. At the time, I was running a quarterly magazine in Scotland, the *New Edinburgh Review*. On one of my regular visits to London, I had come to Gray's Inn Road in the company of a friend who wanted to correct the proofs of his review for the following week's issue.

It was a notable event in my early literary consciousness, to have walked from the offices of the *New Statesman* at Great Turnstile, off High Holborn, where my friend worked, to climb the stairs at the Bloomsbury premises of the *TLS*, there to make the acquaintance of people whose names were familiar only from their bylines, to leave with three books in my grip, with the request from Blake to turn in 1,200 words.

The books are within reach on my shelves now: an assortment of essays, *Was That a Real Poem* by Robert Creeley—the second half of the question being "or did you just make it up yourself?"; an ecology tract by the Californian Beat poet Gary Snyder, *A Place in Space*; and a slim collection of interviews with Edward Dorn, author of the cult long poem *Gunslinger* and Creeley's pupil at Black Mountain College in the 1950s. I can still recall portions of the books. Dorn's response to an earnest question about his readers amuses me whenever I think of it: "I know almost exactly how many they are, and I even know a large percentage of them personally." Blake asked me to write another piece, and then another.

Gross's editorship of the *TLS* is regarded by many as having had the strongest cultural undertow of any in the paper's 120-year-long course. He arrived from the *New Statesman* in 1974 and left seven years later. One of his first acts was to abolish the institution of reviewer anonymity—not a move welcomed by all reviewers and readers—and thereafter to establish a range of contributors whose names would appeal in their own right. It is startling to realize that the *TLS* had rarely enjoyed this advantage before. (A few freestanding essays were printed with the name of the writer attached—that of Henry James, for example.) Virginia Woolf's association with the *Lit Supp* continued until her death in 1941, outdistancing even Bruce Richmond. At stages along the way her reviews appeared weekly, yet every one was printed without a byline.

On Gross's front page, the names of the reviewers were

intended to attract attention, as much as those of the authors and subjects of the books under discussion. Anthony Burgess wrote on music, Anita Brookner on art, Gore Vidal on American affairs, Lorna Sage on literature, Clive James on literature and everything else. Noel and Gabriele Annan formed one hospitable couple, John and Hilary Spurling another. Patrick Leigh Fermor had license to roam the world in typical rococo manner; the name-dropping Alastair Forbes to be shamelessly bad-mannered. The *TLS* as a cultural project was never more assured than under Gross. But the project was often interrupted by strikes, and eventually by the management's decision in 1978 to impose a shutdown on all the journals in the *Times* stable, brought about by an increasingly frustrating sequence of disputes with the printers' unions.

Since 1967, *The Times*, the *Sunday Times*, and the supplements—*The Times Educational* and *The Times Higher Education*, as well as *The Times Literary Supplement*—had been owned by the Canadian media group, Thomson Newspapers. In November 1979, after almost a year of closed doors, the papers came back to life, but the Thomson family had had enough, and in early 1981 sold the titles to Rupert Murdoch's News Corporation. Gross departed, with exasperation and not a little resentment, towards the end of that same year. He moved from one job to another: first as an editor at the publishers Weidenfeld and Nicolson, then as a book critic on the main body of the *New York Times*, and later, back in Britain, as theater critic for the *Sunday Telegraph*. I'd hazard a guess that he never found anything as engaging as his work at Gray's Inn Road. "He saw it as an opportunity to put down a marker for the kind of worldview that he espoused," Roger Scruton told an interviewer in 2015. "He took seriously the question of developing an argument and a philosophy through the journal, just as Sartre had done, to opposite [political] effect, in *Les Temps modernes*."

John Gross was replaced by Jeremy Treglown, until recently a lecturer in the English department at University College London, which was under the direction of Karl Miller. During the *Times* shutdown, Miller, in partnership with Frank Kermode and with the moral support of the *New York Review of Books*, founded the *London Review of Books*, an obvious rival to the wounded *TLS*. The main financial backing came from Mary-Kay Wilmers who, until the *Times* lockout, had been editor of the *TLS*'s Commentary pages. When unions and *Times* management reached an accord that permitted the printing machines to roll again, Treglown left UCL and joined the *TLS* at Gross's invitation. After Gross quit, the editorship was advertised and Treglown was urged to apply. The other candidates on the high-class shortlist were John Gross's deputy editor and foe, John Sturrock; the biographer and literary editor of the *Sunday Times*, Claire Tomalin; and the editor of the magazine *New Society*, Paul Barker. The interview proceedings were overseen by Rupert Murdoch.

"When Murdoch asked me what I would like to do with the *TLS* if he made me its editor," Jeremy told me, "I didn't say I would do my utmost to save the paper from Rupert Murdoch but that was my main hope." The Murdoch takeover of *The Times* and the *Sunday Times* had led to pessimistic speculation about the fate of the *TLS* and the likelihood of its diminished standing in the world of letters—in short, concern about "the brand," though the term was not then in use. Jeremy acknowledges, however, that his editorial decisions, "good and bad," were made in complete freedom. "If, for nine years, I played a part in saving the *TLS* from Rupert Murdoch, neither he nor—until my last few months—any of his managerial underlings took a step against me."

Treglown strove to maintain the intellectual standard of Gross's *TLS*, but in one respect, at least, his editorial ambitions departed from those of his former boss. "The *TLS* had played a small part in the 1970s' British high-cultural turn towards neoconservatism," Jeremy says, "and one of its senior editors still seemed to draw most of his commissioning ideas from the American neoliberal magazine, the *New Criterion*. An element of contrarianism was something I valued in the paper but what had seemed refreshing in Harold Wilson's day was less so now that Margaret Thatcher's Conservatives were in power." Saving the paper from Murdoch "surely meant, among other things, bringing in younger, leftier voices, both among the staff and as contributors."

He was not long in the job when he received a letter from me, now the former editor of the *New Edinburgh Review* and lately removed to London. I was scraping a living by writing articles and reviews for various publications, including the *London Magazine*, the *New Statesman, New Society*, the *Scotsman*, occasionally speaking on the radio—the bob-a-job literary life. I had also been offered a contract with a modest advance from Weidenfeld and Nicolson to write an account of a voyage by thumb and foot through Scotland, with distant echoes of Edwin Muir's book of 1935, *Scottish Journey*. The commissioning editor, recently installed at the firm, was John Gross.

In my letter of approach, I asked Jeremy about the chances of office employment. I knew that the *TLS* had part-time editors who were also aspiring writers, or else academics with an untenured university post (usually at Oxford), who would work in the office for three or two or even one day a week. He lamented that there was nothing available at present, but said that he would bear my name in mind when there was. He hoped, meanwhile, that I would continue "to write for us."

It was a standard polite gesture, but encouraging enough. I had carved a minor niche in the pages of the paper as a reviewer of books on a variety of Scottish subjects: a collection of the literary criticism of Francis Jeffrey, for example, the co-founder and first editor of the *Edinburgh Review* in the early nineteenth century—a few doors down the street from the offices of its reincarnation, which I had just left. I also reviewed an account of the history of writers, magazines and publishers in Edinburgh through the ages; a book of the uncollected criticism of Edwin Muir; the *Selected Poems* of Robert Garioch; a clutch of reissued novels by James Kennaway, the never-quite-but-nearly man of modern Scottish fiction who died of a heart attack at the wheel of his car in 1968, aged forty. Blake Morrison kept them coming my way and, when he left the *TLS* to become Terence Kilmartin's deputy on the books pages of the *Observer,* his successor Alan Jenkins did the same.

One Sunday afternoon in the summer of 1983, while preparing to make a final trip north to fuel the book commissioned by Weidenfeld and Nicolson, I received a phone call at home. Jeremy wanted to know if I was still interested in that part-time editorial post. "Only two days a week," he said, half apologetically. If so, would I like to come in the following afternoon to have lunch and talk about it?

I was still interested—I certainly was—I could come in, and by the time the bill for our café lunch was settled I had a job at the *TLS*. There was no interview with Personnel (or Human Resources—HR—as it would later be known), no paperwork to complete, nothing to sign, no bank details to register. I came to the office, then in Saint John's Gate, Clerkenwell, fulfilled an editing shift of general literary duties on Monday and another on Tuesday, picked up a bundle of notes at the cash desk downstairs, and walked through Covent Garden to Soho to meet someone at the French House or the Coach and Horses in the happy prospect of spending some of it.

My colleagues for the next decade and more—the *TLS* wheel was slow to turn—included Sturrock, the most deeply informed intellectual the majority of us would ever work closely with but still, to his chagrin, deputy editor; Mandy Radice and Elizabeth Winter, usually paired by name, though unalike except in shared congeniality; the Alans, Jenkins and Hollinghurst; Anna Vaux, lately down from Oxford; the naturalist and jungle adventurer Redmond O'Hanlon; the philosopher Galen Strawson; Lindsay Duguid and Holly Eley, the last a sharp-nibbed editor and sharply amusing presence at her desk, from under which her black Labrador sometimes kept half an eye on office proceedings. From time to time, Holly would appear with a plump sack of freshly plucked game, shot by her and shooting pals in Oxfordshire a few days earlier, offered for selection by colleagues. Before long, she became Mrs. Treglown. The senior editor mentioned above by Jeremy, who "seemed to draw most of his commissioning ideas" from American neo-conservative journals, was Adolf Wood, a gentle, witty man with humane and liberal views concerning his native South Africa, and a stubbornly conservative outlook on his adopted land.

On my first morning in the office, I was guided to a desk next to Lindsay, then overseeing the *TLS*'s wide coverage of children's books, soon to be in charge of arts, and later fiction. She presented me with a two-page review in typescript and showed me how to mark it up with a pencil in readiness for the printer. "It's our style to write 'realize' and not 'realise.' 'Premiss,' as in 'the basic premiss,' rather than 'premise,' which is how everybody else does it. Don't ask me why."

Lindsay returned to her seat, leaving me with my first office task. It was *something to do,* the new boy's most desired objective. As Lindsay put it: "Just in case you need an alibi. . . ."

When Sexton was offered a job as literary editor and resident critic on the *London Evening Standard,* in the spring of 1997, Ferdinand Mount invited me to take his place. My two paid days were upped to three, without the obligation to appear in the office on the third, and the keys to NB were handed by D.S. to J.C.

I set out with no mission or plan, not even with a determination to establish a different tone from that of my predecessor. But a column naturally reflects the personality of its author. Paradoxically, it takes practice to let this show. The hardest thing of all in writing is to sound like yourself. And only by writing a lot can you hope to hear yourself as you do sound, to recognize which effects and devices you can control and which remain beyond your reach. In short, why you sound as you do.

The going-against-the-grain habit, evident in that first outing, with Sontag's *Godot,* wasted little time in showing up again. When everyone appears to be of one accord in thinking *the right thing*, go the other way. There is something of this in the *Private Eye* rule, as expressed by the magazine's first editor, Richard Ingrams: So-and-so is up? OK, let's pull down so-and-so. An example was the Women's Prize for Fiction (formerly the Bailey's Prize, and before that the Orange Prize), treated by right-thinking types as indisputably a good thing, a beneficial intervention into the tired and traditional world of publishing, a modest but necessary correction in the rapidly increasing catalogue of male-enabled wrong. No matter what the personal views of the writer behind the initials might be, it is the job of the columnist to be contrary. In NB, the prize was invariably referred to as "the segregationist Women's Prize. . . ." Feel free to say it isn't so.

Another example of going against the grain was displayed in a series which bore the heading "Racial segregation in the literary world." In the late 1990s, renewed attention began to be paid to the status of black and Asian writers in Britain, not a topic I was unmindful of in its wider scope. What failed to appeal to me was consideration of black writers as a group apart from the community at large, with supposedly innate disadvantages and special needs that required help. Wasn't that approach what they (we) were trying to overcome?

In the columns of NB there were regular protests against the idea, and the practice, of "separate-but-equal" treatment of British black writers, which was gradually becoming embedded in the general conversation—a return to the bedrock of pre-civil rights segregation in the United States. Separate workshops for women of Asian origin sprang up in London and elsewhere, often funded by local authority culture departments eager to find worthy ways of spending taxpayers' money. Would a woman of non-Asian appearance be asked to present ethnic certification at the door, on pain of being turned away? Anthologies reserved for black and Asian short story writers (the term BAME, standing for black, Asian and minority ethnic, had yet to come into common use) were announced, as well as prizes restricted to those who consider themselves black. If that condition of entry is broadly acceptable, then the argument is settled: we do live in a society in which people—in this case writers—can be separated according to the colour of their skin.

A question that raised itself in the course of considering these events was: who is black (or brown or white) and who is not? Does the contentious question of self-identification come into it? Not many in the arts world seemed willing to engage with such complications, even to show awareness of them. Rather, the "literary establishment," so disdained by D.S., rushed to offer a new, British form of what Americans had once called "black uplift" to this disadvantaged sector.

It had an unwelcome echo of the one-drop rule that in certain Southern states fixed the racial status of many unwilling Americans, determining their destinies, up until the 1970s and to an extent until the present day (the one drop being that of a single distant African American ancestor, bestowing "invisible blackness"). The scenario seemed to me absurd, the invidious effect being the opposite of the intention. Apart from anything else, it was surely in contravention of the terms of the Race Relations Act. If there could be a book of stories restricted to so-called black writers, what was to stop someone advertising an anthology of work reserved for authors who proudly proclaimed their Aryan purity? In NB, we tried to avoid use of the term "black" to describe writers and their work; and disavowed "white," too, which is vague and misleading in its own way.

We failed, of course, but can at least claim to have tried to do our duty as we saw it. One day a BBC producer rang up with the suggestion of making a radio programme on some aspect of this question. When he gave his name, Tony Phillips, I recognized him as the brother of a friend of mine, the Caribbean-born writer Caryl Phillips. Caz and I shared an acquaintance with, and devotion to, James Baldwin—had met originally, in fact, via Baldwin's introduction. Nothing came of the radio proposal, but I retain a memory of Tony's voice on the telephone, enlivened by a rippling chuckle. "No one else is saying this." Why not? "Because they're afraid." Of what? "Of being seen to be on the wrong side." In view of that response, we didn't fail completely.

ONE OF SEVERAL notional publications the reader will find mentioned in the succeeding pages is *The TLS Reviewer's Handbook*. Its intention was to offer elementary advice to practising writers, and to give guidance to "our style."

House style is something the common reader encounters at every journal, usually without being aware of the steadying hold it exerts over the words on the page. The rules vary from one publication to another—a simple example of house style is the choice between *-ise* and*-ize* verb endings: "recognise" or "recognize"?—but the most important thing is that, once laid down, they should be adhered to.

This would sometimes be lost on the individual contributor. A writer might try to insist on a lower-case m for Marxism, for example, whereas *TLS* house style favors upper case. House style requires First World War, not World War One or the Great War, Muslim, not Moslem, italics for *nom de guerre* but not for nom de plume, Scotch to be used only in phrases involving broth, whisky, mist . . . and observance of numerous other rules, some of which outsiders might regard as paltry, if not eccentric. Upper-case the definite article for *The Times* but not for the *Guardian*; cap T for *The Economist* but not for the *Spectator*. It was once the style of the *New Yorker* (not *The New Yorker*, though they style it that way themselves) to avoid "wig" and "midget." Why? Because the editor of the time, William Shawn, said so. It doesn't take much more justification than that. House style should, however, be open to change, and after Shawn's departure "wig" broke down the barrier and stormed the *New Yorker*'s from then on less decorous columns. Midget, too, probably. In the late 1980s, it was *TLS* style to avoid "gay" and to stick with "homosexual." That changed—the homosexual usage became mainstream—and *TLS* style changed with it.

Good. But a going-against-the-grain columnist might silently insist on a regular non-gay use of "gay," just to draw attention to its continued existence, while not disputing the validity of the newly accepted one. That's good, too. Above all, *The TLS Reviewer's Handbook* wished to be seen as taking a stand against lazy-minded linguistic habits.

Some advice from the *Handbook*: don't use "iconic"—which has come to be applied to anything from Beethoven's iconic Ninth Symphony to a brand of perfume (the iconic Chanel No. 5)—except in relation to iconography; avoid "interrogate"—a fashionable item of sub-academic jargon used to indicate close reading—except in relation to criminal proceedings; do not pursue "the usual suspects," unless in aid of a police investigation. The reader will find more examples in the main part of this book. There is never any need to use "within," a senior colleague once insisted; "in" will always suffice. We gave him a copy of Graham Greene's retitled novel *The Man In*, and promised to add his name to the acknowledgments in the next edition of the *Handbook*.

The TLS Reviewer's Handbook, though real enough in the world of NB, was a notional publication. It never existed beyond the page. From time to time, a reader would write to office general inquiries (not "enquiries") to request a copy, at the same time asking how to pay. Some had tried to order it at a local bookshop. One of many hopeful purchasers was the film director Martin Scorsese. It was pleasant to imagine these loyal subscribers eager to raise their literary level by a notch or two, and to know that they believed possession of *The TLS Reviewer's Handbook* would help. To each of the requesters, including Scorsese, I wrote what I hoped was a good-humored note, receipt of which would not provoke a feeling of being thought foolish.

Both good writing and bad writing come in many forms. It was easy to make a public display in NB of the bad kind—the Incomprehensibility Prize was set up for exactly this purpose—but establishing guidelines for the good is a risky enterprise. Many intelligent, thorough reviewers consistently get tangled up in awkward phraseology. Just about any sentence of more than two clauses is susceptible to objection on some point or other. As the years passed, and peer pressure incorporated more and more politically correct usages into common speech—we don't say "peasant," we say "country people"; we don't say "suicide," we say "took his or her own life"; we don't say "slaves," we say "enslaved people"—the advice offered by *The TLS Reviewer's Handbook* went unheeded, not least by *TLS* reviewers.

AN ESSENTIAL FEATURE in the continuing life of the *TLS* since the Second World War, if not before, has been "the brand." It was, in fact, formulated and broadcast, without recourse to that term, in connection with the first issue in January 1902. A note about the forthcoming launch was inserted in the journal *Academy and Literature,* with which *The Times* had a connection. "A special Literary Supplement is published with *The Times* on Friday. This Supplement is an impartial organ of literary criticism and a comprehensive medium of literary intelligence."

The last sentence is a stirring one. Not only that, it proved to have enduring spirit. Over the next century and more, the paper aspired to live up to it. If you were to be introduced to a group of professors of literature at the universities of Chicago or Paris or Cairo, in the 1970s, 80s or 90s, maybe even later, with the information that you were an editor at *The Times Literary Supplement* in London, your hosts would know immediately where to position you by way of the cultural compass—no matter that they might not have read the paper for years. There would be courteous gestures of restrained awe. There are few equivalent brands in the world of letters. A "comprehensive medium of literary intelligence" may be read as embracing information as well as critical thought, but it nonetheless evokes an element resistant to facile change in a too-fast-changing world, in which the standard bearers of culture, including literary culture, are liable to appear as an array of blurred shapes from one season to the next. "Literary intelligence" holds out a promise of reliability in the realm of the humanities and sciences. Even if the

TLS has been overtaken in recent times by other journals, trading in a richer currency than the much-resented Murdoch shilling (taking it at its most literal: we were seldom able to pay our hard-working reviewers what they deserved), it could still claim to stand for what the poet and critic Geoffrey Grigson called, in another context, "items of best being."

My view, intuitive as it is, is that the brand slipped into the danger zone not when it was taken over in 1981 by News Corporation, which broadly speaking supported the cultural project, but when it receded, in later years, from Rupert Murdoch's individual gaze. There had been scant attempt to exercise direct control from above, as Treglown says, except in the appointment of the editor, which will always be the proprietor's prerogative. After Treglown's departure, in 1991, Murdoch oversaw the appointment of Mount and then, in 2002, of Stothard, formerly the editor of *The Times*, keeping the *TLS* in motion as a medium of literary intelligence. It had changed since those words appeared in the *Academy and Literature* advertisement in 1902—of course it had—but its fundamental purpose remained the same. By the time of the replacement of Stothard, management arrangements at the peak of the company, now known as News UK, had undergone significant reorganization.

On February 12, 2016, my colleagues and I stumbled on a headline on the *Guardian* website: "*Sun* managing editor . . . to become editor of the *TLS*." The instinctive first reaction was to read it as the prelude to a parody. The author of the article was the veteran media journalist Roy Greenslade, and the managing editor in question was Stig Abell. In a follow-up interview with Abell (May 1, 2016), Greenslade described the process by which the new editor had been appointed:

> With the planned retirement after fourteen years of its editor Peter Stothard, there were vague plans to approach a high-profile figure. . . . But they were abandoned when Abell sent a two-page document with ideas for revitalizing the

> weekly to News UK chief executive Rebekah Brooks. She showed it to News Corp's chief executive [in New York], Robert Thomson, who said: "Go for it."

None of those on the shop floor assembling that week's paper had been told about the "planned retirement" of Stothard. All were left out of the "vague plans" to approach someone with a famous name to be our next overseer—blue-pencil experience not essential. We were likewise in the dark about radical ideas, conceived by an outsider but convincing enough to persuade the top people at News Corp, for "revitalizing the weekly."

The new editor made his way downstairs from the *Sun* in due course—the offices of all the papers were now housed in the News Building at London Bridge, with spectacular views of the River Thames—and set about introducing himself to a staff with which he had no previous acquaintance. The passage of 114 years is perfectly captured in the semantics of the transition: from "a comprehensive medium of literary intelligence" to "Go for it."

The three editors who succeeded John Gross in the editor's chair—Treglown, Mount, Stothard—obeyed an identical impulse to that which had carried Gross's project forward. While not necessarily aware of doing so, they were "developing an argument and a philosophy through the journal," as Scruton put it, according to the will of the individual in question. Each would doubtless claim to be different in outlook from the one who went before, but all were fueled in their endeavors by a common energy: the energy of the *TLS* itself; a consciousness, much of the time just a quasi-consciousness, of the combined values of those on whom the project most depends: loyal readers, good writers, able and dutiful desk editors; not forgetting a keen alertness to literary status, "the brand." For an editor of *The Times Literary Supplement* to be inattentive to this status would be tantamount to drawing the cultural project—Richmond's "thing"—to a close.

Postscript

The history of *The Times Literary Supplement* was related in detailed form by Derwent May in *Critical Times*, published in 2001 to coincide with the approaching centenary. It is, as May wrote in his preface, "a history of the paper's editors and staff, from their literary trials and triumphs to the office comedies." *Critical Times* was an official account, commissioned from May "by the publishers of the *TLS*."

This book is, in non-adversarial fashion, an alternative version. Among the humble functions of NB was the largely accidental one of acting as an extended series of footnotes to the history of the paper. One example may be found in the brief obituary notices we included of figures who had played a part, large or small, in *TLS* life. Another can be seen in the series The *TLS* in Literature, which unearths occurrences of the *TLS* in fiction, including detective and romantic fiction; in poetry; also in film (we had a role in *Iris*, based on John Bayley's book about his life with Iris Murdoch); in television soap opera (yes, the *TLS* has featured in *EastEnders*), and in painting. Philip Roth puts the *TLS* at the center of an early short story; Jorge Luis Borges includes it in one of his tales. It turns up in poems by W. H. Auden and John Berryman, in novels by writers as unalike as D. H. Lawrence and Barbara Pym—in the latter case proving useful as wrapping for decayed flowers about to be dumped in the bin. Imaginary books that figure in real novels—novels by Rose Macaulay, Eric Linklater, Ian McEwan and others—receive imaginary *TLS* reviews by imaginary *TLS* reviewers. Never-existing poems are accepted for publication in this never-existing journal which, however, bears the name of our own. The reader will find a selection in the pages that follow. More than once I tried to force the series into abeyance, only to have it revived by a reader proposing an irresistible cameo.

In a parallel fashion, NB provided a way of footnoting my own life, while in the office and out of it. It brought many gifts. The most valuable was the provision of a structure that invited me to exercise my faculties at large over an extended period of time. It gave me a reason to think about external affairs, in the literary realm and beyond, from one day to the next. It was NB that drew me out to poke around in dusty secondhand bookshops in remote parts of London, and over time in Edinburgh, Glasgow, Brighton, across the Channel, in New York, and elsewhere. NB duty led me to ponder grammatical enigmas, such as the potential of "whom" to ignite class war; the invasion of the impertinent preposition ("meet with," "next up"); the anxiety-provoking apostrophe. Seated at work next to genial Etonians and Oxbridge graduates, it was right that J.C. should speak for the benefits of a Poor School education, from which the scholar emerges with qualifications in the Lesser-Used Languages of Britain and Europe (qualifications acquired, for the most part, on the day of writing), as well as Rock and Roll A Levels and much else. NB *was* the Poor School. Writing the column for twenty-three years was a further education all by itself.

Assistance in these researches came from colleagues, naturally, and from readers. The basis for the next installment of the column might arrive on a Monday morning email flight from Greece or New Zealand or China—or, as likely, from Inverness, Cambridge or Cheltenham. To a significant degree, engagement with readers was the raison d'être of the enterprise. One example involves a Scottish woman living in British Columbia, who sent some French-derived words found in Older Scots usage that she remembered from her grandmother's speech. They were added to a brief series on the subject, and she duly became an NB pen pal. In the course of a subsequent exchange, I remarked that the battery charge of the column came from the knowledge that it was read, week after week, in places unfamiliar, by people like her.

During a trip to London, my correspondent came to the News Building and left a miniature, leather-bound volume at reception: *Beauties of the Scottish Poets* (Glasgow, 1825). I was in the office at the time, but she did not attempt to make contact; only asked that the book be delivered to the initialed persona on the fourteenth floor. On reflection, I saw the gesture as representative of the discreet exchange of feeling that connects writer and reader.

Why not say it straight? It was a great job. I hope that some of the enjoyment of doing it is reflected in the pages that follow. The complete NB comes to something like 1.5 million words. This selection from twenty years offers under one-twelfth of that total. If some years seem to the reader to have been fatter than others, it is mainly through an effort to lend variety to the material.

NB

2001–2006

2001

March 23

Anyone nursing a rejection slip is likely to feel better after perusing the current issue of the *Missouri Review.* The latest in its "Found Text" series is a feature on readers' reports from the archives of the publisher Alfred A. Knopf. The list of rejectees is spectacular, and the comments are frank. In 1949, for example, a reader recommended turning down a collection of stories by Jorge Luis Borges, *El Aleph,* with the comment "they are utterly untranslatable, at least into anything that could be expected to sell more than 750 copies." The reader himself found the stories "remarkable," but thought they would appear to the general public as "$50-a-pound caviar." *El Aleph* would not be translated for another twenty-one years.

Anaïs Nin was felt to be "a small, arbitrary, overpraised talent who has been able to hide her emptiness behind a lot of chinoiserie," and *A Spy in the House of Love,* later a Penguin Classic, was kicked out. In 1953, the young Peter Matthiessen submitted "a very bad novel" called *Signs of Winter.* "We had great hopes for this guy," sighed the reader, before stamping "REJECT." The title has never seen the light of day. Two years later, Knopf saw off Italo Calvino, with reluctance, and the young James Baldwin, without it. *Giovanni's Room* merited extended comment, as Baldwin had published a promising first novel with the firm in 1953. *Giovanni's Room* seemed to the first reader "an unhappy, talented, and repellent book," to the second "a bleak little tale," and to the third "hopelessly bad." "We must try to persuade him to put this away; it will do neither publisher nor author any good. It will have bad reviews and bad sales."

Sales to date have probably topped the million mark.

In 1956, it was the turn of *Lolita* ("impossible for us"), followed by a novel by John Barth ("I cannot conceive of a healthy mind produ cing this"), Isaac Bashevis Singer ("not worth Knopf's time and effort"), an apprentice Joyce Carol Oates ("for all I know the long-hairs may single this out as a masterpiece . . . but it is incomprehensible"). Sylvia Plath's novel *The Bell Jar* got a similar reception—"ill-conceived, poorly written, occasionally atrocious"—as did Jean Rhys's *Wide Sargasso Sea* and *The Joke* by Milan Kundera. The last was found to be "a long sentimental wail." Knopf published later novels by Kundera.

Apart from their entertainment value, the reports give an intimate glimpse of the times in which they were written. Knopf readers no longer write reports.

April 13

Carrie Kipling, Rudyard's wife, was "one of the most loathed women of her generation," according to a new book about her. It is also reported there that Henry James called her "this hard capable little person." You may be wondering how it is possible to gauge degrees of loathing for an entire generation; you may even be aware that what James said was "this hard, devoted, capable little person"—somewhat different—but only a pedant would want to spoil good hype.

The book in question, by Adam Nicolson, is part of a new series, Short Lives, published by Short Books. The ninety-six-page life of the devoted and capable Carrie is called *The Hated Wife*. On the back cover, Nicci Gerrard, the *Observer* journalist, joins in: "Adam Nicolson takes Mrs Kipling—for so long despised—and gives her back her humanity." Hated, loathed, despised? Well, you say, at least Carrie had the consolation of being married to a great man. Wrong again. "It was she who provided the backbone that her husband privately lacked."

Even Mr. Nicolson acknowledges that Carrie Kipling could be awkward. Her sister-in-law Mai, as well as certain friends, "thought there was something mad about Carrie." She was jealous of Mai's beauty, and as a result, Mr. Nicolson says, was apt to "patronize" her. She suspected her brother of cheating her financially, and treated him "with a miserliness which any man would have resented." But the time of the great writer's wife has come—Fanny Stevenson, Frieda Lawrence, Nora Joyce, Vivienne Eliot, Zelda Fitzgerald, and others have been receiving their rewards at last. There is no reason to leave Carrie behind.

As part of the process, the great writer himself must undergo revision. Not only did Kipling lack backbone, he was secretly queer. "It was not Carrie with whom Kipling fell in love," Mr. Nicolson writes, "but her brother Wolcott." Does he mean that the two men were lovers? "The way in which, in later life, Kipling wrote and spoke with such frantic loathing of homosexuality as a beastly and bestial business has been taken as a sign that they were." It couldn't, by any chance, be a sign that they weren't?

April 27

Is our regard for literary figures commensurate with our memorials to them? Take Ruskin. He was raised in Herne Hill, in south-east London, and later lived in Camberwell, not far away. Rosemary Hill, a frequent contributor to the *TLS*, lives there, too. As an admirer of Ruskin, she wanted to see how he is commemorated locally, and writes about the experience in the magazine *things*.

Ms. Hill's quest for Ruskin in the stones of Camberwell began on Denmark Hill, at the Ruskin Wing of King's College Hospital. It is, unfortunately, "a building so banal as to be striking." She was reminded of a remark by Ruskin himself: "Who are they who like these things? I have never spoken to anyone who did like them." Neither has Ms. Hill. Neither has anyone at King's. Attempts to discover from the Hospital who designed its Ruskin Wing were in vain. They appear to have disposed of the plans.

Ms. Hill moved on past Ruskin Park ("a noble gesture in a Ruskinian spirit, if a slightly scruffy one") and the graffiti-stained blocks of flats which occupy the site of the villa where, in the 1840s, the Ruskin family kept cows. She came to Ruskin House, a nursery for two-to-five-year-olds, and for a moment Ms. Hill's spirits rose. "The school is in a converted house whose square-headed windows and Venetian details proclaim the influence of its namesake." On enquiring, however, "I was informed crisply that the school 'has nothing to do with Ruskin, we just called it that.'"

Carrying on past Camberwell Green, where Ruskin played as a boy and where today's children compete for fresh air with homeless drinkers, Ms. Hill reached Walworth Road and, eventually, "the wreck of Beresford Chapel," Ruskin's childhood place of worship. He remained attached to it for aesthetic reasons. The entire upper half of the building has been destroyed. Why? wailed Ms. Hill, only to be reminded of Ruskin again: "Of wanton or ignorant ravage it is in vain to speak; my words will not reach those who commit them." In a potent compound of insult and injury, the ruins of Beresford Chapel stand on John Ruskin Street. Ms. Hill could summon the energy only to hail a cab from Ruskin Cars, conveniently nearby, and go home.

June 15

The condemned Oklahoma bomber, Timothy McVeigh, chose for his last words the poem "Invictus" by W. E. Henley:

> Out of the night that covers me,
>   Black as the Pit from pole to pole,
> I thank whatever gods may be
>   For my unconquerable soul.

The gesture put the final touch on what was quite a literary affair. McVeigh was said to have been inspired to blow up the Alfred P. Murrah Federal Building in Oklahoma City, killing 168 people, by a novel, *The Turner Diaries*. It was written by "Andrew Macdonald," the pseudonym of William Pierce, described by the *New York Times* as the head of a "neo-Nazi publishing and music company" in West Virginia. McVeigh copied out Henley's sixteen-line poem in his own hand, and spent his last hours writing letters. He has been complimented as a correspondent by Gore Vidal, who told *The Oklahoman* newspaper: "He's very intelligent. The boy's got a sense of justice." Vidal had been expected to attend the execution but, in the event, other obligations kept him away.

Vidal owed it at least to the condemned man to warn him that his choice of Henley was hopelessly inappropriate, thus rendering his official "last statement" meaningless. It was not the State that Henley was up against, but Fate. He wrote "Invictus" in an Edinburgh hospital in 1875, having had one leg amputated and fearing he would lose the other. The poem might have been more suitably mumbled by maimed survivors of the bomb than by the bomber. The famous line "My head is bloody, but unbowed," evoking courage in the face of dreadful disablement, can scarcely be said to apply to the mass murderer McVeigh, who is anyway not "unbowed" but dead. Even the "unconquerable soul" part does not fit McVeigh, a self-proclaimed agnostic.

To heap further indignity on Henley, the *Sunday Telegraph*'s James Langton described him as "an obscure English 19th century poet," then got the poem's most famous couplet mixed up and unpunctuated, to read, "I am the master of my fate / I am the captain of my scroll." Henley's consuming tuberculosis was reduced in the report to a bout of arthritis. After that, we were unsure whether Mr. Langton was joking when he wrote that McVeigh was denied a last cigarette, because "Federal Death Row does not permit smoking, considered bad for the prisoners' health."

July 27

The fashionable crime writer Elmore Leonard has published his ten rules for writing fiction. Here they are:

1. Never open a book with weather.
2. Avoid prologues.
3. Never use a verb other than "said" to carry dialogue.
4. Never use an adverb to modify the verb "said".
5. Keep your exclamation marks under control.
6. Never use the word "suddenly."
7. Use regional dialect, patois, sparingly.
8. Avoid detailed descriptions of characters.
9. Ditto places and things.
10. Try to leave out the part that readers tend to skip.

We can add an eleventh rule: on coming across lists like this, ignore them. Leonard's rules may sound sensible enough but, with the exception of No. 5, each could be replaced with its opposite, and still be reasonable advice. Leonard complains that, while reading a book by Mary McCarthy, he had to stop and get the dictionary—a painful duty. William Faulkner, who broke all of these rules whenever he wrote, complained of Hemingway that he never used a word you had to look up the meaning of. And what is meant by "leave out the part that readers tend to skip"? If every writer tried to be as exciting as Leonard, there would be no *Brothers Karamazov*, no *Anna Karenina* (remember those exquisitely boring sections on agronomy?), and the shelf reserved for Dickens and Balzac would measure about a foot in length. Banish patois and we lose a library of fiction, stretching from *Huckleberry Finn* to *Trainspotting*. As for dialogue, if Leonard samples Henry James, he will find "remarked," "answered," "interposed," "almost groaned," "wonderingly asked," "said simply," "sagely risked," and many more colorful carriers (these from a page or two of *Roderick Hudson*). Should they all be ironed into a Leonardian "said"?

Our rule for the cultivation of good writing is much simpler: stay in, read, and don't limit yourself to American crime fiction.

October 19

On the 100th anniversary of the Nobel Prizes, the Literature award went to V. S. Naipaul. Born and raised in Trinidad, Naipaul is now a citizen of the United Kingdom. This country may thus share the pride of the Caribbean island, and claim Naipaul as the first British laureate since William Golding received the Nobel in 1983.

But the country has not claimed him, or at least not officially. We rang the Downing Street Press Office to ask if the Prime Minister had commented on the award. "Not that I'm aware of. When was it announced?"

"On October 11—on every news outlet in the world."

"And it's the . . . ?"

He promised to check and ring back but never did, so we went to the government's Department of Culture, Media, and Sport. The following is a transcript of the conversation that ensued:

> "This is the *TLS*. We're calling about the award of the Nobel Prize for Literature to V. S. Naipaul."
>
> Pause. "Let me put you on hold. . . ." Then: "Are you talking about the Booker one?"
>
> "No. The Nobel Prize for Literature."
>
> "Right. Hold on." Long pause. "We don't usually make comments on awards and such."
>
> "It is the most prestigious literary award in the world, and the first time a British writer has won for eighteen years."
>
> "I have a feeling there was a comment from a minister."

She promised to try to track it down, but evidently failed to do so. Over a year ago, Naipaul launched an attack on the Blair administration, “this appalling Government.” He criticized its “philistine” and “aggressively plebeian” attitudes leading to “a culture that celebrates itself for being plebeian.” There was no official response then. Or perhaps the present silence is the response.

2002

January 18

Maya Angelou's proudest moment occurred in 1993, when she received the call to compose a poem for the approaching inauguration of President Clinton. Now an even greater accolade has come her way: she has been chosen to write "sentiments" for Hallmark, the greetings card firm. "Maya Angelou's universal message of hope and inspiration, combined with Hallmark's unique expertise in nurturing relationships, makes for an inspiring new brand." The brand is called Life Mosaic, and it will "serve to uplift, empower and connect everyone who is touched by its spirit."

A typical Angelou sentiment runs along the lines of "Success is loving life and daring to live it"; or "Your life is more important than you think. It is your first treasure." The sentiments are not restricted to cards. You can purchase the "Framed Triple Sentiment," with an Angelou thought on each print. For example, "We spend precious hours fearing the inevitable. It would be wise to use that time adoring our families, cherishing our friends, and living our lives." Or try the "Friendship Fabric," for that friend who has been "an enduring source of nourishment for your spirit." No need to speak to the friend—just hand over the Fabric, and let Maya say it: "Since we met all those years ago, your friendship has been a precious thread."

The most cryptic sentiment comes from the "Inspirational Success Framed Print Series." Here the Pulitzer and National

Book Award nominee, who has been awarded several honorary doctorates, writes: "Success is knowing and being known as a human being." Success is knowing a human being? We're probably missing something.

May 3

The story of F. R. Leavis, *Ulysses*, and the Cambridge Constabulary is set out in the latest issue of the *James Joyce Quarterly*. In a review of the "British Home Office *Ulysses* Files," Carmelo Medina Casado reveals the lengths to which the authorities were prepared to go to protect the reading public from Joyce's novel. Parts of the file read comically now: for example, a circular letter was sent "to the Chief Constables of large British towns with the order to trace any copy of the book in their districts." One was found in a Manchester bookshop. *Ulysses* was thought unlikely to command a wide circle of readers; however, "the fear is that other writers with a love of notoriety will attempt to write in the same vein."

That was in 1922. Four years later, when Leavis asked his local bookseller, Galloway and Porter, to order a copy, the proprietor went straight to the police. "The Chief Constable of Cambridge was informed about the request," reports Mr. Casado, "and he asked the Home Office for instructions as to how to deal with the issue." It was too much for a Home Office official named Harris. "This is an amazing proposition," he wrote of Leavis's request. "A lecturer at Cambridge who proposes to make the book a textbook for a mixed class of undergraduates must be a dangerous crank." The Director of Public Prosecutions instructed the police to find out "who and what Dr F. R. Leavis is," and for personal details to be obtained "discreetly." The DPP then wrote to the Vice-Chancellor of the University, informing him that Leavis intended to introduce students to a book which "concludes with reminiscences of an Irish Chamber-maid, in various parts of which grossness and indecency appear."

When Leavis appeared before the Vice-Chancellor in August 1926, he protested that *Ulysses* was an important book, "with reviews published in periodicals such as the Supplement to *The Times* on March 5 of that year." Presumably this means the *TLS*. Here we have done our own detective work. The *TLS* did not review *Ulysses*, and no mention of Joyce by name occurs in the issue of the week in question, in fact dated March 4. There is, however, an admiring passing reference to *A Portrait of the Artist as a Young Man* in the leading article—which, it turns out, might have saved Leavis's job.

May 10

Members of the excellent British Council Library in Paris were alarmed to receive a letter recently from the Director of the Council in France, John Tod. It began ominously: "Dear Library Member . . . The British Council in Paris has been chosen as the first West European Knowledge and Learning Centre, to pioneer new and innovative information services for the region."

When you hear the words "information centre", you reach for your culture. But too late: they've got you covered. Mr. Tod goes on to reveal that the Council is shutting down the "lending side of our library service from the end of June 2002." After that date, the former lending-library area will host "a Video Conferencing studio and Open Learning zone." What about the terrific stock of books? "They will be donated to French public institutions including the Bibliothèque Nationale." While stressing his esteem for "the British book and the intellectual property it conveys," Mr. Tod makes it clear that the Council is finished with the old relic. "Through imaginative exploitation of the latest technology, the British Council aims to modernize how we deliver information services to our customers."

Literature remains at the center of the British Council's plans, however. "We are creating a literature web portal with Internet reviews and discussion forums on important new publications," Mr. Tod writes. And for those with a quaint taste for the written word and the intellectual property it conveys, the spanking new Knowledge and Learning Centre will provide library members with "guidance about obtaining books."

May 31

"Have ye e'er heard of gallant like young Lochinvar?" Or like young Pierce Brosnan? The actor, best known as a third-generation James Bond, is to play "brave Lochinvar" in a film derived from the work by Sir Walter Scott. The project has a title, "The Legend of Lochinvar," it has a producer, and even a date to begin filming. But does it have a story?

Brosnan and his colleagues are no doubt dreaming of the highly popular *Braveheart*, and of replicating its success. They are probably familiar with sword-clashing films based on *Ivanhoe* and *Rob Roy*. But are they aware that "Lochinvar" is a poem? It occurs in the book-length *Marmion*, as a song sung by one of the characters, and is forty-eight lines long. The action—Lochinvar crashing the arranged wedding between his "fair Ellen" and some dastardly "laggard in love"—would take about five minutes, if played out in real time. The interesting question is whether there is a precedent for a feature film being made from a similarly short poem. Nominations are welcome.

June 21

We have had several responses to our invitation to name poems that have been made into films, in the manner of the forthcoming "The Legend of Lochinvar." William Lee, writing from Maine, reminds us that Edgar Allan Poe's poem "The Raven," published in 1845, was filmed in the mid-1930s, starring Boris Karloff. As it featured car crashes, plastic surgery and a surgeon who is obsessed by Poe, it may be considered a loose adaptation. A 1963 remake provided an early outing for Jack Nicholson.

Vincent Daly from Baltimore nominates *The Charge of the Light Brigade*, shot in 1936, and several people mention the film of Kipling's *Gunga Din* (1939). A contribution to the script (uncredited) was made by William Faulkner.

August 2

A new edition of Nancy Mitford's *Noblesse Oblige* (1956) has just been published by OUP as an "Oxford Language Classic." It contains Mitford's famous essay "The English Aristocracy," which popularized the notion of "U and non-U" usage in writing and speech. U stands for "upper," and Mitford's point was to show that "there are still a few minor points of life which may serve to demarcate the upper class," linguistic usage being one. Her concern was not with upper and lower, however, but with the line between, "on the one hand, gentlemen and, on the other, persons who, though not gentlemen, might at first sight appear, or would wish to appear, as such."

In the interests of separating those from such as those, we rehearse a few snobbisms:

Non-U: cycle; U: bike
Non-U: vegetables; U: greens
Non-U: ill ("I was ill on the boat"); U: sick
Non-U: toilet; U: lavatory
Non-U: sweet; U: pudding
Non-U: to take a bath; U: to have a bath
Non-U: bedspread; U: counterpane
Non-U: wealthy; U: rich

Also disliked by Mitford were "the ejaculation of 'cheers' before drinking, or 'it was so nice seeing you', after saying goodbye." The proper response is silence. It may be rude, but at least it's U. When visiting friends, we take care not to say of our trusty raincoat that "we bought it at Fenwick's"; one should refer to it rather as a "mac" which comes from "Fenwick." We know to pronounce forehead to rhyme with "horrid"; when teeing off, not to sound the l in golf; to avoid exclaiming "Really!" as if it rhymed with mealie.

The other day we came across a little-known follow-up to *Noblesse Oblige*, called *What Are U?* Edited by Alan Ross, it contains his essay "U and Non-U Today." The book was published in 1969, and we were curious to see how many examples stipulated by Ross, in the spirit of Nancy Mitford, remain applicable. Determine your status with reference to this selective list:

Non-U: debutante. U: deb
Non-U: ever so. U: very
Non-U: phone. U: telephone
Non-U: settee or couch. U: sofa
Non-U: relative. U: relation
Non-U: mansion. U: house

There are levels of refinement destined to remain beyond our reach. "Lather: non-U to rhyme with 'father'; U to rhyme with 'gather.'" You are probably unlikely to say nowadays, "We are going out to cocktails," but you might, in greeting someone you've invited *in* for cocktails, ask, "Will you have a whisky?" That's non-U. The U form is, "Will you have some whisky?" When discussing the children's achievements, avoid "He's at university." If Oxford or Cambridge, the U form is: "He/she's up at Oxford"; otherwise, "He/she's at Edinburgh/Leeds."

It requires only a short time spent with either book to make every step treacherous. Do we say we "paid" £3 for *Noblesse Oblige* from a second-hand bookshop, or "were charged" £3? Where would Nancy stand on "stumped up"? It should prove to be a useful—we just stopped ourselves saying U-seful: puns are non-U—investment.

August 30

Clive Birch, of Oxfordshire, has written a book and now would like to see it published. It is a "true story" about wartime Siberia, Samarkand, SOE, smuggling in Poland and the like. He is not entirely without experience, having once run his own small publishing business. Since he has no wish to put out his own work, however, Mr. Birch sent his manuscript to an agent of his acquaintance. "Writing is very good but literary," the agent wrote back. Clinging to the notion that "literary" was something a literary agent might like, Mr. Birch sent his book to another agency, then another. Altogether he tried more than twenty: half bounced his manuscript back at him with unsigned form letters; seven gave him the old not-taking-on-new-clients routine. The nearest he got to a personal note read, "We do not have the time or staff to comment."

September 27

Following the story of Clive Birch and the literary agent who considered his book too literary, we have received plaintive letters from fellow sufferers. A writer with an extensive collection of rejection slips is Carlos Amantea of California. Author of a number of published books, he has yet to find an agent willing to represent his latest, *A Geezer in Paradise.* The excuses Mr. Amantea has received are varied. One agent, regretting that she had "a very full list," invited him to a conference to listen to her speak, but cautioned: "Listening to me lecture is not enough." She added a riddle for Mr. Amantea to ponder: "I really need to have time on a one-on-one with you to have actually asked for your manuscript."

Another agent suffered from a similar syntactical deficiency: "We've reviewed your submission, however, regrettably it's not deemed appropriate that this agency represent it." J. J. Hawkins & Associates sent a form letter saying they would "personally like to thank you for sending in your query. It is indeed a worthy creative endeavour and one that will get a lot of attention." Not from J. J. Hawkins, though.

At least these responses were made on a literary basis. Susan Herner replied that Mr. Amantea's book had arrived at an inconvenient time, "as I am moving both home and office to Connecticut. I hope you can empathize with the amount of sorting and packing I must do." Robert H. Liberman couldn't take on *A Geezer in Paradise* because he was "busy promoting my own novel *The Last Boy*." Considerate to the last, he told Mr. Amantea where to buy a copy.

November 15

A rule of biography holds that the author should not despise his subject. Roger Lewis, author of *Anthony Burgess*, is beyond that: he detests his subject. In a newspaper article written to attract attention to his book, Lewis tried to tempt readers by accusing Burgess of being a "pathological" liar, a "charlatan," an "intellectual vaudeville act." He also calls Burgess a "pretentious prick" and a "complete fucking fool." Lewis spent twenty years on his book, and loathed Burgess more with every minute. "Desiccated in his urn in the cemetery above Monte Carlo, he is almost forgotten," Lewis writes. People to whom he mentioned his project thought he was writing about the Cambridge spy Guy Burgess.

We are reluctant to believe all this, not least because Burgess was a spirited contributor to this paper over many years, chiefly on musical subjects. Lewis claims that Burgess's alleged proficiency in languages was exaggerated, but evidence of a prodigious musical output exists. He was also a poet whose collected works would run to several hundred pages. Burgess sometimes wrote poetry under another name, then criticized the results, as if they were written by someone else. Kevin Jackson has edited a small selection of his verse, *Revolutionary Sonnets*, which shows Burgess ranging in style from high allusive to frivolous. He sought rhymes for unrhymable words, sometimes (as here) in a song.

A concert, Hugo?
By all means *you* go,
But the very first note of a fugue-o
depresses me, like all polyphony.
I'd rather have a diamond from Tiffany.

In his musical, *Blooms of Dublin,* written for the James Joyce centenary in 1982, Burgess set about finding rhymes for "Ulysses" and "Guinness." Buck Mulligan sings:

> Let's find some naked goddesses
> To deck our native odysseys—
> Every man his own Ulysses
> Sailing seas of kicks and kisses
> Ouzo-drinking will spell *finis*
> To the wealth of Arthur Guinness.

It is anything but detestable. Could it be that the desiccated remains in that urn above Monte Carlo are actually those of Roger Lewis, and that the author of the new biography, *Anthony Burgess,* is Anthony Burgess? It is just the sort of literary hoax he would enjoy.

2003

January 3

Happy New Year. With this issue, the *TLS* sees off its centenary. On January 2, 1903, the masthead bore the legend "Second Year," no doubt expressing the relief felt at having survived that far. Readers were promised enlightenment on various topics, including "the inveterate drunkenness of the Royal circle in the days of Charles II" (see Pepys's *Diary* for confirmation). The Letters page carried a long despatch by the novelist H. Rider Haggard about "cattle-sickness," or foot-and-mouth disease. And on page 7, there was Notes, the NB of its day, which the paper had run from the first issue.

It was a lively week for Notes. The lead item was an analysis of the output of books during the previous year. A total of 7,381 volumes appeared, an increase of more than 1,300 over 1901. As today, the most popular genre was fiction: 1,743 novels were published in 1902 (we give you thirty seconds to name more than one of them). After that came theology (567 titles), with poetry, history, and biography all burgeoning; legal books, belles-lettres, and books of travel showed a falling off.

The column contained a number of intriguing stories: "Mr Heinemann will shortly publish a book by Lord William Nevill entitled *Penal Servitude*. The author, after dealing briefly with his own trial, conviction, and life in prison, deals fully with many problems arising out of the present prison system, such as the food, exercise, punishments and daily routine of the convict." The harmless *TLS* drudge who wrote the note did not wish to say so—or perhaps Mr. Heinemann himself declined—but the crime was fraud; the sum involved, £11,000.

Mr. Walter Stephens wrote to the author of Notes to say that "in view of the Censor's refusal to grant me a licence for my drama, *Paradise Lost*, it is my intention to produce the play privately in the West-end of London regardless of expense." The reason for the ban was that the play was "Scriptural," therefore against the rules of theatrical licensing. Mr. Stephens's dramatization of Milton is not entirely forgotten: it was performed at a festival in Williamstown, Mass, in 1976, with characters in the roles of Sin, Chaos, and Death, as well as "Voice of the Almighty."

Then there was the odd case of Miss Stone: "After the interest created last year by Miss Stone's capture by brigands, disappointment will be felt at the non-appearance of her book, the publishers having been compelled to announce that the publication has been deferred indefinitely."

Incidentally, among the novels published in 1902 were *The Wings of the Dove*, *The Hound of the Baskervilles*, and *Youth* by Joseph Conrad.

February 21

A few weeks ago, Frieda Hughes, the daughter of Sylvia Plath and Ted Hughes, complained volubly about a forthcoming BBC film on the two poets' lives. The role of Plath is taken by Gwyneth Paltrow, who was seen swishing through Islington during the filming. Ms. Hughes is wounded by the appropriation of her parents' lives, particularly of that of her mother, who took her own life in 1963. "My feelings were not taken into consideration," she said. "I want nothing to do with the film." Ms. Hughes wrote a poem on the subject, "My Mother," which contains lines such as, "The peanut eaters, entertained / At my mother's death will go home." She imagined viewers of the video version pressing the pause button while putting on the kettle, so that "my mother holds her breath on screen / To finish dying after tea."

Unconnected to the film, but part of the same cult, is *Wintering*, a novel by Kate Moses, published this week. Ms. Moses revealed in a glossy magazine feature last weekend that Sylvia Plath was a terrific baker of cakes—and so is she. Sylvia had to juggle children and writing—and so does she! What's more, Ms. Moses told us, Frieda Hughes does a lot of baking, too. We learned what she baked to honor the unveiling of a plaque on her parents' house in Chalcot Square. Ms. Hughes may wish to stay out of the film, but she can't avoid the baking group.

How much she would have enjoyed Ms. Moses's recipes, one can only wonder. Among them we find "Tomato soup cake à la Sylvia Plath":

2 cups sifted cake flour
1 tbsp baking powder
1 can condensed tomato soup
1/2 cup chopped walnuts, etc

Set the oven at gas mark 5 (190C). Don't forget to light it.

August 1

Racial separatism in the arts. On July 26, the *Guardian Weekend* color magazine devoted seven pages to "black and Asian women" in British theater. There are more of them than ever, which ought to please everybody, not least the women themselves. Most sounded bitter, however. The author of the piece, Helen Kolawole, told a story of cruel exclusion on the one hand, inspirational black women on the other, with a white male theatrical establishment in the middle. The specter of "subtle censorship" was raised, as was, naturally, the "institutional racism" of the British theater. In spite of the oppression in what was once known as the entertainment world, the excluded are now being included. So what's happening in the new Theaterland?

Tanika Gupta, whose play *Fragile Land* was recently performed at Hampstead Theatre, shone a little light on freedom. There is a point in *Fragile Land* "when a character raises his fist and says, 'My Muslim brothers.'" Ms. Gupta explained that, at that moment, "the Hampstead faithful" would "go very quiet." By contrast, the children at an afternoon performance reacted differently. "Half of them had their fists in the air—including the white boys."

In our unreconstructed way, we are trying to puzzle out how we are supposed to react to this. Or indeed why the Hampstead faithful (faithfully shelling out at the box office, in the bleak hope of being entertained) should be publicly mocked for not raising their fists at a rallying cry for radical Islam. Or why the introduction of rallying cries for radical Islam into once-oppressive British theaters should be regarded, even by the *Guardian*, as social progress. You don't get it either? Then you're probably part of the problem.

August 22

If you study at the University of Colorado, Boulder, you might benefit from the teaching of Frederick Luis Aldama, Assistant Professor of English. Mr. Aldama's new book, *Postethnic Narrative Criticism* deals with the work of Salman Rushdie, Hanif Kureishi, Oscar Acosta, and other writers. Dig that postethnic rhythm: "The Acosta-as-character's hypervisibility as abnormal/unreal ethnosexual object ironically leads him into an empowered ethnosexual position that playfully resists hegemonic structures." The chapter on Rushdie is equally playful:

> Rushdie's magicorealism gives texture to a culturally and racially complex and comprehensive fourthspace; rather than invent story-worlds and narrators that reproduce a binary opposition between a firstspace—coded as racial Other, prerational, magical—Rushdie uses magicorealism as the form to invent fourthspace narratives that critically revise such divisions.

But hold on there. It's time to stop mocking this kind of thing, and to ask what tragedies have befallen the Aldamas of academe to have caused their minds to melt. We were just getting into our new compassionate mode when we read the preface to Aldama's book—and there discovered that his misfortune is all our fault. The author tells us that, as a boy in the 1980s, he journeyed "far from my Mexican / Guatemalan-American family" and arrived in London, a city "filled to the brim with Marmite-eating xenophobes." His sojourn "coincided with Mrs Thatcher's reign of terror." The Prime Minister had begun "to 'sweep up' Britain's impure Others . . . council flats were levelled and the urban poor displaced." When young Aldama and other Others "wandered too deeply into London's moneyed West End, police would inform us of a city curfew and escort us to the nearest underground station."

Distracted by reigns of terror in Chile, Uganda, Cambodia, not to mention the social upheavals in parts of Mexico and Guatemala, we missed our own. Things have picked up, though. The Marmite-eaters are in retreat, the moneyed West End curfew has been lifted. As for the displaced urban poor, they are in place again, and numerous enough to please even an Assistant Professor. Come back, Mr. Aldama. Let us help you learn to write the English of the new impurity.

September 26

The Preposterousness of Maya Angelou: An inexhaustible series. Last week, the *Independent* invited readers to question the Great One by email. A reader asked about Her preferred mode of travel. It is by custom-built bus with "king-size bed" (for guess who) and "two bunks for my drivers." Air travel is no longer possible, She explained, for the simple reason that She cannot set foot in airports. "I'm very well known and people often run up and put their babies in my arms."

Did She, at the age of seventy-five, feel beautiful? "I think I'm doing very, very well. True beauty may be found in kindness, courtesy, generosity and courage." Another reader asked about the white people She had known when younger. "They were brutal, crass and ignorant," the Great One replied. Through Her writings, however, Her mottoes on gift-cushions, Her appearances on the Oprah Winfrey show, She has made the world a better place. "There are thousands of young white, Asian and Latino children who are named after me. Thousands. It's a great blessing."

November 21

Publishers were forced to sit up and listen last week as the novelist and book reviewer Amanda Craig complained about the number of free books she receives in the post. "More than 100 books a week flood into my house," Ms. Craig wrote in the *Bookseller.* "This is bad enough during a weekday, when I am rushing to get the kids to school. But on a Saturday morning, being woken at 8 am puts me in a foul mood."

Her mood gets fouler if the publishers haven't packaged the 100 free books in a way that suits Ms. Craig. "Securing the flap of a recycled envelope several times is helpful to the environment but murder on my tendons. By the time I've found my Stanley knife and hacked through a big brown envelope from OUP, I'm not happy." Should she find herself "showered with grey fluff," then the Craig children probably wish it wasn't a Saturday and that they were at school. Incidentally, the box of books received regularly from Penguin goes "straight to my local school library."

As if things weren't bad enough, publicity staff phone Ms. Craig at all hours to ask about her next consignment of free books. She's not happy. "Like all reviewers I am insanely busy writing my own novels and doing the kind of journalism that, unlike reviewing, pays some bills." London publishers are no doubt trying to devise a way to get Ms. Craig the free books without disturbing her. They'd better make a good job of it. "What I want are the right books sent on time in bound proof and with a useful press release."

Ms Craig is one of the "critics who count" and the consequences of phoning her at the wrong time, sending her the wrong book, sending the right book but in the wrong envelope, are serious. "I was asked to write a leader for *The Times* about this year's Booker shortlist. I had to refuse because I had only been sent two of them." Don't upset the critics. "We don't want to be driven crazier than we already are," Ms. Craig says.

2004

January 9

In one of the most famous lines in modern drama, Blanche DuBois in Tennessee Williams's play *A Streetcar Named Desire* says, "I have always depended on *The Kindness of Strangers.*" The phrase made an impression on the BBC journalist Kate Adie, whose memoir *The Kindness of Strangers* is currently on the bestseller list.

On the other hand, it is just possible that Ms. Adie intended a playful allusion to her late BBC colleague Bernard Braden, whose memoir *The Kindness of Strangers* came out in 1990. Or she might have meant to evoke Mary Mackey's novel *The Kindness of Strangers* (1988). Or Laurey Blight's romance *The Kindness of Strangers,* which comes with this tempting synopsis: "Ysande had a fiancé that is vegetating and feels guilty about wrestling with Rufer." Or Julie Smith's Skip Langdon mystery *The Kindness of Strangers* (1997).

Then again, perhaps Ms. Adie's book is an *homage* to Donald Spoto, the biographer of Tennessee Williams (see his book, *The Kindness of Strangers,* 1985). It seems less likely that she had *The Kindness of Strangers: Adult Mentors, Urban Youth, and the New Voluntarism* by Marc Freedman in mind; less likely still *The Kindness of Strangers: The Abandonment of Children in Western Europe* by John Boswell. And if she thought for a moment of *The Kindness of Strangers: Penniless Across Amer-*

ica by Mike McIntyre, the 200,000 copies sold so far of *The Kindness of Strangers* (by Kate Adie) will have helped her forget.

On January 23, Kate Adie replied:

> Sir — J.C. wonders whether any of a number of works account for the title of a book about my life as a reporter, *The Kindness of Strangers.* How to nail a title so that the publisher breathes a sigh of relief? I remember crawling around in a sea of unnumbered pages grumbling that one's friends were less than helpful. "A Grenade in My Bra" was one of the more appetizing suggestions. Yes, I had seen *A Streetcar Named Desire* and yes, in the course of some vaguely esoteric research, I had come across *The Kindness of Strangers: The Abandonment of Children in Western Europe.* No, neither the drama, the romance, nor even the memoir of identical title had ever crossed my consciousness. What I chose had no illustrious progenitors. I had merely recalled the seconds of sharp awareness when an anonymous figure had shoved me though a doorway as the snipers grew active or delivered a drink of tea or wine from a near-empty larder. It just popped up out of experience.
>
> KATE ADIE
> London

2005

February 25

If you are a writer on the make, you want your name to be memorable. For example, if you are a young novelist called Nicholas Royle, endeavoring to write a plain, readable prose, it might be disheartening to discover that there is a literary critic called Nicholas Royle who writes tough stuff on critical theory, with all the usual trimmings.

There is a journalist called Duncan Campbell on the staff of the *Guardian*, who writes mainly about old-fashioned crime, and another Duncan Campbell, who writes on surveillance and official secrets. Occasionally, this Duncan Campbell also writes for the *Guardian*. At least we think he does—unless it's Duncan Campbell (the other one) branching out. How can anybody tell?

Presumably both men (and both Royles) have considered the introduction of an initial and rejected the proposed intruder. Keith Walker, who worked at the *TLS* until his death in 2003, wrote two novels in the 1960s, and thereafter turned to reviewing fiction and drama. Then came Keith Walker, who wrote on eighteenth-century literature. Keith Walker—our Keith—politely asked Keith Walker if he would consider the initial. Keith Walker replied that he would not, whereupon our Keith Walker became J. K. L. Walker.

There is a Nicholas Wroe and a Nicholas Roe, and there are all sorts of John Williamses. And now there is the Richard Holmes problem. Richard Holmes is a military historian, not to be confused with Richard Holmes the biographer and travel writer, author of the book *Footsteps*. He is, let's say, Richard "Footsteps" Holmes, whom no one would mistake for a military historian. The military Richard Holmes is about to publish his latest book. To make sure everyone knows it is by him, and not by Richard "Footsteps" Holmes, he has called it *In the Footsteps of Churchill*.

April 1

Edmund Keeley and Eugen M. Bacon are front runners for the 2005 Kate Adie Award for the year's most unoriginal book title. Ms. Bacon's *Borderline*—"a fast-paced thriller sensual and sublime"—has just been published by Troubador of Leicester; *Borderlines* by Mr. Keeley will be coming from White Pine Press in June.

When ordering the latter from your bookseller, be careful not to finish up with *Borderlines* by Peter Hoeg, or *Borderlines* by Archer Mayor, or *Borderlines* by Axel Marsden. *Borderlines: A Memoir* by Caroline Kraus may be an enjoyable book, but it is not Mr. Keeley's *Borderlines*. Charles Nicholls's *Borderlines* is likely to be a superior account of a journey in the Far East, but it is not to be confused with *Borderlines* by Mr. Keeley.

Ms. Bacon's *Borderline* is not the same as Mr. Keeley's *Borderlines*. Nor is it the same as *Borderline* by J. C. Keener, or *Borderline: A Jack McMorrow Mystery* by Gerry Boyle, or *Borderline* by Janette Turner Hospital. Whatever you do, don't end up with *Borderline Personality Disorders: The Concept, the Syndrome, the Patient* by Peter Hartcollis. *Borderline Personalities: A New Generation of Latinas Dish on Sex, Sass and Cultural Shifting* might sound like fun, but it is not the "sensual and sublime" *Borderline* by Ms. Bacon.

June 10

How Your Money Is Spent, part 99. The Arts Council is funding a survey to be conducted among "poets from Black and Asian communities across the UK," in order to "improve the opportunities" available to them. In order that the improvements may begin, the Arts Council needs to know to which ethnic grouping the poet considers him or herself to belong: "Asian or British Asian, Asian Bangladeshi, Asian Indian, Asian Pakistani, Any other Asian background, Chinese, Black or British Black, Black African, Black Caribbean, Any other Black background, Black African and white, Black Caribbean and white, Chinese and white, Asian and white."

Then there is the matter of the poet's education. Question 23 demands to know, "Which of the following qualifications do you have: 1 or more O Levels / GCSE's (any grades), 5 or more O Levels, CSE's (grade 1), GCSE's (grades A-C), School certificate, 1 or more A levels / AS levels, NVQ Level 1, Foundation GNVQ, NVQ Level 2, Intermediate GNVQ, NVQ Level 3, Advanced GNVQ, NVQ levels 4-5, HNC HND?"

With your racial pedigree established and certified proof of braininess in hand, you ought to be making waves in the poetry world. If not, the reason is likely to be uncovered by Question 12: "What has been the biggest obstacle to developing your career as a poet? Individual prejudice within the poetry world? Individual prejudice within the publishing world? Institutional racism in publishing companies?" Owning up to lack of talent is not an option. Poets are asked if their main ambition is to "become an established poet" or to "have a collection of work published" or to "win a competition."

The main obstacle to developing a career as a poet, in our experience, is a failure to write poetry that sufficient numbers of people are willing to read. Don't expect it to be stated in quite that way when the results of "Research into Publishing Opportunities for Black and Asian Poets" are published.

July 22

Arthur Crook, who has died at the age of ninety-three, was the editor of the *TLS* for fifteen years, between 1959 and 1974, and the last link with the paper's earliest days. His rise to the top job was an unlikely one. When Crook began working for *The Times* as a messenger boy in 1926, aged fourteen, Thomas Hardy and Arthur Conan Doyle were still alive, Kafka had recently died, Hemingway's first book was receiving kind notices, in the *TLS*, among other places. Crook's association goes back even further than that, since his father was a member of the printing staff. As Derwent May writes in his history of the *TLS*, *Critical Times*, the teenage Crook was known for his speed in delivering messages around London "and for the correctness of his spelling." His first position at the *TLS*, which he joined in 1930, was in the reference library, then called the "Intelligence Department."

Among the bright people Crook appointed during his editorship were Alexander Cockburn, Ian Hamilton, Martin Amis, Piers Paul Read, John Sturrock and John Willett. In a letter Crook wrote to the *TLS* in 1992, he was happy to echo another's statement that the paper had "expanded and prospered" under his direction. He clung to the policy of anonymity in reviewing, when others believed its time had passed (it finally did in 1974, when Crook made way for John Gross). When Amis and Hamilton wrote lightheartedly about this and other quaint practices in a celebration of the *TLS*'s ninetieth birthday, Crook responded on the Letters page by saying that "their now pointed objections to certain policies were not always manifest at the time in the internal debates that often enlivened working hours."

Crook's *TLS* might surprise browsers of back issues now: in addition to the general weekly coverage, he published special supplements on experimental literature (including one with a cover by Jean Tinguely), from Concrete Poetry to the Beats. Not only did Allen Ginsberg appear in the *TLS*, but Ginsberg's father Louis did too. Later, Crook persuaded Valerie Eliot to let the paper publish facsimile pages from the early drafts of *The Waste Land*, in Eliot's handwriting, and in his typescript, with Ezra Pound's written annotations. It is rumored that Mrs. Eliot turned down an American publication's lavish offer, in favor of Crook's £100. May ended his chapter on Crook in *Critical Times* by saying that "he gave the *TLS* more of his life than any man in its history".

July 29

A bibliomane friend from North of the border has sent us *The Singer Passes,* a collection of poems published in Glasgow in 1934. The author is Harry Potter. Greater Rowlingologists than we have no doubt pondered the question of how the bespectacled boy got his name, but none, so far as we know, has considered the likelihood that the original is an early twentieth-century poet from Scotland, the country in which J. K. Rowling now makes her home.

The poet Harry Potter was not completely obscure. The *TLS* reviewed both *The Singer Passes* and an earlier Potter collection, *In Thy Heart's Garden* (1919). Harry, said our reviewer, "heard the still small voice amidst the storm of life," and was in close and fervent touch with spiritual things. Even we, who know as little about Ms. Rowling's books as anyone alive, are minded to suspect that this sounds not a little like the youthful wizard who came into being in neighboring Edinburgh. Like his namesake, the original Harry Potter has a tendency towards things mystical even though the manner of expression is different.

> O God, in Whom alone we have the gift
> Of conscious life, of Whom our very need
> For constant upward rise is born, heed
> Our cry . . .

In addition to this kind of thing, of which there is a fair bit in *The Singer Passes,* the poet Potter wrote curiosities such as "Ode to a Gas Meter": "Thou scurvy knave, thou register of lies. . . ." He also made borrowings from exotica such as *The Rubaiyat of Omar Khayyam,* which he rendered into couthie broad Scots, substituting for "a loaf of bread, a book of verse, a flask of wine, and thou beside me" a more temperate menu: "A bowl o' brose, a cosy fire-end, sate, / O' buttermilk a reamin' jug, and fast / Within ma haun' a weel-thumb'd Rabbie Burns." Stop complaining that your kids won't read anything but Harry Potter. Give them some Harry Potter to read instead.

November 25

Norman Mailer was honored at the National Book Awards in New York last week for his "distinguished contribution to American letters." The presentation was by Toni Morrison. Was Mailer pleased at the award? Yes and no. "In the literary world today, passion has withered," he said. The author of *The Armies of the Night, A Fire on the Moon, The Fight, The Executioner's Song* and other works of fiction and journalism, thinks literature is in danger of becoming "a footnote to our technological and commercial culture."

Mailer is in his eighties, and Morrison is getting on. Just as we were wondering who would carry the flame, the *Observer* turned up with "New York's new literary lion." The Review section of last Sunday's paper promised the "first interview" with Benjamin Kunkel, author of *Indecision*, published in the UK this month. He is "the new sensation of literary New York." In an earlier first interview with Kunkel, he was "the darling of the New York literary scene."

Surely this is the man to roar that the novelist is still king of the jungle, and prove Mailer wrong. "We're angrier than Dave Eggers and his crowd," Kunkel told the *Observer.* Well, that's promising, kind of. Angry about what? The war? Religious fundamentalism at home and abroad? Race and its discontents?—the big, Mailerite subjects. No. Kunkel is angry at the listlessness of the latter-day lad. He's angry about dating. "The idea is that dating should lead toward mating, and spread out before us is this array of choices that should lead toward a choice you can feel secure in. But I think the opposite happens. You become familiar with disposable relationships."

No wonder the guy is furious. "To be constantly exposed to people whom you are unworthy of to begin with, yet who want you more than you want them is confusing." Don't get him started. The *Observer* carried some quips from *Indecision*: "In my experience when a person doesn't know what to do with himself, he will check his emails." Could you keep the roaring down, please?

2006

August 11

The following two passages have something in common:

i) I showed Jody *Cain's Book.* Something prevented her from having any response whatsoever. She said she couldn't understand it.
ii) Last night, oddly enough after his disturbing conversation with Adams, Ingham had thought of a title for his book, *The Tremor of Forgery.* It was much better than the two other ideas he had had.

The first passage comes from *Cain's Book* by Alexander Trocchi (1960), the second from *The Tremor of Forgery* by Patricia Highsmith (1969). The common factor is that, in both, a character is writing a novel with the same title as the novel the reader holds in his hand. "*The Tremor of Forgery*" which Ingham is writing in Highsmith's story has nothing to do with *The Tremor of Forgery* in which Ingham himself is the lead character. Trocchi's book is autobiographical, but the quotation from "*Cain's Book*" that is read out to Jody appears nowhere else in *Cain's Book.* The device would now be called "metafictional," but it is a surprise to discover it in a tale of suspense such as Highsmith's. Readers may be able to supply other examples.

August 18

The Seven Deadly Sins get a lot of publicity—Pride and Lust are thoroughly approved of, Avarice encouraged, Sloth nothing to hide (the others are Envy, Gluttony, and Wrath)—but what about the Seven Virtues? Many sinners out there would be hard-pressed to give their names, never mind practise them: Charity, Chastity, Generosity, Humility, Meekness, Moderation, Zeal.

The lists come from *Whitaker's Almanack Pocket Reference*, sister to the larger *Almanack*, which gives all the facts and figures you need to call on in the course of a year. The names of male, female, and young animals, for example: we now know that the male ferret is a hob, the female a jill, and that together they make a kit. Who would have guessed that the male hamster is a buck? With donkeys, the forms of address are jack, jenny, and colt. Apes are among the few species known simply as male, female and baby. Is it because they are so like us? Another species so known is the slothful, gluttonous louse.

The *Almanack* offers a catalogue of over sixty phobias, all relating to things you felt fine about until you learned of their existence. Here are some:

vensaphobia	fear of beautiful women
pogonophobia	fear of beards
oenophobia	fear of wine
peladophobia	fear of baldness
chorophobia	fear of dancing

Ergasiophobia (fear of work), dentophobia (the dentist), and gamophobia (marriage) are more plausible; given that rhytiphobia (fear of getting wrinkles) is practically universal, we are surprised not to have seen the word before.

October 13

On the subject of metafictional references, in which a character in a novel is writing or reading a novel of the same name as that in which he features (see above), Patrick McGrath, who works at Christie's, reminds us of the scene in the film *The Third Man*, written by Graham Greene (1949; the film treatment was later published as a novel), in which Mr. Popescu appears at Holly Martins's talk at the British Cultural Centre. Before he sends a pair of thugs to try to kill Holly, Popescu engages him in some banter:

> Popescu: Can I ask . . . is Mr Martins engaged on a new book?
> Martins: Yes, it is called *The Third Man.*
> Popescu: A novel, Mr Martins?
> Martins: It's a murder story.

Benjamin Friedman of New York draws our attention to *A Clockwork Orange* by Anthony Burgess, in which Alex's robbery victim is a writer.

> "What is this, then?" I said, picking up the pile like of typing from off of the table. . . . "It's a book", I said. "It's a book what you are writing." Then I looked at its top sheet, and there was the name—A CLOCKWORK ORANGE—and I said, "That's a fair gloopy title."

A former editor of the *TLS*, Jeremy Treglown, sends us a double example from Henry Green's last novel, *Doting* (1952). Mr. Treglown (who is Green's biographer) writes: "The central character, Arthur, is infatuated with a nineteen-year-old, Annabel, one of whose boyfriends is an aspiring poet. Annabel teases Arthur with the information that her boyfriend is editing an anthology of love poetry called Doting. Arthur replies, 'Well, you know doting, to me is not loving.'" As Mr. Treglown points out, "Loving is the title of an earlier novel of Green's."

Another reader cites *Monsieur* by Lawrence Durrell, in which the novelist Blanford "is writing a novel called *Monsieur,* containing a novelist called Sutcliffe who is writing a novel called *Monsieur,* with a character called Bloshford (based on Blanford)." They don't come more metafictional than that.

November 3

One day soon, we will get round to updating *The TLS Reviewer's Handbook,* adding prohibitions on words such as "interrogate" (except in legal contexts), "robust" (except in sporting contexts) and "limn" (in any context). The *New York Times* critic Michiko Kakutani has a particular fondness for "limn." Alice Munro creates tales "that limn entire lifetimes in a handful of pages"; Robert Olen Butler has the ability "to limn an entire life in a couple of pages"; Ann Beattie's early works show her "ability to limn her characters' inner lives."

John Buchan never limned a life, inner or outer, in a couple of pages, or even more. He only dislimned. Here he is, in *The Thirty-Nine Steps*: "The plump man's features seemed to dislimn, and form again." Here he is once more, in *Mr. Standfast*: "Mary saw the figures of Ivery and the chauffeur, and then they dislimned into dreams." And again, in *The Path of the King*: "the landscape framed in the doorway began to waver and dislimn." In the Autumn issue of the *John Buchan Journal*, a certain Mr. Hepworth, "bookseller of erudition," points out other dislimnings in Buchan, as in *Witch Wood*—"it dislimned the outlines of horse and rider"—*The Island of Sheep*, and *Midwinter* ("the tangible bounds of life dislimned and he looked into outer space").

"Dislimn" will not be prohibited in the forthcoming *Reviewer's Handbook*, for the good reason that no one else but Buchan and Shakespeare—"The Rack dislimns, and makes it indistinct" (*Antony and Cleopatra*)—uses the word.

INTERLUDE

How It Was

I LEARNED MANY THINGS about the writing of a column as the years went by, some of them quickly. Writing of almost every kind demands reconsideration and redrafting to bring it within reach of the writer's original conception. But the weekly columnist's desire to play his or her best shot is at the mercy of the mundane timetable and the production manager's imperative: to meet the appointed deadline for the paper's place on the printer's schedule.

This should seem obvious to all involved. But imagine: the deadline for putting the paper to bed in the office, before the pages are delivered to the printer—in the early days by a messenger on foot, later digitally—is five o'clock on Tuesday afternoon. This was the typical arrangement during most of the years I worked at the *TLS*. The jejune diarist, although short of inspiring material, has nevertheless cast his net and landed a column, consisting of three separate items, amounting to about 1,200 words.

Most of it will have been written, in the office, on Monday. At first glance on Tuesday morning, it is clear that two of the items are vague or dull or unoriginal or—usually as a consequence of one or all of those faults—are trying too hard. Good prose wraps itself around a sturdy subject; without it, the words are apt to sag and stray. Poor jokes and punchlines (beware of punchlines) further cheapen the effect. Attempts to steer clear of the commonplace and say something attention-grabbing has had the effect of making the story seem artificial. Sarcasm has been given its deadening license. What's more, in several places, facts and citations need to be checked (internet a long way off), necessitating telephone calls to publishers and publicity agents. A chore to have to make, even at the best of times, the calls are likely to elicit that easily given promise, equally easily broken: "I'll get back to you." In between, you might resort to ringing up a friend. "You haven't by any chance got a copy of Heaney's *Collected* to hand . . . ?"

This is the predicament of the inexperienced columnist at noon on Tuesday. He makes a further revision, cutting what he had treasured as his brightest jokes, now gray and unfunny, sets off for the sandwich shop—"If someone phones from Faber and Faber, could you . . ."—then returns to read through yet again while enduring the damp sandwich. By two o'clock, the editor of the *TLS* will expect to have a first look at the column, to see if—to put it at its most blunt—it is fit to be printed. There might be a minor libel doubt to settle (the columnist's least favorite deadline-day announcement: "We'd better have this legaled"). In regard to the confidence it injects, the editor's initial response means a good deal. "Lovely, lovely," was Ferdy Mount's typical approval. Peter Stothard was gratifyingly enthusiastic. Stig Abell's reaction, to material that was sometimes likely to provoke a shudder of woke anxiety, was rarely discouraging.

By the time it came to negotiating with the second and third of that trio of *TLS* editors, I had firm control over the delivery of my copy. But in earlier days I could imagine a scenario in which colleagues hovered behind my chair, talking in whispers at four o'clock on press day, while I wrestled with yet another draft of what was intended to be that week's column (the earliest NBs were written on an office manual typewriter). "Do you know how it's going with Jim?" "I thought he'd spoken to *you*." I remember my desk neighbor Mick Imlah, having heard one exaggerated fear too many from me, asking if I'd noticed any white mice in my top drawer. Meanwhile, the minute hand moves to four-thirty.

The most important lesson I learned as a weekly columnist was slow in dawning. When it did so, I realized that it is the key to the enterprise: the secret of writing a regular column is not so much having something to say as having a space to fill and a deadline to meet. If the editor were to ask: "Have you got much to say? Do you need a full page?", you might be inclined to answer no. If he says: "You have a full page. We need it by two o'clock," the copy will be delivered on time, and the page will be filled. Once you've got your chops, as jazz musicians say—once you are on first-name terms with your instrument—necessity will see you through. After a while, you can rely on it.

In twenty-three years of writing NB, I took time off for holidays, naturally, but was hardly ever absent on account of common ailments. When the telephone brought the news from Scotland in the early hours of May 30, 2002, that my father had died, I went into the office later that morning and got the next NB ready, knowing I would be gone throughout the following week. It seemed not just the right thing for the paper, but the best way of occupying the time for me. A column is a friend as well as a dependent.

NB

2007–2009

2007

January 5

Where are the poets of the war? This was the question posed in a leading article in the *TLS* of August 8, 1942, when Britain and other nations were three years into the struggle against Germany. The leader writer contrasted the current situation with that of "the last war" which "threw up a fair amount of notable poetry." To the names of soldier-poets from the First World War, such as Owen, Graves, Sassoon, Brooke, and Rosenberg, could be added Kipling, Bridges, Hardy, and others who were "not soldiers," but who viewed the conflict "through the accumulated knowledge and wisdom of years." Indeed, our editorialist said, "the singers of war have been for the most part not soldiers," even though the poetry of Europe is "full of war."

We have now been at war for over five years, first in Afghanistan, then Iraq. Where are the poets of the war? We exclude, for the moment, poems gathered together in collections such as *100 Poets Against the War*, edited by Todd Swift, and *101 Poets Against War*, edited by Matthew Hollis and Paul Keegan, the very titles of which amount to a political agenda (the former contained new work; the latter, poems from all ages). The kind of war poetry you want, as a reader, challenges your assumptions with doubt, pity, glory, even gore.

Our most distinguished living war poet is probably Christopher Logue, but his *War Music*, a wonderful modernist assembly kit based on a selective chart of the *Iliad*, can only be applied to the present situation in the sense that practically anything can. Under no reading could it be classed as anti-war. James Fenton has written about a previous war; Seamus Heaney and others have addressed themselves to the Troubles in Northern Ireland (at least one poem in Heaney's latest collection glances in the direction of Afghanistan). But no writer of distinction has borne down on the wars in Afghanistan and Iraq with the authority of direct experience and few, if any, with "the accumulated knowledge and wisdom of the years." An exception might be Harold Pinter. No writer has ever been so belligerent about belligerence.

One explanation for the paucity of war poetry lies in the ending of National Service. Another in the present-day unfashionable standing of nationalism and militarism. "Is there no such thing as righteous indignation?" our editorialist wrote in 1942. "May not a dear homeland be in imminent danger?"

As it turned out, the Second World War threw up "a fair amount of notable poetry" by Keith Douglas, Sydney Keyes, Alan Ross, and others. In 1942, they appeared to our leader writer as the reserves (the first two were killed; the third seriously wounded). Yet he conceded that war had given them that much-desired thing, a subject. "Were there no war, they would still be poets, but poets compelled, like all children of this age, to think, observe, and write within a narrow living-space."

February 2

Whenever we let fall our intention to update *The TLS Reviewer's Handbook,* some helpful soul is sure to let us know that, while sharing our dismay at a wrong-footed "enormity," a lazy "disinterested," a plain ignorant "fulsome," he or she was distressed (they mean "delighted") to encounter an example in the same issue of the *TLS.* When we suggested recently that the overused word "robust" be restricted to sporting contexts, Theodore Rabb was among the first to spot a transgression. "Despite your entirely justified condemnation, there is a glaring instance of it on p 8." With heavy heart, we turned to the page in question, expecting to be blinded by the glare: "He is writing in a robust tradition," our reviewer wrote of a new book about Satan. In this case, the usage seems suitable.

The point nevertheless seems worth making—readers seldom tire of making it—that it is wise to inspect your own elegance before objecting to the style of others. The most fluent writers can be reduced to helpless sputtering. Try digesting this sentence:

> Mrs Wharton not only owes to her cultivated art of putting it the distinction enjoyed when some ideal of expression has the whole of the case, the case once made its concern, in charge, but might further act for us, were we to follow up her exhibition, as lighting not a little that question of tone, the author's own intrinsic, as to which we have just seen Mr Conrad's late production rather tend to darken counsel.

The author of this fulsome enormity is Henry James, writing in the *TLS* of April 2, 1914. Even now it elicits the pained cry: "Who subbed this?"

February 9

Henry James and the *TLS*, contd. Last week, we presented a sentence from James's article, "The Younger Generation (Part II)," with the suggestion that it was incomprehensible. So far, no one has put forth their comprehension. We now find ourselves confronted with a tangential problem. A respected colleague, who retired some years ago, was fond of quoting a communication from James to Bruce Richmond, editor of the *TLS* from its early days until 1938. The story goes that James returned proofs of his essay on Balzac (June 19, 1913), from which one-and-a-half sentences had been cut. As our elder would cheerily recount, the proofs arrived on Richmond's desk with a note: "Here's the bleeding corpse. Yours is a butcher's trade." It became customary in this office, when a wordy script was about to go under the knife, to utter in sepulchral tone, "Yours is a butcher's trade."

We now find, on consulting a volume consisting of letters between James and Richmond (*Pardon My Delay*, Foundling Press, 1994), that what James actually wrote as he surrendered the Balzac piece was, "My dear Bruce! I have done it *tant bien que mal*—though feeling it thereby bleeds. But it's a bloody trade."

The bloodthirsty subs around here would be distraught to lose "butcher's trade," but we can find no documentation to authenticate it. The printer's proof has gone, and our archivist tells us that "none of this correspondence survives in the archive." Richmond, alas, discarded the letters he received. Meanwhile, the reader turning to James's Balzac essay might feel that My dear Bruce was not bloody enough. No butcher got close enough to this sentence:

> So it comes that his mastership of whatever given identity might be in question, and much more of the general identity of his rounded (for the artistic vision), his compact and containing France, the fixed, felt frame to him of the vividest items and richest characteristics of human life, can really not be thought of as a matter of degrees of confidence, as acquired or built up or cumbered with verifying fears.

March 23

Where are the poets of the war? When we asked this question at the beginning of the year (see above), reminding versifiers that the nation had been fighting in Afghanistan and Iraq for over five years but you wouldn't know if you depended on them for news, we expected the protest poems to rain down. But scarcely a word.

Discovering that the Wilfred Owen Poetry Award for 2007 was to be given out last week, we contacted the sponsors, the

Owen Association, to ask if theirs had been a difficult task. No, not really. The choice was between Owen Sheers, Tony Harrison, and an American whose name the kindly secretary of the Association could not recall. In the event, the honor went to Harrison, partly for his work as "the *Guardian*'s poetic war correspondent during the 1992–94 Bosnian conflict," and partly for his poems about the first Gulf War:

> Now with noonday headlights in Kuwait
> and the burial of the blackened in Baghdad
> let them remember, all those who celebrate,
> that their good news is someone else's bad . . .

Harrison is the fifth recipient of the award, following Christopher Logue, Seamus Heaney, Michael Longley, and Harold Pinter. As it happens, the *Collected Poems* of Tony Harrison has just arrived, and we opened it hoping to find something to help us make sense of the current conflicts. The closest he comes is "The Krieg Anthology," which seems to have been written before the fighting began in earnest. It includes "Holy Tony's Prayer": "Sometimes I wake up in a sweat / they've not found WMDs yet!" etc.

In fact, Harrison is in a constant state of belligerence. He gets into a scrap each time he picks up a pen. He is fighting a war against taste, in which rhyme is his military strategy. In the Harrison world, it is a political gesture to rhyme "books" with "fucks" (you have to know he is a Yorkshireman), "count" with "cunt," "Eng Lit" with "shit." There are poems about vomiting, poems about pissing and getting pissed, poems about being revolted at not smelling a "realistic" turd in the theater, and a poem wondering whether "you've not yet wiped your arse" with "my verse." The battle against gentility in the Harrison household is conducted on a daily basis. Harrison gets a virulent poem out of the innocent linking of his name with the Laureateship in the press. No one has been more ruthless with nobility: "Dames and Knights" provides a convenient rhyme for "parasites." A four-liner about Prince Charles and Camilla Parker-Bowles is unrepeatable, but if we tell you that it rhymes "whore's" with "menopause," you might agree that real fighters don't hit girls.

April 13

In our last note on the subject, we said we had expected readers and writers to propose the names of poets who had used the war in Iraq and Afghanistan as subject matter in verse. A. E. Stallings, who lives in Athens and is herself a poet, draws our attention to Brian Turner, whose book *Here, Bullet* was published in 2005. Turner did a year-long tour in Iraq, beginning in November 2003, as an infantry team leader with 3rd Stryker Brigade Combat Team, 2nd Infantry Division. Before that, he was deployed in Bosnia-Herzegovina with the 10th Mountain Division. What follows is part of "Here, Bullet":

> If a body is what you want,
> then here is bone and gristle and flesh.
> Here is the clavicle-snapped wish,
> the aorta's opened valves, the leap
> thought makes at the synaptic gap.
> Here is the adrenaline rush you crave,
> that inexorable flight, that insane puncture
> into heat and blood. And I dare you to finish
> what you've started. Because here, Bullet,
> here is where I complete the word . . .

Ms. Stallings adds: "I cannot say if the rest of the collection lives up to the promise of this poem. But it does seem to me there is at least one real Poet of the War." *Here, Bullet* is published by Alice James Books, which recommends it "for anyone who cares about the war, regardless of political affiliation."

June 1

Walking on Air, effectively the first posthumous publication by Muriel Spark, who died last year, is a "cahier" of forty pages, consisting of nine short items. Most are previously published—including the poem "What?", which appeared in the *TLS* in 2002—but some notebook entries are seeing the light of day for the first time. One describes a dream in which the author "started walking on air, about six inches from the ground." In a note that is characteristic to the point of pastiche, Spark expresses delight in her newfound ability, not only for its novelty but because "I remembered hearing of Popes and other special people who 'seemed to walk a few inches above the ground' when they appeared in public, and I thought maybe I could do so too. . . ."

Also included is a five-day journal log, commissioned by the online magazine *Slate,* and possibly hitherto published only in that medium. In the entry for July 11, 1996, Spark muses on the pronoun "one," after an acquaintance had remarked, "One feels that this is earthquake weather, doesn't one?" She finds the exclusivity of "one" objectionable, preferring the "friendlier" formulation, "You feel . . . don't you?" or even "We feel. . . ." Then, too, Spark goes on, "we have to consider if we want to be included in that presumptive 'doesn't one?' Generally, I don't, and I think it presumptive on the part of the speaker to suppose that I do."

In our view, it all depends on the mood of the conversation. Aren't there cases where "one / one's / oneself" are useful, where the use of "you" and "yours" might be too direct, or cause confusion? For example, Ms. A, feeling low, meets a doctor at a party. "What is the way to fight depression?", she asks, not wishing to disclose particulars. His reply, "One should stay active," is both helpful and discreet. With a pinch of irony, "one" is a useful ingredient of style (as Spark surely knew). To the question, "What age is Ms. A?", the reply "One's age" answers the question while sidestepping the thorny subject of people's numerical age. At the same time, it offers sympathetic rather than "presumptive" complicity between the two speakers (i.e., We're both getting on). We invite readers to join the Defenders of One, to supply a sentence in which no other pronoun could do the job as well.

June 8

Our newly formed association, the Defenders of One, dedicated to preserving the pronoun "one" against attacks by Muriel Spark and others, has drawn widespread support. The request was for sentences in which "no other pronoun could do the job as well." Anthea Ingham of Leamington Spa draws attention to several instances in Nancy Mitford's novel *Love in a Cold Climate*. The first—Cedric Hampton's declaration, "In Paris I have an apartment of all beauty, one's idea of Heaven"—seems to us not to pass the test. The first-person possessive would be as effective, and would sound less "pompous" (Spark's objection).

Ms. Ingham's second example of Cedric's speech—"What one does so love about love, is the time before they find out what One is like"—hits the mark. Here, the first-person singular would dampen the comic touch, while "what you are like" would risk offending Cedric's interlocutor.

John North provides an example from Jane Austen: "Everybody is always supposing that I am not a good walker; and yet they would not have been pleased, if we had refused to join them. When people come in this manner on purpose to ask us, how can one say no?"

Perhaps the best example we have seen of a passage in which "I" or "you" would fail to work in the same way as "one" occurs in a novel written in 1959, in which the elderly Godfrey Colston muses on his senile wife, Charmian:

> "Why can't one be kind to her?" he asked himself. . . . Why can't one be more gentle?" He himself was eighty-seven, and

> in charge of all his faculties. Whenever he considered his own behaviour he thought of himself not as "I" but as "one". "One has one's difficulties with Charmian", he told himself.

It comes from *Memento Mori* by Muriel Spark, who is hereby elected president (posthumous) of the Defenders of One.

July 6

The new Prime Minister, Gordon Brown, is a dour Scot. If you don't know this, you haven't been reading the newspapers, and you don't know your Scots. Chambers defines dour as "obstinate: sullen: grim," and gives the root as "L. *durus*, hard." So while it would be quite feasible to identify a Russian as dour, or a Portuguese or Jamaican, no one except a Scot is ever so described, just as nothing is ever "mordant" but wit, dudgeon is always "high," and only hussies are "brazen." These days, the only Scot described as dour is Gordon Brown.

On the day of the handover of the keys to No. 10 Downing Street, Michael White of the *Guardian* saw Mr. Brown as "the dour Scot who was steadily moving to the spotlight." In the same paper, William Keegan told us to drop our "old-fashioned" notions that Brown was "a dour Scot who smiles," and to see him as "easy going and witty." But Keegan's warning came too late to prevent news of the PM's dourness spreading across the globe: even the *New York Times* has Mr. Brown down as "dour and often awkward in public."

Nowadays, Jews are rarely rapacious, blacks are no longer distinguished by their sense of rhythm, and the Irish are stupid in that Irish-joke way only if you're an Irishman yourself. But it remains acceptable to state that economic thriftiness and dogged dourness are innate Caledonian characteristics. Loyal readers will know that we are revising *The TLS Reviewer's Handbook*; you may be sure that "dour Scot" will come with the advice, "We avoid." And while we're at it, don't ever again say of an irony that it is "delicious" or of a crime that it is "heinous" or of praise that it is "fulsome" (a double fault, that). It just makes us more and more dour.

August 3

We like the *Gissing Journal,* published quarterly by the Gissing Trust; so much so that we pay out of our miserable Grub Street earnings to have it delivered at home. Where else would we learn that the Persian translation of *New Grub Street,* Gissing's best-known novel, is *Mārāiyān va Jāspir* (Tehran, 1998), and that the cover sports a portrait of a sullen, modern-looking girl next to an oriental table with an inkpot and quill?

We are beginning to wonder, however, if our scribbler's earnings might be better deployed. The heart leapt when we opened the July issue of the Journal to find a long essay on "Mass Literacy and the Complexity of Reading and Writing in *New Grub Street*" by Ryan Stephenson, but sank when we realized it contained much complexity and little literacy. You might consider it a cheap shot to quote a chunk and then ask: What would Gissing have made of this? But there's nothing cheap about being a subscriber, so that's what we are going to do.

The burden of Mr. Stephenson's essay is Marian Yule's presence in the Reading Room of the British Library, and the nature of her activity there as reader and writer. That's one way of putting it. Here is Stephenson's way:

> While the consumption of print through reading is a practice that draws attention to the reader's physical body . . . the production of print through writing in a male-dominated field and within a predominantly masculine space requires a form of self-abstraction and a denial of the body which Marian finds painful.

Stephenson is keen on the terms "public space," "library space," "space of reading," "discursive space," leading to the climactic "masculine space of the study and the public space of the Reading Room." The argument is guided by "the public sphere," as conceived by Jürgen Habermas: "a discursive space for rational-critical debate between individuals determined to be guided by argument rather than status." Not clear? Let Mr. Stephenson explain:

> The "utopian" principle of negativity when it came to bodies in the public sphere—a principle that said that the validity of one's public statement "bears a negative relation to [his or her] person" so that an utterance carries force despite and not because of one's personal status—continued to mark discursively certain features of bodies that were not modes of whiteness, and wealth "as the humiliating positivity of the particular".

If the *Gissing Journal* is to continue to attract the positivity of our particular subscription, it might show a little mercy. Occasionally, it still does: we learned from the July issue that the Chinese translation of *The Private Papers of Henry Ryecroft* is *Si ji sui bi.* You know where you are with that sort of thing.

IT IS A peculiarity of our linguistic experience that, while we often read of the ascendancy of "chavs," we have never heard the word used in speech, except ironically. The chav is seldom a bookish type, but the chav in book-making is thriving: so far we have had *The Little Book of Chavs, Diary of a Chav,* and *Chav!: A User's Guide to Britain's New Ruling Class.* Now there is *Buttering Parsnips, Twocking Chavs* by Martin Manser, a bright book that pretends to be dim.

The jacket copy tells us that there are "self-styled guardians of the 'correct' way to speak and write," but that books such as *Buttering Parsnips, Twocking Chavs* "throw open the prison doors and allow our language to run free." If you skip this tosh, you might find some interesting stuff inside. A section on "silent letters" in words—for example, the "l" in calm—observes that almost every letter of the alphabet can be used silently. Here we go, alphabetically: a: clinically, b: bomb, c: indict, d: handsome, e: bridge, f: halfpenny, g: gnat, h: exhaust, i: business, j: marijuana, k: knack, 1: yolk, m: mnemonic, n: damn, o: people, p: psalm, q: lacquer; s: isle, t: castle, u: tongue, w: answer.

The book also provides examples of pangrams, "grammatical sentences containing every letter in the alphabet," the most economical of which are "Quick zephyrs blow, vexing daft Jim" (twenty-nine letters) and "The five boxing wizards jump quickly" (thirty-one). Even more interesting is the curious phenomenon of words with contradictory meanings: cleave (stick together/split apart), clip (cut/fasten), fast (fixed/moving), left (gone/remaining), sanction (approve/ban), screen (show/conceal) and weather (withstand/wear away).

Finally, there is the tried-and-tested "Me, Myself, I," offering real names next to better-known pseudonyms: Daryl Walters, Amandine-Aurore Lucille Dupin, John Griffith, Marie-Henri Beyle are, respectively, Enid Blyton, George Sand, Jack London, Stendhal. See what happens when you throw open the prison doors? One thing we could not find in the book was any reference to chavs.

September 27

Perambulatory Christmas Books. In a ten-part series, culminating at Yuletide, we intend to recommend admirable but more or less forgotten books by notable writers. Each will have been picked up for under a fiver, at one of London's second-hand bookshops, which lazy reports deem an ailing species.

We kick off with Edmund Blunden's delightful book *The Face of England*, published by Longmans at 3s 6d seventy-five years ago. (Blunden had a long association with the *TLS*; he joined the staff in 1945.) The first thing to strike us about this series of sketches on the subject of the turning year is that it would be impossible to write in such a way today, without irony:

> The new almanac has begun work. If we still, as by instinct, feel that a New Year is a sort of personality, a shape, we are at this time staring at shadows and sharp rain; the vision, a few paces off, is grey smoke. Its voice proceeds from some unseen mouth. All day long there sounds the wrestling of the wind in the trees. Thus comes our fabled Infant.

The question is not whether the quality of composition is good or bad (we tend towards the former); simply that the tune has been lost. The Englishness of Blunden's prose sounds improbably foreign. There are numerous memorable touches in *The Face of England*, including a description of youths bullying a cow at market; they were "almost ferret in eye, nose, mouth and action. Their white faces quivered. They became almost beside themselves because the cow, terrorized, took wrong turnings." A strange thing, Blunden muses, "that all our social education seems incapable of preventing degeneracy." He thinks that better diet might help. People are saying the same today.

Every now and then, the author inserts an oblique mention of his First World War experience, which marked him indelibly. "The definite seems past," he writes as spring approaches; "all that is permitted me as I stand bewildered in this carnival is to live over again the corresponding weeks and weather, which were so minutely charactered in me, of the 1916 war in the wild-grown fields of Festubert." We picked up *The Face of England*, complete with dust jacket, at one of our favorite London bookshops, Any Amount of Books in Charing Cross Road, for a pound.

October 5

The most famous poem of the twentieth century begins:

> First we had a couple of feelers down at Tom's place,
> There was old Tom, boiled to the eyes, blind

(Don't you remember that time after a dance, Top hats and all. . . .)

At least, that's how it went in its early version. Following the intervention of Ezra Pound, the opening of *The Waste Land* picked up a rhythm: "April is the cruellest month, breeding / Lilacs out of the dead land," and so on.

This is one of the stories in Gary Dexter's book, *Why Not Catch-21?*, an examination of fifty literary works and their origins. It is easier to get going with *The Rape of the Lock* if you know beforehand that, in 1712, "the 7th Lord Petre committed a gallant little rape" by snipping a lock of hair at a card party "from the head of a young beauty, Arabella Fermor." The Fermors and the Petres stopped talking. Mr. Dexter tells us that Alexander Pope's account of the affair—in which Arabella is cast as "Belinda" and Lord Petre as "the Baron"—was intended to reconcile the families.

The title of Dexter's book refers to Joseph Heller's arithmetic. Conceived as Catch-18, his novel sank to Catch-11, caught up a bit by becoming Catch-14, before making the decisive leap to Catch-22. A theory advanced for the derivation of *Waiting for Godot* is that Samuel Beckett saw the 1936 film of Balzac's play, *Le Faiseur*, in which creditors wait anxiously for the stock-market trader Godeau to arrive with their money. An English-language version was made in 1949 (the year *Godot* was being written), starring Buster Keaton, whom Beckett admired. The last line of Balzac's play is "Let's go and see Godeau." The last line of Beckett's *Godot* is "Yes, let's go."

A good Dexter story concerns Edward Albee and Leonard Woolf. After seeing Albee's famous play, featuring the name of his late wife, Woolf wrote to the playwright about a short story by Virginia called "Lappin and Lapinova," in which a husband and wife indulge in a fantasy existence at home (like Albee's George and Martha). He, Lappin, is a rabbit, and she, Lapinova, a hare. As Dexter puts it, the game "is dealt a cruel *coup de grace* by the husband, standing behind his wife with his hands on her neck"—just as George does with Martha at the crucial moment in Albee's play. Virginia Woolf wrote:

> "Oh, Ernest, Ernest!" she cried, starting up in her chair. "It's Lapinova. . . . She's gone. I've lost her!" . . .
>
> "Yes," he said at length. . . . "Caught in a trap, killed."
>
> So that was the end of the marriage.

Albee claimed that he had never read the story.

November 9

The reader about to embark on *War and Peace* is advised to pause before selecting a suitable translation. Until recently, the standard choice was between Louise and Aylmer Maude's 1923 rendition and the 1957 version by Rosemary Edmonds. Lately, however, two new versions have appeared in succession: the first, in 2005, by Anthony S. Briggs; and now the much-heralded translation by Richard Pevear and Larissa Volokhonsky, who have already produced a bestselling *Anna Karenina.*

Briggs gave us an ordinary bloke's *War and Peace,* dispensing with the French (Tolstoy's story is rich in French conversation) and making the lower-rank soldiers speak in a typical-Tommy, dropped-aitch cockney: "One shows up, so I grabs 'im. He starts yellin' 'is 'ead off," etc. The soldier Denisov, with a minor speech impediment, was given to saying things like, "We don't get them by tomowwow they'll gwab the lot fwom under our noses." Then there is Kutuzov's cursing. Briggs put into the refined General's mouth at the battle of Krasnoye the words, "They asked for it, the fucking bastards," where previous translators had followed Tolstoy and opted for dashes.

The unprepared reader comparing Pevear and Volokhonsky (P&V) with Briggs might think they are reading a different book altogether. On the French question, P&V do not just retain the famous opening, "Eh bien, mon prince, Gênes et Lucques ne sont plus que des apanages," but allow Anna Pavlovna to carry on for pages, with English translation in the form of footnotes. Briggs's Dad's Army types wouldn't be understood by P&V's soldiers, who speak in standard English: "One of them came along. I grabbed him like this. He started jabbering." Denisov's speech impediment is suggested by a Russian guttural "gh": "If we don't take it tomoghrrow, they'll snatch it fghrom under our noses."

In the vexed matter of General Kutuzov's swearing, P&V stick close to the original. Tolstoy has the General say, "M . . . ee . . . v g", an old-fashioned curse which (we are told) refers to the mothers of the unfortunates in question, and for which "fucking bastards" is a poor substitute. P&V leave it as "It's their own doing, f . . . th . . . in the f . . ." which is vague (like the Russian) and leaves the unspeakable properly unspoken.

War and Peace is often thought by unfamiliars to be a "heavy" book. On the contrary, it skips along. However, P&V's *War and Peace* is heavy in another sense: it weighs 3¼ lbs. For that reason, among others, we are sticking with the excellent Rosemary Edmonds, available in two volumes from Penguin Classics.

In advance of Remembrance Sunday, we find ourselves wondering how the poets of the First World War were received by the *TLS*. The war was just two months old when a reviewer felt moved to commend "the finest poem which the war has so far produced." It was "Thou Careless Awake!" by Robert Bridges, the Poet Laureate. The occasion was the publication of *Poems of the Great War*, consisting of work written since the outbreak:

> Thy mirth lay aside
> Thy cavil and play:
> The foe is upon thee.
> And grave is the day.

The general tone of the collection was of patriotism and duty. Within a year, the first discrete volumes of war poetry had appeared and the mood had darkened. *Battle* by W. W. Gibson "speaks for the perplexed soldier under orders," according to the *TLS* reviewer (October 14, 1915), "and, doing so, illustrates the other side of the medal." It is possible that Gibson's short, plain-speaking verses mark the birth of the modern protest poem. Battle was "a monument to the wantonness of it all . . . the disregard alike of promise and performance." Our reviewer quoted "Hill-Born":

> I sometimes wonder if it's really true
> I ever knew
> Another life
> Than this unending strife
> With unseen enemies in lowland mud
> And wonder if my blood
> Thrilled ever to the tune
> Of clean winds blowing through an April noon.

By the time of Siegfried Sassoon's first reports, the notion that young men should put aside mirth and "Die gladly for thee" (Bridges) was tarnished. "What Mr Sassoon has felt to be the most sordid and horrible experiences in the world he makes us feel to be so in a measure which no other poet of the war has achieved"—so wrote our reviewer of *The Old Huntsman and Other Poems* in 1917. Several stanzas are quoted, which we dare not repeat, for fear of the litigious Sassoon estate which habitually guns down innocent commentators. But disappointment is modified by the discovery that the anonymous reviewer of *The Old Huntsman* was that *TLS* stalwart, Virginia Woolf. Issued when the war had a year and a half to run, her praise applies equally to Sassoon's poetry today:

> As these jaunty matter-of-fact statements succeed each other such loathing, such hatred accumulates behind them that we say to ourselves "Yes, this is going on; and we are sitting here watching it", with a new shock of surprise.

December 7

Like others, when abroad, we enjoy paddling in the shallows of foreign languages, blithely dipping into our phrasebook to ask a Cycladean goatherd for directions to the Parthenon, or to argue with an Italian policeman about the price of fish. We have, however, yet to discover the magic phrasebook that will unscramble the language of academic theory. Try making this comprehensible:

> Displacing queerness as an identity or modality that is visibly, audibly, legibly, or tangibly evident—the seemingly queer body in a "cultural freeze-frame" of sorts—assemblages allow us to attune to movements, intensities, emotions, energies, affectivities, and textures as they inhabit events, spaciality, and corporealities.

That is one sentence from *Terrorist Assemblages: Homonationalism in Queer Times*, by Jasbir K. Puar. It may be a characteristic of people who speak in a private language that, once they get going, there is no stopping them, even though no one can understand. Here goes Ms. Puar again: "This ontogenetic dimension that is 'prior' but not 'pre' claims its priorness not through temporality but through its ontological status as that which produces fields of emergence; the prior and the emergence are nevertheless 'contemporaneous.'"

Occasionally, in this 335-page semantic riot, the reader stumbles on a word or two from other languages, including English. Before one can detect the sense, however, the sentence spins off on its own course. Have another try. You think you know what a turban is? Here is Ms. Puar's view:

> The turban is thus always in the state of becoming, the becoming of a turbaned body, the turban becoming part of the body. In all its multiple singularities it has become a perverse fetish object—a point of fixation—a kind of centripetal

force, a strange attractor through which the density of anxiety accrues and accumulates.

Jasbir K. Puar is Associate Professor of Women's and Gender Studies at Rutgers. If you hear a strange dialect being spoken on campus, you'll know who it is. We would suggest asking her for details of the proper phrasebook. But how to phrase the question? *Terrorist Assemblages* is published by—who else?—Duke University Press.

A DISLOCATION OCCURS in the reader's mind on witnessing a writer largely associated with the nineteenth century bumping into things more common to the twentieth. Robert Louis Stevenson first spoke on the telephone in California in 1880, in a hotel that would look good in a Wild West film. In 1898, George Gissing and H. G. Wells darted missives back and forth from Rome to Surrey, with a speed that matches Federal Express. Recently, we reported Thomas Hardy's admiration for early American high-rises.

Henry James also had a giddy experience of the skyscraper, as revealed in *Henry James's Waistcoat*, the recently discovered cache of letters sent to a neighbor in Sussex. In 1910, James visited New York, where he stayed at the Hotel Belmont, on the corner of Park Avenue and Forty-second Street. "I write this from the 12th storey of my hotel," he told Mrs. Francis Ford with bemusement, "& there are many more above." The letter was written on hotel notepaper. James scribbled a postscript: "This colossal pile isn't so hideous as the picture, partly because it isn't detached but colossally surrounded." The Belmont was demolished in 1930.

Like RLS, James enjoyed chatting on the phone. The first fictional occurrence of the request, "May I use your telephone?", is surely in RLS's novel *The Wrecker* (1892). What are the earliest literary mentions of the motor car, television, and other newfangled machines?

December 14

The Literature of Newfanglement, contd. Last week, we discussed RLS on the telephone and Henry James in a high-rise, and wondered about early literary records of other obnoxious contraptions. John Fuller, author of *W. H. Auden: A Commentary*, passes on a sentence from that curious mixture of poetry and prose, *The Orators*: "My first memories of my Uncle were like images cast on the screen of a television set, maternally induced." This is from 1932, Mr. Fuller tells us, "published about three months before regular BBC transmissions, though Baird Television had been transmitting for a few years via the BBC." It is probably not a coincidence that, during the writing of *The Orators,* Auden was teaching at John Logie Baird's old school, Larchfield Academy in Helensburgh.

Peter Barlow, from nearby Dunoon, suggests that the "earliest book inspired by the motor car was *La 628-E8* by Octave Mirbeau (1907), an account of a tour in France and the Low Countries." *La 628-E8* (the title derives from the registration number) was published one year before *The Wind in the Willows,* in which motormaniac Mr. Toad drives pastoral road-users into the ditch. "The real way to travel," he exclaims, gleefully imagining "dust-clouds" rising behind, "as I speed on my reckless way!" Inching back in the literature of the internal-combustion engine, Jonty Driver nominates Kipling's story "They" (1904), as one of the first in which "the motor car plays an important part." So far no one has mentioned an even earlier celebration of the automobile: W. E. Henley's *A Song of Speed* (1903), a breathless paean to "This marvellous Mercedes, / This triumphing contrivance."

The TLS Reviewer's Handbook: an update. Visitors to the Basement Labyrinth, where teams of lexicographers toil, pass under a stone arch on which is carved the motto, "Abandon 'Hopefully', all ye who enter here." The naff usage—"Hopefully, it will snow on Christmas day"—is sometimes known as "the dislocated adverb." For example, the dedication to *Forever and Anon,* a collection of prose and poetry by "Anonymous," edited by Gerry Hanson, reads: "For Jill, who, happily, is anything but anonymous." Jill is probably happy not to be anonymous; it is equally probable that Mr. Hanson means "fortunately." A visit to the labyrinth (under escort) is being arranged.

Meanwhile, more memos have surfaced from the subterranean team.

We avoid:

"Let's be clear about this" (especially when the sense is clear, as it usually is when thus prefaced);

"So that's all right, then" (in cases where it isn't);

"So that's that sorted" (may be used in connection with DIY, not otherwise);

"But hey—," "I know, I know," "Surprise, surprise," "Whisper it," and similarly matey interjections.

We have previously cited Team *Handbook*'s memo: "We avoid: 'ironically', except in reference to metals." Edward Lovering writes with the following comment: "Since one would use 'metallically' for metals in general, I suppose you propose to use 'ironically' if the metal in question is iron. If so, 'ferrically' would be a more appropriate term." To which there is simply no reply.

December 21 & 27

Previous winners of the Nicholas Mosley Award for the year's most unappealing book title include *Pox Americana* by Elizabeth Fenn, *How To Shit in the Woods* by Kathleen Meyer, and *Old Filth* by Jane Gardam. A special citation was made to Raymond Sederman, author of the novel *Return to Manure.*

The shortlist for the 2008 Mosley Award has just been announced. The bookies' frontrunner is *Dirtbags* by Teresa McWhirter, published by Anvil of Vancouver. The cover photograph of a distressed girl clutching a beer bottle while squatting on the lavatory gives it an edge over *Random Deaths and*

Custard by Catrin Dafydd (Gomer Press). Quick to appreciate lack of appeal in every form, the judges took into consideration Ms. Dafydd's opening sentences: "It's not that I'm superstitious or nothing. It's just that magpies really do give me the shits." *Bog Child* by Siobhan Dowd is also shortlisted. It gains an advantage from being published by David Sickling Books. Volume II of the "literary memoirs" of John Metcalf, *Shut Up He Explained* (Biblioasis, Ontario), is in with a chance. Mr. Metcalf begins: "Friends have begged me not to entitle this book *Shut Up He Explained*. . . . Their responses astonish me." Whether that is enough to sway the judges in Mr. Metcalf's favor remains to be seen. The winner will receive a copy of *The Uses of Slime Mould* by Nicholas Mosley.

2008

January 4

The TLS Reviewer's Handbook: New Year update. As we emerge into 2008, hopes rise that the team of lexicographers toiling in the Basement Labyrinth will issue sufficient directives to permit preliminary consultation on future production of Volume I, Part One, Section A, of the *Handbook*. Meanwhile, another memo has surfaced from below:

> We avoid: Idle talk about a subject of which the talker is evidently ignorant.

The reference for this typically sensible piece of advice reads, "*Guardian*, Dec 18; Carey, Professor John; subject: lit crit." On making a beeline for the stacks, we found, already laid out for perusal by an invisible hand—such are the mysteries of Labyrinth life—a copy of the *Guardian*'s *Education* supplement of the date in question. It was open at an article on the function of literary criticism, and its future. Some remarks in an interview with Professor Carey had been highlighted. They included the following: "If we can get away from the wilful obscurantism of a few academics talking to each other in the pages of *The Times Literary Supplement* it can only be a good thing." The journalist interviewing Professor Carey observed: "He laughs."

Professor Carey has been writing book reviews for the *Sunday Times* for a quarter of a century. Readily we admit that ignorance disqualifies us from making polite remarks about his contributions; by the same token, it prevents us being impolite. Were we to say, on being asked about the value of Sunday supplement criticism, "If we can get away from the wilful obscurantism of John Carey talking to himself in the pages of the *Sunday Times* it can only be a good thing," you might "laugh," while feeling it was a low blow on our part to have thus provoked your mirth. We would be indulging in "idle talk about a subject" of which we are plainly ignorant.

Fairness is to be our guide in this New Year, and so we invite Professor Carey to put forth examples of "the wilful obscurantism of academics talking to each other" in the pages of the *TLS*. Half a dozen from the past six months will be enough for us to concede the point.

The Literature of Newfanglement, contd. In NB, December 7, we wrote that the first occurrence in fiction of the polite request, "May I use your telephone?" is to be found in *The Wrecker* by R. L. Stevenson and Lloyd Osbourne (1892). Peter Rowland writes from East London, to say that one year earlier, in *Hôtel d'Angleterre and Other Stories,* Lanoe Falconer (aka Mary Hawker) has the "tall and beautiful blonde" Belinda Gray entering the dining room of a Mediterranean hotel and announcing that she has been "busy ever since I got up, telephoning all over the place for two south rooms."

Thirteen years before that, in the octet of Gilbert and Sullivan's *HMS Pinafore,* the Boatswain, Dick Deadeye, and Cousin Hebe sang: "He'll hear no tone / Of the maiden he loves so well! / No telephone / Communicates with his cell!" This was in 1878, according to David Hawkins of New York, "two years after the telephone was invented."

What was the first mention in literature of the railway? James Connelly from Hingham, Mass, reminds us of Clifford Pyncheon in *The House of the Seven Gables* (1851) by Nathaniel Hawthorne: "These railroads—could but the whistle be made musical, and the rumble and the jar got rid of—are positively the greatest blessing that the ages have wrought out for us. They give us wings; they annihilate the toil and dust of pilgrimage; they spiritualize travel!" Few feel that way about the railways now; but then few reading this have faced "the toil and dust of pilgrimage" when trying to get about.

January 18

The salient aspect of Sir Brian McMaster's government-sponsored review, *Supporting Excellence in the Arts,* published last week, is his belief that "excellence" can be cultivated, and that it is worthwhile to do so. "Excellence in culture occurs when an experience affects and changes an individual," Sir Brian writes, with no logic whatever. Matthew Arnold has been invoked—"the best that has been thought and said"—and the Secretary of State for Culture, Media, and Sport, James Purnell, says in his foreword to the report that "the time has come to reclaim the word 'excellence' from its historic, elitist undertones." An alien visitor might have the impression that British artists are throwing off the chains of socialist-realist tyranny.

It is difficult to know when "excellence" acquired its historic, elitist undertones, or how undertones differ from overtones, but safe to say that Arts Council England, which answers to Mr. Purnell's department, has encouraged the process. The culture secretary's use of the fashionable "reclaim" concept gives even this novel meritocratic gesture a politically correct tinge. The failure to recognize that excellence (good) is inseparable from elitism (bad) has been at the heart of the diversity-driven grief of the past decade.

Simple observation shows that the art produced by the greatest artists is inherently democratic; or—to reclaim a few terms which politicians would understand—great art is always inclusive; all "excellent" culture, from Homer to Hemingway, Plato to Picasso, Shakespeare to Chopin, Dante to Dylan, is popular culture. Art has never been more accessible to more people; you simply choose whether to accept the "cultural offer" (another of Sir Brian's terms) or not. It is the imposition of a culture in which "music" is widely supposed to mean pop, and television "drama" to mean soap, that is tyrannous. It is too much to hope that Sir Brian's review will shake from their somnolence those who choose to live an art-free life; but it might help to reclaim the concept of taste for others, who know not only what they like, but why.

February 8

How senior politicians find the time to write, while shouldering the burdens of office, is a mystery to us all. Take Gordon Brown, for example. Since September 2006, he has published three books, two of them since becoming Prime Minister: *Courage: Eight Portraits*; *Britain's Everyday Heroes*; and *Moving Britain Forward: Speeches*. These are added to his existing bibliography, which includes biographies of the socialist MPs James Maxton and Keir Hardie.

Mr. Brown has also contributed to other people's books. Readers of the *TLS* of January 18 may recall the review of several studies of the great economist Adam Smith, one of which, *Adam Smith, Radical and Egalitarian* by Iain McLean, came with a foreword "written specially" by the Prime Minister. Our reviewer, Richard Bourke, quoted a sentence from the introduction: "Coming from Kirkcaldy as Adam Smith did, I have come to understand that his *Wealth of Nations* was underpinned by his *Theory of Moral Sentiments*." Mr. Bourke pondered this, and wondered "how exactly has coming from Kirkcaldy enabled the Prime Minister to arrive at his understanding?" Mr. Brown's introduction then indulged in some fine feeling about Adam Smith's civic virtue and "neighbourliness," which left Mr. Bourke, a senior lecturer in history at the University of London, unimpressed.

This curious claim to intuitive geographical sympathy rang a bell. In December 2005, Mr. Brown delivered the Hugo Young memorial lecture at Chatham House, London, in which he said:

"Coming from Kirkcaldy as Adam Smith did, I have come to understand that his *Wealth of Nations* was underpinned by his *Theory of Moral Sentiments.*"

The Prime Minister has now written an introduction to the first British edition of *The Roads to Modernity* by Gertrude Himmelfarb, which tackles "such thinkers as Adam Smith, David Hume and Edmund Burke." First Brown tells us that "the British Enlightenment" was "not just the province of the privileged," but was, in New Labour style, "accessible to all." He then writes: "Coming from Kirkcaldy as Adam Smith did, I have come to understand that his *Wealth of Nations* was underpinned by his *Theory of Moral Sentiments.*" There follows some fine feeling about civic virtue and "neighbourliness." Having two arms and two legs, as George Santayana did, we have come to understand that those who do not remember their own waffle are condemned to repeat it.

February 22

Reading obituaries of the French chansonnier Henri Salvador, who has died in his ninety-first year, we were struck by the literary quality of his collaborators. One obituarist noted that "a meeting with André Maurois led to Salvador setting a verse that the famous novelist gave him, 'Les Oiseaux et les raves.'" In the 1950s, Salvador teamed up with the novelist Boris Vian, a friend of Jean-Paul Sartre and a regular contributor to his journal *Les Temps Modernes.* Vian wrote in all about 500 songs, which were taken up by many singers, including Juliette Gréco (the gentle "Musique Mécanique"). Other novelists wrote songs for Gréco, then known as "la chanteuse existentialiste": Françoise Sagan ("Sans vous aimer"), Raymond Queneau ("Si tu t'imagines") and allegedly Sartre himself (his lyrics no longer exist). Gréco also recorded songs by the poet Jacques Prévert, as did many others. Georges Brassens, who composed most of his own chansons, collaborated with the novelist Louis Aragon to produce "Il n'y a pas d'amour heureux."

A striking thing about this inventory is that it has no equivalent in English or American popular music. Our Freelance neighbor Hugo Williams wrote recently about contemporary poets, himself included, teaming up with rock-and-roll musicians, but as for a classic songbook of the 1950s and 60s, in which Kingsley Amis might have penned the words for a finger-snapping number by Alma Cogan, or Helen Shapiro belted out some lyrics by Anthony Powell . . . it appears not to exist.

February 29

Our suggestion that while Jean-Paul Sartre had allegedly written songs for Juliette Gréco, "his lyrics no longer exist," has created a flurry of protest from the nation's Grécophiles. One of the first recordings by *la chanteuse existentialiste*, we are reminded, was "La rue des Blancs-Manteaux," featuring words by Sartre and music by Joseph Kosma:

> Dans la rue des Blancs-Manteaux
> Le bourreau s'est levé tôt
> C'est qu'il avait du boulot
> Faut qu'il coupe des Généraux

(Briefly: the executioner rises early to do the job of cutting off the generals' heads.) Sartre certainly wrote it, and Gréco sang it, but the song originally featured in the play *Huis Clos* (1944), where it is given to the character Inès. We were referring to songs that Sartre "wrote for Gréco," which are said to have disappeared.

As for the English-language songbook we hope to establish, involving songs by leading novelists sung by golden-age pop singers, we are still searching. Christopher Hawtree tells us that "Graham Greene always hoped the lyrics in his novels would be set," but that no one did so. He mentions a poem by John Hollander, "An Old-Fashioned Song," which was appropriated by the group The Eagles. It may be good, it may be bad, but it's not what we had in mind.

April 25

What is the wisest thing ever said? Not "It is impossible to live without poetry," the view of Pyotr Kapitsa, Nobel laureate in Physics (1978), since millions of people prove it to be possible every day. Certainly not "You can have it all!", as Rosalyn Yalow (Medicine, 1977) believes. A wise person would consider it unwise to try. These remarks and 998 others are contained in *Nobel Wisdom: The 1000 wisest things ever said*, edited by David Pratt. Mr. Pratt has ploughed through the wisdom of the 768 people who have won Nobel Prizes. Some of the wisest things ever said turn out to be plain daft. A few of the chosen sayings were probably not even said, such as the enquiry made of W. B. Yeats by J. J. Thomson (Physics, 1906): "Been writing much poetry lately, Mr Keats?", but most are from written sources.

An interesting feature of a collection of what are essentially one-liners is how people tend to speak in character. When Ernest Hemingway says, "There is no friend as loyal as a book," you know he might have said the same about a dog, a good pencil, a shotgun, or a bottle of Champagne. Toilers in the trade probably won't think V. S. Naipaul wise for saying, "People who call themselves publishers are no better than people who sell books off a barrow," but nor will they be surprised. T. S. Eliot's advice, "Genuine poetry can communicate before it is understood," could have been directed specifically at readers of his own work. Like the poetry in question, the remark is at once gnomic and clear. The wisest thing that can be said of Pablo Neruda's utterance, "In the house of poetry nothing endures that is not written with blood to be heard with blood," is that Spanish is kinder to fancy rhetoric than English.

It is tough luck on Jean-Paul Sartre to be branded a Nobel laureate, since he refused the prize in 1964. He is quoted in *Nobel Wisdom* as saying, "Any anti-communist is a dog." Sartre said many silly things, some on the theme of communism, but this one didn't sound right. Checking the references, we discovered that the remark did not derive from a written source, nor was it ever recorded from Sartre's speech. It comes from an interview in the *Paris Review*—not with Sartre but with Claude Simon. It is not Nobel wisdom, it is not wisdom, it is not Sartre; it is hearsay. Sartre made a genuinely wise remark about the Nobel Prize itself—"The writer must not allow himself to be transformed into an institution"—but it goes unmentioned. Poor Claude Simon, Nobel winner in 1985, is otherwise not quoted.

Mr. Pratt attributes to that unlikely laureate, Sinclair Lewis (1930), the wisdom, "A man takes a drink, a drink takes another, and the drink takes the man," which we reclaim for the wittier non-Nobelist, F. Scott Fitzgerald: "First you take a drink, then the drink takes a drink, then the drink takes you." You might prefer the wisdom of a medical man, Alexander Fleming: "A good gulp of hot whisky at bedtime—not very scientific but it helps." For the common cold, he meant, but it works as a general remedy even if you skip the "hot."

May 16

To celebrate the fortieth anniversary of the Man Booker Prize for Fiction, the Victoria and Albert Museum is mounting an exhibition which "tells the visual story of the prize over its forty years." The show will coincide with the announcement of the shortlist for the 2008 Booker Prize. Throughout June, the Institute of Contemporary Arts offers screenings and talks, entitled "Booker at the Movies." The Booker publicists tell us that it will be "a season featuring films from Booker Prize-winning books": namely, *Possession* by A. S. Byatt; *The Van* by Roddy Doyle; *A Month in the Country* by J. L. Carr; and *Atonement* by Ian McEwan.

Readers not preoccupied with generating relentless publicity related to the Booker Prize know that only one of the above novels won the Booker (*Possession*; the others made the shortlist). However, before you have time to check your facts, there is the

"Best of the Booker" to announce—for the second time. Salman Rushdie's novel *Midnight's Children* won the first, in 1993; it is shortlisted again on this occasion, alongside *The Ghost Road* by Pat Barker, *Oscar and Lucinda* by Peter Carey, *Disgrace* by J. M. Coetzee, *The Conservationist* by Nadine Gordimer, and *The Siege of Krishnapur* by J. G. Farrell.

Is that enough Booker prizes for you? Not at all—don't forget the Man Booker International Prize, the Man Asian Prize, the Russian Booker. An article in the latest issue of the *Bookseller* reads: "Children's 'Booker' mooted," while in the same issue another headline announces "'Terrible cock-up' by Booker," referring to the fact that the winner of the 2008 award will be announced on the eve of the opening of the Frankfurt Book Fair. Don't believe it—the only cock-up would be failing to provoke another mention of the Booker Prize.

Our own contribution to the fortieth anniversary celebrations, sponsored by Man Group plc, is to remind you that Booker is "a leading global provider of alternative investment products and solutions for private and institutional investors worldwide, designed to deliver absolute returns with low correlation to equity and bond market benchmarks." As a second contribution, we propose another article in the *Bookseller*, under the headline: "The more Booker there is, the less bookish you get."

June 6

One thing got better in the Soviet Union under Communism: the humor. In the days just after the Revolution, they used to laugh at jokes like this:

> An old peasant woman is visiting Moscow Zoo, when she sets eyes on a camel for the first time. "Oh my God," she says, "look at what the Bolsheviks have done to that horse."

As things got progressively worse, however the jokes—*anekdoty*—became better. Ben Lewis has written "a history of communism told through Communist jokes," under the suitably ridiculous title *Hammer & Tickle*. Many of the jokes were about people being sent to prison camps for telling jokes:

> A judge is sitting in his courtroom, convulsed with laughter. "What's so funny?" asks the clerk. "I just heard the funniest joke of my life." The clerk asks him to repeat it. "I can't. I just sentenced someone to five years' hard labour for doing that."

A transferable joke concerns the completion of great feats of engineering. For example:

> The right bank of the White Sea was dug by those who told anti-communist jokes. And the left? By those who listened.

Another favorite topic was food shortages and the queues that formed outside shops.

> "The problem of queues will be solved when we reach full Communism."
>
> "How come?"
>
> "There will be nothing left to queue up for."

Jewish jokes are particularly popular among Jews. "How does a clever Russian Jew talk to a stupid Russian Jew? By telephone from New York." Yet another sort derives from the difficulties of publishing, and the resort to samizdat:

> A woman brings a good edition of *War and Peace* to a typist. "Why do you want me to copy this? You can buy it in the shops." "I know, but I want my children to read it."

The Khrushchev era was a good one for jokes—"Is it possible to wrap an elephant in a newspaper? Yes, if it contains a speech by Khrushchev"—and by then the worst of the joke terror was over. Mr. Lewis reports that in the spring of 1953, when the death of Stalin was reported, a man called Toth was gossiping among friends about how cold the weather was. "Never mind," said Toth, "it will be warm in Hell because Stalin is already there, and wherever he is things are always hot." One of his listeners betrayed him to the police, according to Mr. Lewis, "but all he got was a warning."

June 20

Writing in the *Guardian Review* last month, the novelist Hilary Mantel recalled her life in Botswana in 1978. The country had one road, no television, and little in the way of a free press. Ms. Mantel "subscribed to the *TLS*, which came late after many overland adventures." The investment might appear sensible, but Ms. Mantel found it "hardly a publication to get you excited." For what seemed to her "like months" during that year, the letters columns "were dominated by a fraught, increasingly savage set of exchanges about Gray's *Elegy*." The correspondence "centred on the line 'And drowsy tinklings lull the distant folds', which—some lamented—Gray wouldn't have written if he had been less ignorant about sheep farming."

Unlike Ms. Mantel, we find the idea of an exchange on eighteenth-century sheep farming a diverting prospect. When we rummaged the *TLS* index for 1978 in search of Thomas Gray, however, we drew a blank. Nor is there any reference to the poet or his *Elegy* in 1979. We did find a well-informed piece about the manuscript of the poem in the issue of May 27, 1977, but there is not a word in it about sheep farming, and not a single savage reader wrote in response.

Now there has landed on our desk something to get Ms. Mantel properly excited: *Elegy in a Country Churchyard: Latin Translations*, a collection of forty-five versions of Gray's poem, starting in 1762, eleven years after its original publication, concluding with that of Donald Gibson, one of the book's editors, made in 2001.

The opening lines of the *Elegy* are among the best-known in English poetry:

> The curfew tolls the knell of parting day,
>   The lowing herd winds slowly o'er the lea,

The ploughman homeward plods his weary way,
And leaves the world to darkness and to me.

Robert Langrishe's version, made in 1775, takes an enjoyably straightforward approach:

Vespertina notat finem campana diei,
Pigra armenta boant, tarde tenduntque per agros,
Passibus erga domum lassis se vertit arator,
Et totas terras tenebrisque mihique relinquit.

As for the line mysteriously engraved in Ms. Mantel's memory—"And drowsy tinklings lull the distant folds"—Langrishe offers "Tinnitus ad somnum pecudes ducitque soporans," which even she might think neat and to the point.

For music, as well as meaning, Langrishe's rendering of the famous opening beats many others. John Wright (1786) gives us the tongue-twisting "Triste dat occidui signum campana diei," while William Woty (1789) offers just as much of a mouthful, with "Decessum graviter pulsat Campana diei." Henry Latham's 1864 attempt seems positively discordant: "Jam campana diem morituram plangit." Latham's rendering of the drowsy tinklings—"aut qua / Languescente procul tinnit ovile sono"—likewise misses the soporific substance, his daring caesura notwithstanding.

Our hope is that these samplings will inspire Ms. Mantel to recall the real name of the journal in which she read the savage exchanges, and that she will pass it on. No one should have cause to think her one "in aeternum se ad muta oblivia tradens"—or to turn from Langrishe's eloquent rendering back to the original, "to dumb forgetfulness a prey."

July 25

In an item about the Oxford literary magazine *Areté* in July 2006, we mentioned Harold Pinter's dramatic sketch "Apart from That," the briefest yet in a series of shrinking dramas by the Nobel laureate. Two characters make repeated small talk on mobile telephones:

> Gene: How are you?
> Lake: Very well. And you? Are you well?
> Gene: I'm terribly well. How about you?
> Lake: Really well. I'm really well.

In recklessly speculative mood, we hazarded that the suppressed subject—the "that" of the title—might be the war in Iraq, to which Sir Harold is violently opposed. Everybody is "really well" here and in the US—apart from that.

This prompted an uncongenial letter from Pinter, complaining that it was "absurd" to read political meanings into "Apart from That." Despite its calling to mind the view, expressed by his mentor Beckett, that the playwright is the last person to ask about his own work, it seemed simpler to leave it there.

Now the Spring-Summer issue of *Areté* arrives, with a new Pinter poem. It begins,

> Do you fuck him
> And he fucks me too
>
> But did she fuck you
> But she fucked you too

and continues in that vein over the course of a page, ending "But you say she fucks you / And she fucks you too // But you say she loves him / She's as fucked as you // But I love him dearly / And she fucks me too," leading to the broader finale: "And fuck you too."

Don't ask what it's about. It's about what it says it's about.

August 22 & 29

Poetry babble is the quotation on the back of a nosegay of verse that purports to illuminate the contents, but in practice obscures them. For the Golden Age of poetry babble, you need to go back to 2004 and *Ring of Fire* by Lisa Jarnot. A typical stanza reads, "ding dong / dug dirt / ditch dib / chimp chore"—in which Alison Cobb found "both Dante's suffering and the Johnny Cash song's self burned away by passion".

Recently, poetry babble has been in recession. There are still occasional flashes—W. N. Herbert describing the Chinese poet Yang Lian as "like MacDiarmid meets Rilke with Samurai sword drawn," or Scott Thurston praising Robert Sheppard's achievement as "nothing short of a re-education of the reader's desire, constantly turning from the said to the saying." Mr. Herbert merits a D plus in poetry babble, Mr. Thurston possibly a C. Neither approaches the level of Peter Riley on the back of John Seed's *New and Collected Poems*: "The world is authentically before us, caught at its personal point of disclosure and held in a gerundive suspension which is always open, stripped to 'the dreamlessness of time.'" That's the real thing.

The nearest you get to quality babble nowadays is from the cover of *Hard Reds* by Brandi Homan, published by Shearsman Books. Ms. Homan is herself a publisher, specializing in "transsexual, transgender, genderqueer, and female identified individuals." Her work includes a sequence called "Red Dress"—"I put on that dress and that is all / I ever did for poetry"—and some riddles along the lines of "The best thing about a sandwich / is not the pickle next to it." Of these and other poems, Simone Muench says, "They sizzle and shimmy: from firebirds to firebreathers, legato to pizzicato, Harleys to Kawasakis, they dazzle with their light show. Homan's work is gunslinger-sure." Not bad; but, like most other things, poetry babble isn't what it used to be.

September 12

We're no dimmer than the next dimwit, generally speaking, but the effect of James Walton's "literary quiz book," *Sonnets, Bonnets & Bennetts* is to make us feel dimmer than thou. The book, which is derived from the genial Radio 4 programme *The Write*

Stuff, of which Mr. Walton is host, is divided into ten rounds. Here is a question from Round Ten: "Can you link the following literary people or things? *The Wasp Factory*; *The Lonely Passion of Judith Hearne*; Brother Cadfael; twice over, the birthplace of Walter de la Mare."

Think carefully. No luck? Okay, the link is England's 1966 football World Cup winning side. *The Wasp Factory* is a novel by Iain Banks, as in England's goalkeeper, Gordon Banks; *Judith Hearne* is by Brian Moore, as in the team's captain, Bobby; Cadfael is the crime-solving monk in the novels of Ellis Peters, as in Martin Peters; de la Mare was born in Charlton, as in Bobby and Jack. If you got all that before reading the answers, you have our deepest sympathies.

On the assumption that difficulty increases as the book progresses, we turned back to Round One, hopeful of scoring a dimness-alleviating point or two. Here are the first half-dozen, on which to test your knowledge:

1. Which literary character's first words to whom are: "How are you? You have been in Afghanistan, I perceive."
2. Which writer's first names were John Ronald Reuel?
3. Who was the first British writer to win the Nobel Prize?
4. Who was the first winner of the Whitbread First Novel Award?
5. What was the first Harry Potter novel?
6. What's the only book for children by Ian Fleming?

Without checking, we guess that No. 3 is Kipling, and No. 1 involves Sherlock Holmes, though we can't name the story. Nos. 2, 4, and 5: don't know. As for No 6, surely the answer is that all his books are for children.

2009

January 2

Volume 5 of *The Essays of Virginia Woolf* covers the period 1929 to 1932, years in which she wrote fewer pieces for the *TLS* than previously. Only five out of some fifty articles in the book, published this month, first appeared here.

There is, however, an odd story concerning an essay Woolf wrote on George Gissing. It was reprinted in 1932 as the introduction to an edition of his Italian travel book *By the Ionian Sea*. When the volume appeared, Gissing's son Alfred contacted the *TLS* to dissociate himself from Woolf's contribution. "I am in no way answerable for the errors it contains," he wrote (April 13, 1933). First, he cited a passage about a rejection of his father's novel *Workers in the Dawn*. Woolf had written: "So, dining off lentils, Gissing paid for the publication himself. It was then that he formed the habit of getting up at five in the morning." Not so, Alfred pointed out. His father had given up lentils the year before. Nor was it then that Gissing began rising at five in the morning, "but some time previously."

Woolf also claimed that Gissing had bought an edition of Gibbon at a second-hand bookstall, "and lugged the six volumes home one by one through the fog." Wrong again, said the son. Gissing took only two journeys to the bookstall, and made no mention of fog. It was furthermore incorrect to suggest, as

Woolf did, that he uttered "Patience, patience" to a friend "as he died." The request was made a full two days before expiry.

Replying, in the days of anonymity, as "Your reviewer," Woolf wrote: "I regret that I may have led the reader to suppose that Gissing dined off lentils a year after he had given up eating them; still got up at five when he had stopped getting up at five; took six journeys to a bookseller when in fact he took only two; referred to a fog when there was not a fog; and used the phrase 'as he died' instead of 'two days before he died.'" Alfred Gissing asked Woolf "not to make further use of her introduction." It is, however, in Volume 5 of *The Essays*.

January 16

Mick Imlah, who has died aged fifty-two, was a poet, poetry editor, and popular member of the *TLS* staff. His final year was mired in debilitating illness, which he bore with almost military fortitude, but it was also a time of literary triumph. In the spring of 2008, Faber issued Imlah's second full collection of poems, *The Lost Leader*. In October, it was awarded the Forward Prize for Best Collection, rewarding an effort that had occupied more than a decade.

Over the years, Mick wrote a substantial amount of literary criticism, most of it published in the *TLS*. The center of his enthusiasm gradually migrated from English literature of the nineteenth century—the voices of Browning and Tennyson are marked in his poetry—to Scotland, where he was raised (the family moved south when he was ten). Typically, he had a liking for writers who had dropped out of fashion: Barrie, Crockett, Buchan, and—a particular love—Scott.

His first contributions to the paper came in 1982. In the same year, he made his debut as a poet, with a pamphlet, *The Zoologist's Bath and Other Adventures*, published by the small Sycamore Press of Oxford. It was run by the poet and Oxford don John Fuller, who was perhaps the closest Mick had to a mentor. In this little sheaf of unnumbered pages, he tested the forms that continued to serve him: dramatic monologue and narrative, with literary allusion, personal opinion and gothic incident mixed in the same pot.

Mick was often to be seen at his desk after hours or at weekends, endlessly revising the verse that would make up *The Lost Leader.* He seldom spoke about work-in-progress; rather, he liked to talk about sport. He played rugby and cricket, passionately following the fortunes of Scotland in the former, and of England (dispassionately) in the latter. To say that we miss the sight of him curling his forelock while deep in a piece of writing or editing is to make an inadequate gesture in the direction of his absence.

January 23

To who it may concern: In a letter published in the *Guardian* (January 17), headed "Whom is doomed," the children's author Michael Rosen rebuked an earlier letter writer, Andrew Papworth, for insisting on the correct use of whom. The paper's error occurred in a headline, which read: "Signed, sealed, delivered: by who?" Mr. Papworth described this as poor usage. Mr. Rosen objected: "It could only have been called 'poor' if the usage had created difficulties for the reader. . . . Neither the *Guardian* nor anyone else should let themselves be cowed by the grammar bullies."

In Mr. Papworth's eyes, the headline-writer appeared to be a person in who he had no trust, to who he would not entrust his journalistic copy, for who he would not write nothing. Far be it from we to wag the fingers at Mr. Rosen. His point—no usage is "poor" that makes itself understood—is common enough, and neglects the advantages of style and elegance. If writers theirselves are heard declaring that it doesn't matter what you write, only that you are understood, then we feel impelled to put a fight up. Ask not who the bell tolls for, Mr. Rosen, it tolls for thou.

February 27

In January 2007, we asked, "Where are the poets of the war?" Five years of military engagement by Britain and America, first in Afghanistan and then Iraq, had produced few examples of contemporary war poetry. There was plenty of anti-war verse about, some of it worthy, but where was the poetry by serving soldiers, "that challenges our assumptions with doubt, pity, glory, even gore"?

Some good poems came to light. Our investigations inspired a two-page article in the *Guardian* ("In the Line of Fire," September 8, 2007). This in turn appears to have prompted the *Sunday Times Magazine* to seek out members of the armed forces who had written poetry, and to publish some of it in time for Armistice Sunday last year. Now there is to be an event at the Imperial War Museum, at which two of the poets, Lieutenant Colonel Jonathan Brown and Major David Hamilton, will take part.

One of Lieutenant Colonel Brown's poems describes "the boneyard at Taji," where "the detritus of war" is dumped:

> Lost and dangerous toys, skeletons
> Seeking their previous owners,
> Whose stories are embedded
> In the rusting metal,
> Just as metal was embedded
> In them.

Skeletons in search of their owners is a striking image, but the danger stalking war poetry is over-emotionalism, which bleeds into hackneyed language, the commonest cause of death in all poetry. Brown, who is still on active service in Iraq, does not avoid it: "the broken toys / Would weep if they could . . . / And they would speak of fragility / And honour, / And furious pain."

Hamilton's work is more conservative, but strong feeling in strict form is potentially explosive. His long poem, "Battalion Headquarters," is reminiscent of Sassoon:

Assuredly, impressive in his chair
The Colonel shuffles paper with disdain,
Resenting being tied to this campaign.
He knows his way round dogma, showing flair;
No question, this man's tactically aware.
Responsibly compelled, now and again
He shows seat-shiny trousers to the men
Stood rigid to attention on the square.
He loves his private soldiers and they know
He owns the right to mirror in their boots
And poke the youth who ties a twisted lace.
He sees himself as a father to recruits.

Hamilton has also written from the point of view of a dead American soldier. "I've kicked the butt of old Saddam, so wrap me in the flag," the poem begins, continuing, "Place fifty stars above my head, that I may see their light. / I'll take my seat amongst the dead on this eternal flight." Another, "Soldier with a Tattoo," plays with rhyme and refrain in a skillful pattern:

"Unscarred", his belly boasts in blue.
Be mindful! If not him then you
Could head the surgeon's inventory.
Ink mocks the shredded flesh anew.

We know of only one collection of current war poetry from an established publisher: *Here, Bullet* by Brian Turner (Carcanet), who will also be at the War Museum. David Hamilton's *Manic Verse* is available from Author House.

April 17

Wole Soyinka's play *Death and the King's Horseman*, originally staged in 1975, is currently in revival at the National Theatre in London. The action, set in Nigeria during the Second World War, calls for a large cast of both African and European characters. Instead of doing the obvious thing and employing a troupe of English actors in the roles of district officer Pilkings and other old-school colonials, the director, Rufus Norris, has asked black actors to play them, wearing white make-up. In the course of an interview on *Front Row* on BBC Radio 4, the playwright declared himself "not the slightest bit bothered" by the strategy, despite efforts by the interviewer to stir up controversy. "It's intriguing to see what effect it will have, both intellectual and emotional," Soyinka said. African actors in Nigeria and elsewhere are used to performing Shakespeare and Bernard Shaw, he continued. What's the problem?

In the same way, European actors slip into the character of Ancient Greeks, Romans and other exotics in English theatres every night, and no one thinks of objecting. Not even the adventurous Mr. Norris, however, would dare to use blacked-up Europeans to enact the African roles in Soyinka's play. Internal censorship prevents the very thought of it; actors would resile from it; in the unlikely event of a production reaching the stage, protests would be mounted in the street outside. The defence of Brechtian alienation would get you nowhere, even on *Front Row.*

We have long wondered why this should be the case. What assumptions lie behind it? For that matter, why is the role of Othello withheld from white actors? It is politely accepted that it would be the wrong thing to do. Perhaps a Shakespearean can tell us who the last leading Caucasian actor to take on the role was, and how the performance went down with audiences.

May 15

We love humanity as much as the next idealist, but the thought of being trapped in a room full of nodding comrades, affirming sentiments such as

> Socialism says it can
> Improve the lot of common man.
> Capitalism says: Oh no,
> I amass, you forgo

seems like a punishment not even Stalin or Mao could have devised. "Marx v Smith," the work of Martin Green ("Adam Smith's *Wealth of Nations,* / Capital's firm foundations"), appears in *Well Versed*, an anthology of poems from the *Morning Star*, "the only English-language socialist daily newspaper," and one of the few of any stripe to publish poetry regularly.

Not all the poems in *Well Versed* urge us to work towards "the achievement of an earthly paradise," as one of them does, or declare that "bosses despise / workers." There are verses by Dannie Abse and Alan Brownjohn, as well as by Antonio Machado and Robert Burns, but the majority are of the kind that bring readers news they already know, seeking to stir a sense of injustice that is surely never far from *Morning Star* hearts. When a poem ends with a picture of comrades, "tossing down vodka, clenching our fists / we drank to Trotsky, Lenin, Marx, mother's jokes," as "Left Rites" by Hylda Sims does, you ought to know what kind of company you are in. Roque Dalton's "Headaches" begins, "It is beautiful to be a Communist," and continues with a complaint that would make fellow believers and unbelievers alike reach for the vodka bottle, though for different reasons:

> Under capitalism our heads ache
> so they just take off our heads . . .

The veteran Labour politician Tony Benn has supplied a preface to *Well Versed*. "It is important to understand the close link between art and socialism," he writes,

> for both speak across the barriers of language and local culture. The poet expresses his or her perception of life in a form that speaks directly to us, whether in rhyme or not, because it escapes the rigid discipline of grammar that is so tightly imposed by our educational system, which can deny us an understanding of what the author really feels and wants to express freely.

This is harder to comprehend than most of the verses—poets speaking "across the barriers of language," speaking "directly," moreover, having evaded the repressive coils of grammar. We must put it down to Mr. Benn's own experience of the educational system, first at Westminster School and later at New College, Oxford.

WE ASKED WHO was "the last Caucasian actor to take the role of Othello." Learned readers have responded by citing everyone from Shakespeare's contemporary, Richard Burbage, to Orson Welles, who played Othello in 1952. According to Russell Jackson of the Department of Theatre Arts, University of Birmingham, other Othellos include Emil Jannings in a German silent film (1922) and Sergei Bondarchuk in the Russian cinema in 1955.

Very interesting, but we were reflecting on the past quarter-century or so, during which time, uniquely among Shakespearean roles, the part has been subject to racial profiling, in advance of the auditioning process. It would be far-fetched to insist that Macbeth be played by a Scot. Up till now, the most recent liberated Othello we have been able to find is Ben Kingsley, who played the Moor as an "accented Arab" at the RSC in 1985. Helaine Smith writes from New York to recommend a television version, directed by Jonathan Miller, with Anthony Hopkins as the Moor (1981). "It is an extraordinarily difficult role to get right," Ms. Smith says, "and therefore a shame when casting is determined by criteria other than dramatic ability."

Several readers have protested that Patrick Stewart took it on in a production at the Shakespeare Theatre, Washington, DC, in 1997–8, in which the rest of the cast was made up of black actors. A worthy concept, no doubt, but it comes into the category of novelty, and is not what we have in mind.

May 22

Julian Barnes is sixty-three, and his memory is getting faulty. He doesn't remember where he was when President Kennedy was shot, and cannot recall the Lord's Prayer. He doesn't know his height in metres, though he can still manage feet and inches. "I would say six foot one." When gauging the temperature, he thinks "more in Fahrenheit, though I can do Centigrade." He talks "out loud" to himself in the street. There is consolation in the thought that this doesn't look as bad as it used to, because of the people speaking on mobile phones (he has one but doesn't know his number).

The information comes from an interview first published in *The Oldie*, now reprinted in *Conversations with Julian Barnes*. For the benefit of overseas readers, we should explain that *The Oldie* is a journal devoted to making readers whose memories aren't what they were feel better about it. What were we just saying? Wasn't it just the other day that Julian Barnes was one of the country's finest young novelists?

> *Oldie:* Do you find that Old Age Pensioners are starting to look young to you?
>
> *Barnes:* If they looked young to me I wouldn't know they were OAPs, would I? I absolutely don't believe in saying absurd things like, "Sixty is the new forty". I think that's a sign of a person in deep denial.
>
> *Oldie:* What's wrong with deep denial?

Interested readers will learn from this collection of eighteen conversations that Barnes made so many last-minute revisions to his first novel, *Metroland*, that he received a bill from the publishers; that he contributes to the fanzine of Leicester City FC, "which is full of other nutters writing"; that he has been tempted to have cosmetic surgery—"I'm not going to tell you what, though"—and that when he received the penultimate volume of Flaubert's Correspondance for review, the commissioning editor put in a note saying, "Could we have a million words, please?"

You might think his memory is failing him here, but we can vouch for it, because the journal was the *TLS* and we saw the note. Apart from falling short of the word length, the piece was everything we hoped for. *Conversations with Julian Barnes* is edited by two Barnes nutters, Vanessa Guignery and Ryan Roberts.

OTHELLO FOR ALL, contd. Our quest to find the last non-racially profiled actor to take the role of Othello has advanced by a few years with the information that Michael Gambon played the Moor at the Stephen Joseph Theatre, Scarborough, in 1991, directed by Alan Ayckbourn. Until receiving this news, we had been misleading readers that "the last Caucasian" to play Othello was Ben Kingsley, who performed the role as an "accented Arab" at the RSC in 1985. However, we have been put right by the Shakespeare scholar Jonathan Bate. Not only is Gambon's performance more recent, but

> Kingsley was born with the name Krishna Pandit Bhanji. Even the dreaded Wikipedia knows that "Kingsley's father, an Ismaili Muslim, was born in Kenya of Indian Khoja Gujarati descent, as Kingsley's paternal grandfather was a spice trader who had moved from India to Zanzibar, where Kingsley's father lived until moving to England at the age of fourteen". How Caucasian is this?

Not very, Mr. Bate. In fact, we dislike the term Caucasian, and only used it in preference to "white," which we don't like either. At least a lot of uninformed people (ourselves included) now know more about Othello in black, white, and all shades in between. Which is how it ought to be.

August 21 & 28

We wondered, with what now seems unaccountable ignorance, "if there are writers still at work in Cornish, and for whom they write." Our introduction to the bountiful world of Cornish poetry began straight away, when the publishers Francis Boutle sent us "Geryow Kernewek" (Cornish Words) by Donald Rawe, part of which we printed last week. We now have the anthology in which it appears, *Nothing Broken: Recent Poetry in Cornish*, edited by Tim Saunders. It reveals a neighboring literary world of which we knew next to nothing.

Mr. Saunders's anthology contains work by poets born between 1917 and 1977. One bears the surname Chaudri; another is American, author of probably the first gay love poem in Cornish. We have always favored writers having real jobs, and these poets' professions range from revenue officer for Penzance (Mick Paynter) to clergyman (Michael Palmer) to chemical engineer (Jowann Richards). Several have alternative bardic names, such as Freckled One, Worm's Fool, Moor of Thorns, or, in the case of Ann Trevenen Jenkin, Bryallen—"Primrose." There are long poems (one by Mr. Saunders himself), love lyrics, political verse ("Kows Kernewek . . . Na wra omblegya"; "Speak in Cornish . . . No surrender") and many poems about the sea (mor), its sailors and creatures. Thanks to Neil Kennedy's "Brilli a Clappia," we know that the vivid Cornish word for mackerel is brilli.

As for a readership, Mr. Saunders tells us that the magazine *An Gannas* (The Message), "created a new public for Cornish poetry" in the 1980s. He believes there is a significant group "who think and feel in Cornish. The language articulates their personal experience, gives voice to national aspirations." The implication is that some Cornish speakers have separatist intentions, expressed by Cliff Stephens (b. 1961) in his poem about the death of Diana, Princess of Wales. In translation—what Stephens calls "the foreign tongue"—it begins: "England mourns the death of a princess, / And so we must mourn too, / For the ex-wife of an uncaring Duke / Who used Cornish money. . . ."

December 4

Authors regard it as a bonus when the painstaking effort of the past year is selected by a fellow writer in one of the books of the year round-ups. Some are chosen more than once, multiplying the pleasure. Hilary Mantel is in favor all over the place, as is Colm Tóibín, for his novel *Brooklyn*. Such fortunate souls open one journal after another to a round of festive applause.

Mantel and Tóibín are not the only ones. In last week's *New Statesman*, for example, the first book by Mary-Kay Wilmers got a salute from Andrew O'Hagan. "I always want to cheer when something truly singular comes along," Mr. O'Hagan wrote. "Such a book is *The Eitingons* by Mary-Kay Wilmers . . . a small masterpiece of indirection." In case any doubt remained, he added: "I loved it."

That would have delighted the author, and it must have pleased her again to see her book chosen in the *Guardian*. "My prose book of the year is without a doubt *The Eitingons* by Mary-Kay Wilmers," Andrew O'Hagan wrote. "A completely riveting story of the author's wider family. . . . Patience, irony, indirection." To dispel any lingering doubt, he added: "All the great prose virtues are here."

Could Christmas look any brighter? Yes, it could, for *The Eitingons* turned up yet again, this time in the *Daily Telegraph*. "It was many years in the making," Andrew O'Hagan wrote, "but *The Eitingons* by Mary-Kay Wilmers was worth the wait. Readers will feel rewarded from the first pages, when the author begins to tell the story of her family." No attentive reader could possibly remain in doubt, but just in case he added, "*The Eitingons* is the non-fiction book of the year."

Ms. Wilmers, who is the editor of the *London Review of Books*, must be thrilled. If she wishes to thank Mr. O'Hagan, she won't have far to look. He is a contributing editor of the *London Review of Books*.

December 11

Perambulatory Christmas Books, 3rd series. Last Friday afternoon, we took the Tube to North London and perambulated to Highgate Village, home of Fisher & Sperr, an Old Curiosity-type bookshop, complete with bottle-glass bay window, on Highgate High Street. The proprietor, admirably ancient, regarded us stonily and declined to respond to greetings. When asked if the business had been there long, he paused before yielding: "Yes." Could we look in the basement? Silence. A magnifying glass with a small lightbulb inside was produced for the purpose of scrutinizing accounts, and the prospect of further conversation disappeared.

In this series we seek a neglected work by an established author, from one of London's bountiful second-hand bookshops, for about £5. Heading undaunted for the basement, we found stacks of mainly hardback fiction, from which we selected *Young People* by William Cooper, author of the proto-Angry Young Man novel *Scenes from Provincial Life*. Published in 1958, *Young People* was unknown to us. Our researches suggest that it was never reissued. Upstairs, we handed it to our new friend, not omitting to add that it was unpriced. "Seven pounds," he announced, with barely a glance. After our banknote had been found not to be a forgery, we were breathing the healthy air of Highgate again.

Cooper died in 2002, aged eighty-two. He wrote twenty novels (four of them under his real name, H. S. Hoff), including *Disquiet and Peace* and *The Struggles of Albert Woods*, which inspired the room-at-the-top generation but are little read now. His topic was "ordinary life," the toil of the self-made man, sexual longing in the suburbs. The charms of *Young People* (Macmillan, 1958) are of the period sort. "And what about you?" one of the group of university friends at its center asks another. "You're in love with this girl of a higher social class than yourself, and where is it leading you? To no sexual life at all." A friend of ours who was acquainted with Cooper in the 1980s remembers his dislike of modernism, and his delighted comment on the work of Milan Kundera, then in fashion: "The clothes have no emperor!"

Our initial feeling was of having been overcharged for the unjacketed but otherwise good copy of *Young People*. It turns out to be quite rare, however, with only three listed on the internet bookselling collective Abebooks. One, with "minimal bumping to corners, cloth stained at rear board, sun damage to spine and edges, marks of ex lib"—blemishes not affecting our copy—is available from Yatton of Bristol at £140.

A CURIOUS DEGREE of excitement has attended the sale of Cormac McCarthy's Olivetti Lettera 32 manual typewriter. The novelist recalls having bought it second-hand in 1963 for $50. "I have typed on this typewriter every book I have written," said McCarthy, author of *All the Pretty Horses* and *The Road.* "Including drafts, I would put this at about five million words." The scuffed, blue-green machine was auctioned at Christie's, New York, and sold to a private collector for $254,500, ten times its estimate. The proceeds will benefit the Santa Fe Institute, an interdisciplinary research organization.

The most intriguing aspect of the affair was the comment of Glenn Horowitz, a book dealer who organized the auction. He was awestruck that "some of the most complex, almost otherworldly fiction of the postwar era was composed on such a simple, functional, frail-looking machine." It was, he said, "as if Mount Rushmore was carved with a Swiss Army knife." Who could fail to be similarly moved? It is as if the complete works of Shakespeare were written with a quill pen.

Whenever news breaks that a successful author uses a typewriter, non-literary types appear confused at the discovery that not all technical equipment requires frequent updating. Many writers compose in longhand, only later transferring the results by means of a keyboard, whether belonging to a computer or a typewriter. One who clings to the latter is the *TLS*'s Freelance correspondent Hugo Williams, whose immediately recognizable hand-corrected typescripts are welcomed here each fortnight. We asked the recalcitrant Mr. Williams for an interview.

Q. Why do you use a manual?
A. Simpler.

Q. How many do you have?

A. Five.

Q. Which is the best?

A. Adler Gabriele 25.

Q. How much have you typed on it?

A. Every book I've ever written—about fifteen, including three prose books.

Q. Why don't you update your equipment?

A. There's never time between assignments to learn a new method. That's why the only people who still have typewriters are writers. Everybody else has time.

Q. Do you ever feel you are carving Mount Rushmore with a Swiss Army knife?

A. Not in his sense of the phrase. Life is like that, but not typing.

INTERLUDE

Poor J.C.

"What sort of column do you write?" The question was asked often, usually by people unlikely to read the *TLS*. I didn't know how to reply, and still don't. "A weekly look at literary life" has just the blandness I hoped to avoid. Above all, perhaps, I was eager from the start to avoid any resemblance to a gossip column, and disliked hearing it described that way. I rarely attended literary lunches and went to few book launch parties for working purposes; when present at one or the other, or chatting to literary acquaintances encountered in the street, I never thought of myself as "a chiel amang ye taking notes," in Robert Burns's phrase. "I've got a good story for your column" is a well-intentioned offering but it was seldom indulged, however amusing the tale might sound when related in person. I had no interest in Ian McEwan's (briefly dramatic) family life or Salman Rushdie's arrogance, or Will Self's drug taking—only his alarmingly recondite vocabulary. I used to say that "Martin" and "Amis" were two words unlikely to be found in that order in the NB column. And stuck to the pledge, more or less, breaking it only for a trivializing biography of the writer, which gave much information about his *TLS* love life. There have to be exceptions.

In *The Letters of Thom Gunn*, published in 2021, I came across a note from Gunn to Clive Wilmer. "Do you know James Campbell? He is . . . also 'J.C.' who is unkind and sarcastic about a lot of people I don't like and a few I do in the *TLS* every week." That was written in September 1998, by which time J.C. had been in residence for only eighteen months, and was still finding his voice. One evening at the Poetry Society, while I was talking to Ian Hamilton—himself an old *TLS* hand, and on occasion a diarist (Edward Pygge) at his own little magazine, *the Review*—a woman poet interrupted us.

"Are you James Campbell?"

She stepped back, maintaining a hostile stare, as if devising a spell. "I just wanted to see what you look like."

"Who was that?" Hamilton asked when she had retreated. I told him something had recently appeared in NB in connection with remarks she had made about poetry and her domestic life that had struck me as ridiculous.

"It seemed she didn't like it."

A Hamiltonian snort.

"I'm not surprised!"

I can't recall now what had been said to make her so annoyed, but before issuing a retrospective apology I turn my mind to the words of Christopher Logue, who as well as rendering Homer into English in an original way was for many years a *Private Eye* employee. Sometimes he oversaw the entries into Pseuds Corner, the magazine's pillory of pretentiousness. When I mentioned that my name had recently appeared there (not in connection with NB), Logue shot back without hesitation: "You must have *deserved* it!" (Twice, in fact; the first time I did, the second less so.)

Hamilton himself once wrote a grumpy letter to the editor of the *TLS*, grousing about something that had appeared in the column (neither unkind nor satirical, but inaccurate on a point of detail). My predecessor David Sexton also complained, more severely, in a telephone call, about a piece in NB on the subject of a review that was published in the books pages of his new home, the *Evening Standard*. I thought the NB comment was fair—the editor, Ferdinand Mount, agreed—and argued, Logue-like, that former colleagues shouldn't expect special protection. Sexton was not to be assuaged and wrote a letter to the editor, beginning, "Poor J.C." I asked the letters editor, Adrian Tahourdin, to be sure to make that the heading if he intended to use the letter, which he did. After that, "Poor J.C." became Adrian's way of alerting me to the fact that another frowning letter on the subject of NB was about to appear on the page.

I mention it in the hope of showing that I wished to be open to the rough and tumble of the column-writing enterprise. Dish it out, if you feel that something pretentious or self-regarding "deserved it"; but be ready to take it in response. Give the reader the right of reply. Maybe someone else will answer in turn, even—who knows?—speaking up for Poor J.C. On we go. As time went on, J.C. persuaded himself—by dint of widening experience rather than by others' arguments—to be less unkind and to cut down the sarcasm.

NB
2010–2013

2010

February 5

The death of J. D. Salinger on January 27, aged ninety-one, overshadowed that of another American writer the day before, Louis Auchincloss. Separated by a year in age, they represented different worlds: one the voice of a new, loose-mouthed youth ("If you really want to hear about it, the first thing you'll probably want to know . . ."); the other a representative of New York's patrician elite ("Daddy was always spoken of as one of the best lawyers downtown, and was a rich man, too . . ."). Salinger's name was among the most famous in modern literature, though he wrote only one novel. Auchincloss produced more than thirty, as well as numerous nonfiction works. Many readers will claim their favorite Salinger works were his short stories; but no obituary led with the information that the author of *Nine Stories* had died.

The Catcher in the Rye was reviewed, briefly, in the *TLS* of September 7, 1951. Our reviewer, while put off by "the endless stream of blasphemy and obscenity," found Holden Caulfield "really very touching" and concluded, "One would like to hear more of what his parents and teachers have to say about him." This is itself touching, and prefigures the tendency of cultists to regard Holden as "real," with a life beyond the novel.

Auchincloss's British debut came two months earlier. The *TLS* review of *The Injustice Collectors*, a book of stories, perceptively noted the resemblance to Edith Wharton—Auchincloss's grandparents were friends of Wharton, and he later wrote an appreciation of her—and enjoyed the "unmerciful" tone in which the moneyed classes were described.

The complaint about obscenity and blasphemy in *The Catcher in the Rye* came as a surprise. We had a vague memory of once reading that the book's British publisher, Hamish Hamilton, had airbrushed some offending terms. The recollection was reinforced by a note on the back of the 1994 Penguin, which boasts "for the first time in Penguin books, the original American text." In short, we would have assumed that our reviewer in 1951 was reading a bowdlerized version—which upset him none the less.

Placing this newly released "original American text" beside the Hamilton edition, we set ourselves the task of earmarking the changes. But where were they? In the first paragraph of the book as originally published by Hamilton, "all that *David Copperfield* kind of crap" is there, as is "serious as hell," "shoot the old bull," "sonuvabitch," "very sexy bastard," and "goddam." A continued search revealed no excisions, leaving us in the dark as to Penguin's claim to be reproducing "for the first time" the uncut text. We won't call you a Salinger cultist if you can supply a list of alterations.

A footnote. Having heard a rumor that Salinger was a reader of the *TLS*, we asked our subscriptions department to check the list, and received the following reply: "We do have a subscriber with the name J. D. Salinger who lives in Cornish, New Hampshire. I'm assuming it is the same J. D. Salinger." He most recently renewed in October 2009.

February 12

J. D. Salinger and *The Catcher in the Rye*, contd. Last week, we raised the issue of the allegedly censored UK edition of Salinger's novel, published in 1951. Reports say that obscenities and blasphemies had to be removed to avoid prosecution, and that American speech was altered to suit English ears. Our hasty comparison of the American and British editions failed to reveal any discrepancies.

Hopes were raised by a letter in the *Guardian* of February 3. It came from Tim Bates, a former editor at Penguin Classics, who was responsible for overseeing the reissue of Salinger's novel in 1993 in its original US form. "The existing text of *The Catcher in the Rye* had been heavily edited by Hamish Hamilton in the 1950s," Mr. Bates wrote; "profanities and swearing had been censored, and Caulfield's US colloquialisms had been anglicized." Penguin wished to correct the situation. Mr. Bates prepared a new UK edition, he told readers of the *Guardian*, which would reproduce "the unbowdlerized American text."

But not a single example of this bowdlerization did he give. Last week, we stated that Salinger's "hell," "old bull," "sexy bastard," and "goddam" had all been approved for a British audience in 1951. Further scrutiny of the two editions since then has revealed six instances of "Fuck you" in Chapter 25 of the US text, a message which angers Holden when he sees it written on a wall at his sister's school. In each instance, in the Hamish Hamilton version, it has been reduced to "—you."

That's all we've found. If Mr. Bates or anyone else can supply further instances of "profanities and swearing" being removed, colloquialisms being anglicized and Thomas Bowdler being asked to run riot throughout, we would be pleased to hear of it. Otherwise, the myth of the "heavily edited" UK edition should be laid to rest.

March 12

Perambulatory blues. Late last year, we visited Fisher & Sperr, the old curiosity bookshop on Highgate High Street, complete with bottle-glass bay window. Walking past last week, we found the shop locked, a curtain drawn across the window and a vase of flowers placed there. John Sperr, who had run Fisher & Sperr since 1947, died in February. According to a passer-by who saw us peering in, the shop is likely to remain closed.

Our perambulatory experience there (December 11, 2009) was out of the ordinary. Mr. Sperr declined to make small talk. On being asked a question, he continued to peer at invoices through a magnifying glass with an inbuilt lightbulb. When we went to pay for an unpriced book, he plucked a figure from the air, then scrutinized our banknote. We regretted that such an appetizing bookshop was so deprived of customers.

An offended reader wrote to say that "had you known that the bookseller was ninety-six, you might have made more allowances," and he is correct. Others wrote to tell of being refused requests to look at books in the back room, where the treasures were said to be. One had the experience of presenting a book at the till, only to have the price rubbed out and replaced with a higher one. As the obituarist in the *Camden New Journal* wrote: "Stories of his idiosyncrasies are legendary." You only miss them when they're gone.

March 19

We opened *Infinite Difference: Other Poetries by UK Women Poets* at the statement by the editor, Carrie Etter, that "this is an exciting time for women's Other poetries in the UK." Ms. Etter complains that "the cliquishness and vocal dominance of men at past poetry readings surely repelled some [women] from attempting to be part of such a collective," and she may be right. She cites "the still dismissive and gendered critical language often used to describe women's poetry."

We're all for doing away with that, but not so Frances Kruk, one of the poets here. She observes that "my position as a female body composing a text frequently seeps into what I write." It isn't charming, but it's certainly gendered. For Ms. Kruk, "the material body and its contents are both the nervous source and the intended result of these poems":

> read and do words they say lie
> shameful in unfashionable tomeyards

little zombie spines yapping silly
revolution silly say silly with mcstuffed mouth

Another contributor to *Infinite Difference* is Marianne Morris, who writes, "it depresses me when someone says, 'I don't get poetry', as if it were locked in a box." We agree. All you have to do is read it, right? We started to read Ms. Morris's poem "Turquoise." It begins like this:

not knowing anything or her name. Rich
susurration of words at soil's thumby reach
as he gluey gibbers, love is here . . .

If you get it, there's more. If not, there's Carlyle Reedy: "I have not pursued the way of language which speaks of poetics of today in a language." While you're trying to get that, you might figure out this: "Bring yr mind back from overpowerance, pinch / Hard if you think her heart has stopped, and rub / The smallest finger of the victim— / That little pinkie represents ether."

The effect of reading through the twenty-five poets in the anthology is that if you come across one that is prepared to meet shared human experience halfway, you catch yourself thinking you've got it.

April 2

We have been alerted by the Fiction editor of the *TLS* to a common thread running through three novels published in the past year: *Final Demands* by Frederic Raphael; *The Pregnant Widow* by Martin Amis; and *Afterlife,* a first novel by the poet Sean O'Brien. In *Final Demands,* the third part of the trilogy which began with *The Glittering Prizes,* Adam Morris is in conversation. Adam

> stood by the low table, which now had a vase of dahlias on it, and opened the latest *TLS,* at the letters page. . . . "Dear God, someone else complaining about how the Jews are ganging up on T. S. Eliot. . . ."

In Amis's novel, Keith, while still at university, had "written to the *Literary Supplement* earlier in the summer and asked to be given a book to review." The *Supplement,* later referred to as the *Lit Supp,* sends him an 800-page book, *Antinomianism in D. H. Lawrence* by one Marvin M. Meadowbrook. Keith has read "a third of *Sons and Lovers*" and the racier parts of *Lady Chatterley's Lover.* As a journalistic debut, it sounds unpromising, but Keith then lands a job at the *Lit Supp* in the mid-1970s—as did his creator.

O'Brien's novel features literary life of the same period. The narrator, a budding poet, sits down in the university library

> to examine the latest edition of the *TLS.* There it was, "Visitation" by Jane Jarmain, looking as if it belonged perfectly with other poems in that issue, which I remember—still—were by Fleur Adcock and Peter Porter. . . . Young poets would give a lot to get a poem in the *TLS.*

The citations came our way at the same time as a reader directed us to the correspondence of the New York poet James Schuyler (1923–91), who, it turns out, was a devoted *TLS* reader. Among many references to the paper is one in a letter to John Ashbery in 1964. Schuyler promised to "root out the snippets about you from the *TLS.* I know what a joy it is to see one's name in print, especially when it's a Stanley Morison font." Morison, of course, is the former editor of the *TLS,* who was responsible for designing Times Roman, in which the columns of this paper are set.

April 9

The *TLS* in modern literature, contd. Anthony Thwaite writes from Norfolk with a passage from *Foreign Affairs* (1984) by the American novelist Alison Lurie. "Among the topics discussed" at a dinner party in London, "are the Common Market, growing exotic bulbs indoors, the films and love life of Werner Fassbinder, the novels and love life of Edna O'Brien, the current mass murder case . . . the financial and staffing difficulties of the *TLS*, and hotels in Tortola and Crete."

Ms. Pip Savage from Belsize Park, London, directs us to Somerset Maugham's *Cakes and Ale* (1930), which features Edward Driffield, thought by many at the time to be Thomas Hardy in disguise:

> The cultured reader of these pages will remember the leading article in the Literary Supplement of *The Times* which appeared at the moment of Driffield's death. Taking the novels of Edward Driffield as his text, the author wrote what was very well described as a hymn to beauty.

Further instances are welcome. With chapter and verse, please.

April 16

When asking for occurrences of the *TLS* in literature, we did not anticipate so many citations from poetry. Jeffrey Aronson writes from Oxford with a reference from Oliver Reynolds's "Auden Hotel":

> "Well, she's more *TLS* than *LRB*:
> attractive, but formal. More tea?"

The late Vernon Scannell wrote a poem called "Aide-memoire," which might have cast him in disfavor if we had seen it earlier:

> Write that review for the *TLS*.
> I've read most of the book—well, more or less.

Katherine Duncan-Jones draws our attention to John Berryman's "Dream Song, 208," in which the poet's alter ego Henry checks the mail:

> A special number of the London *TLS* came
> and he studied the Asiatic & European
> brains of late, across the water . . .

Some of the contents "were spectacularly stupid," but Henry reflects that "Voznesensky was good on watermelons."

A quick search of the archive leads us to conclude that the number in question was "Sounding the Sixties—3" (September 30, 1965), which considered experimental literatures. Voznesensky's poem—"Moscow is milling with watermelons. / Everything breathes a boundless freedom" (translated from the Russian by Edwin Morgan)—appears on a page with others from Eastern Europe.

Mr. Aronson has also sent "The Deconstruction Co to Jeremy Reed" by Jeremy Reed, a poet known for his extravagant personal manner. A spokesman for the Deconstruction Co advises Mr. Reed to write "clean literature, / nothing controversial or near the truth":

> it's the best way to get reviewed,
> we hope you'll consider the *TLS*,
> and give up wearing mascara, lipstick . . .

Perhaps he did so.

April 16

The Figes affair

Readers who depend on Amazon for reviews of new books might have stumbled on one in response to *Molotov's Magic Lantern* by Rachel Polonsky. The Amazon reviewer did not like it at all, as these comments show:

> This is the sort of book that makes you wonder why it was ever published. . . . We learn very little about Molotov. Nor do we learn much about the real Russia . . . her travelogue is written from the viewpoint of her chauffeur-driven car . . . her writing is so dense and pretentious . . . that it is hard to follow.

The reviewer's chosen nickname is given as "Historian"; also as "orlando-birkbeck." He or she appears to be something of an authority on Russian subjects, having already posted notices of books on Stalin, Trotsky, and Robert Service's *Comrades* ("awful"). Orlando-birkbeck has also tackled *The Whisperers: Private life in Stalin's Russia* by Orlando Figes, Professor of History at Birkbeck College, London. With this, orlando-birkbeck was mightily pleased:

> A fascinating book. . . . Beautifully written . . . leaves the reader awed, humbled, yet uplifted . . . a gift to all of us. Orlando Figes visits their ordeals with enormous compassion, and he brings their history to life with his superb story-telling skills.

Some Amazon commenters are under the impression that Orlando Figes and orlando-birkbeck are one and the same. W. Cohen, for example, says of the harsh notice of *Molotov's Magic Lantern*: "This review is clearly by Orlando Figes, whose own book on Russia was famously roasted in the *TLS* by Polonsky." Another, H. Crawley, says: "read his own review of his own book, in which he extolls his very own 'story-telling skills'. . . . Hilarious!"

We find those suggestions implausible, and are confident that Professor Figes will tell us they are mistaken. *Molotov's Magic Lantern* will be reviewed in next week's paper.

April 23

The headlines have been blazing since the weekend: "It was the wife". . . . "Mystery is now history," etc. We are entitled to say that you read it here first. Last week, based on information supplied by the writer Rachel Polonsky, we reported on a series of reviews which had appeared on Amazon under the pen name "Historian." One of the notices was hostile to Ms. Polonsky's book, *Molotov's Magic Lantern* ("This is the sort of book that makes you wonder why it was ever published"); another was rude about Robert Service's *Comrades.* A third, however, was full of praise for *The Whisperers: Private life in Stalin's Russia* by Orlando Figes.

Some Amazon commenters concluded that the author of the reviews was Figes himself. Ms. Polonsky shared the suspicion. Staggering under the drubbing he had received from "Historian," Mr. Service was of the same view. The commenters treated the matter as a joke; Polonsky and Service did not. From our point of view, it was simply a story too good to pass over. Could Figes, one of the country's bestselling historians, be attacking fellow Russianists—comrades, indeed—from behind the protection of a mask? "We find those suggestions implausible," we wrote, purposefully cautious, "and are confident that Professor Figes will tell us they are mistaken." The *TLS* went to press.

Twenty-four hours later, journalists across Fleet Street received legal notices warning them off the Figes-Polonsky dispute. Such notices are common, though they usually refer to stars of the screen or sports field. It has unfortunately been the case for many years that Figes's standing as a historian is undermined by a reputation for rushing to law when feeling under attack. Readers might recall a previous quarrel with Polonsky, which began in the *TLS* (she questioned the lax use of sources in his book *Natasha's Dance*, 2002) and ended in legal proceedings. Now, David Price, Figes's lawyer, was threatening to sue anyone who connected him to the reviews written on Amazon by "Historian."

Our story was already in print and the paper was on the newsstands. Through the week, no other journal touched it. The *London Review of Books* reproduced our item on its blog; otherwise the web stood back in silence under Historian's repressive glower.

On Friday afternoon, we heard the inevitable knock on the door:

> I have advised my client that the *TLS* article is actionable. He wants a corrective publication and not to be out of pocket. For the record, I am confirming in writing that he denies having any involvement in the reviews. . . . I have advised my client that he is entitled to damages.

Our objection that we had stated that the claims were "implausible" was apparently not a defence. A judge would regard it as tongue-in-cheek.

As the world now knows, Figes has since acknowledged involvement in the machinations of Historian—not his own direct involvement, but that of his wife. On Friday night, just a few hours after advising our legal department that his client was entitled to damages, David Price issued a statement: "My client's wife wrote the reviews. My client has only just found out about this, this evening. Both he and his wife are taking steps to make the position clear." The story broke in the papers on Sunday morning. Mrs. Figes, Stephanie Palmer, is a Fellow of Girton College, Cambridge, and a barrister at the human rights specialists, Blackstone Chambers.

The *TLS* was not the only party to receive a lawyer's letter. Robert Service did, too. His week went something like this: on April 13 he circulated a letter to colleagues, including Geoffrey Hosking and Antony Beevor, in which he complained about Historian's comments. To Service, it was reminiscent of the system of *anonimki*, prevalent in the pre-glasnost Soviet Union. "Gorbachev banned *anonimki* from being used in the USSR as a way of tearing up someone's reputation. Now the grubby practice has sprouted up here." On April 15, Service received a personal email from Figes, who addressed him as "Bob," and claimed to be "very sad that you chose to start a campaign against me without asking me to comment first. . . . I cannot understand what I have done to you to deserve that. I hope that we can mend our relations."

The next day, the knock came to Service's door, preceding the letter from David Price. His email had been forwarded to newspapers, which were threatening to print the story. The fact that Service might claim not to have sent the email himself was of no importance. Mr. Price wrote: "Whether or not it was supplied directly by you, it was a foreseeable consequence of you sending the email [to the historians mentioned above]. In such circumstances, the originator, ie you, is liable for republications by the media (see for example McManus v Beckham [2002] EWCA Civ 939)." Mr. Price did not call him "Bob."

Rachel Polonsky is the heroine of the story. It was she who employed an expert in computer forensics, who established practically beyond doubt that "Historian" lived under the Figes family roof. As Ms. Polonsky put it to us, "a hoaxer would have had to set up an account pretending to be Orlando Figes in 2001 or earlier with a view to bringing the insane hoax to fruition in 2010."

Before the dramatic announcement—"My client's wife wrote the reviews"—Figes had contacted all the historians originally emailed by Service, denying involvement. "Virtually anybody could have written the Amazon reviews," he said, contradicting the expert's findings. "To those of you who have circulated Bob's email, I'd be grateful if you did the same for mine, in the interests of glasnost." In fact, the spirit of glasnost—openness, debate, fair comment—was precisely what Figes, through the offices of his lawyer, worked frantically to extinguish.

April 30

A fortnight is a long time in the literary world. On April 16, we were weighing the costs of having run an item about Orlando Figes and the anonymous Amazon reviews which certain people believed were his mischievous work. In our hands was an unwelcome letter from David Price, Mr. Figes's lawyer. His client was seeking our acceptance that he was not the author, and damages.

By Monday, the narrative had taken a twist: the comments about books by Rachel Polonsky and Robert Service were not the work of a hoaxer, as implied. "My client's wife wrote the reviews," said the abject Mr. Price. "My client has only just found out about this."

No doubt he believed his client this time. Stephanie Palmer, Mrs. Figes, is a barrister and Fellow of Girton College, Cambridge. Within a few days, however, the story had changed again. Mrs. Figes was not the author, after all. It was the original suspect, Figes himself. Shocked, anyone? Mr. Price probably was.

Figes hired the public relations firm Financial Dynamics to liaise with the press on his behalf. His actions—anonymous malice, lies, legal threats when his denials were questioned—were the result of a "deep depression," he claimed, brought about by immersion in Stalin's crimes while researching his book *The Whisperers.* One day, Figes is wielding "the sword of truth" (Jonathan Aitken's phrase, before his conviction for perjury), the next he is pointing a finger at his wife. Now it's all Stalin's fault.

Eventually, Figes will face his employers at Birkbeck College and the whodunnit which diverted the public for a couple of weeks will be closed. He has apologized for telling lies to Price, and said sorry to Service for sending him a woeful "Dear Bob" letter one day and setting Mr. Price on him the next. He has expressed regrets to Rachel Polonsky. As for the *TLS* . . . we must assume his apology is held up in the post.

It is worth noting that neither Service, in his email to fellow historians, nor our "tongue-in-cheek" report on April 16 went so far as to name Figes as the person who posted the reviews on Amazon under the pen name "Historian." Yet both Service and the *TLS* were threatened with the law. Something, or someone, is an ass.

May 14

French words in Scots. We sought clarification of a quirk of Scots English, namely that it is rich in French-derived words. A number of readers wrote to say, "Och, it's the Auld Alliance," as if that explained everything. More helpfully, Roy Love sent us some pages from *The Guid Scots Tongue* by David Murison, former editor of the *Scottish National Dictionary.* He states that it is "a common mistake to ascribe all this [French] vocabulary to . . . the Auld Alliance," which was "effective from about 1330 until the Reformation of 1560." Equally important, according to Murison, was "Norman French," brought to England by William the Conqueror, "from where it percolated northwards over the next hundred years." The trade resulting from the Auld Alliance only cemented on the Scottish tongue words which had faded from its Sassenach neighbor.

We hereby list some of the Franco-Scottish words we have collected so far. Others will be welcomed, so long as they are in more or less common use.

aumri	wardrobe (cf. armoire)
ashet	plate (cf. assiette)
bonny	good
bouls	(child's game of) marbles
cowp	capsize
douce	sweet
fashious	angry (cf. fâcheux / -euse)
gigot	lamb chop
pettycoat tails	shortbread (cf. petites gautelles)
pooch	pocket (cf. poche)
row	street (cf. rue)
serviette	napkin
scrivener	writer (cf. écrivain)

Every Scottish schoolchild knows the Edinburgh expression "Gardyloo!", which preceded the dumping of slops into the street from high tenement windows, short for "prenez garde à l'eau." They still say it, though they no longer (mostly) do it.

THE *TLS* IN LITERATURE, contd. Paul Birch from Somerset has alerted us to Graham Greene's short story "A Shocking Accident":

> Jerome's father had not been a very distinguished writer, but the time always seems to come, after an author's death, when somebody thinks it worth his while to write a letter to *The Times Literary Supplement* announcing the prepa-

> ration of a biography and asking to see any letters or documents. . . . Most of the biographies, of course, never appear.

This brought to mind a letter which appeared in the *TLS* of June 24, 1949:

> I have been commissioned to write a biography of Robert Louis Stevenson, and I should be very grateful if any of your readers who have unpublished letters of Stevenson's would allow me to inspect them.

The biography never appeared. The author of the letter was Graham Greene.

Peter Parker alerts us to Justine Picardie's novel *Daphne* (2008). The time is June 1959 and Daphne du Maurier is writing *The Infernal World of Branwell Brontë* (1960). She discovers that the Brontë scholar Winifred Gerin is at work on a similar book:

> Daphne threw down her copy of *The Times Literary Supplement* with such force that it skated off the polished table. . . . "Well, that's it," she said, though there was no one in the dining-room to hear her. "I'm done for now." The headline that caused her such distress still glared up at her from the floor. "Gerin Goes Head to Head with Du Maurier."

Mr. Parker asks whether the *TLS* in 1959, or ever, ran items about rival books under headlines like this? As Daphne herself might have said (or something of the sort): We wouldn't have thought so, Mr. Parker.

June 4

Lesser-used languages of the British Isles, contd. The number of different tongues spoken up and down the land keeps growing. Everybody knows about the varieties of Gaelic spoken in Wales, the Western Isles of Scotland and, presumably, in pockets of Northern Ireland. There is a rich literature in Scots, or

Lallans, dating from the fifteenth century. We have written about the revival of Cornish. The leading publisher in this area is Francis Boutle of London, which produces handsome anthologies catering for readerships which are small but enthusiastic. Here's a piquant paradox: in 2009, a UNESCO report declared the Manx language to be extinct; this month Boutle publishes a new anthology of Manx literature.

Manannan's Cloak: An Anthology of Manx Literature includes a brief section of work produced since 2000, the decade in which the language was pronounced dead. Since then, Manx has been introduced to schools by, among others, the editor of *Manannan's Cloak*, Robert Corteen Carswell, also a broadcaster in Manx. His former wife led a "Manx-language playgroup." Presumably they spoke it occasionally at home. Is it possible for a language that was alive in the Carswell household to be extinct?

We shouldn't be surprised that one recent Manx novel is about the living dead. An extract from *The Vampire Murders* by Brian Stowell (2005) appears in *Manannan's Cloak*, together with an extract from Agatha Christie's *Murder on the Orient Express*. Early on, Poirot meets the general:

> "Ta shiu er hauail shin, mon cher", dooyrt yn kionfenee dy toghtagh, as yn farveeal mooar bane echey craa myr v'eh loayrt. . . .
>
> (You have saved us, mon cher", said the general emotionally, his great white moustache quivering as he spoke. . . .)

Poirot replies: "But of course am I not mindful that you saved my life once upon a time?" Or, as they say in the Manx capital Douglas nowadays, "Agh dy jarroo nagh vel cooinaght aym dy ren shiu sauail yn vioys aym keayrt dy row?"

Last year, we asked: is there a single Manx speaker or reader who is also a reader of the *TLS*? A correspondent, Robin Moroney, writes to tell us that the local government "is putting Manx on more and more official products: driving licences, passports, road signs. I was surprised to see last year that even the destinations of buses are now written in Manx." Though a native of the Isle of Man, however, he doesn't speak it.

In his Freelance column last week, the book dealer James Fergusson drew attention, with due modesty, to his catalogue "of books and manuscripts that are by Scottish writers, or have something to do with Scotland." It has just landed on our desk: *Spicilegium Scoticum*. Inside, the prefatory matter offers mysterious information of a kind that appeals to members of the perambulatory brotherhood: "The codeword for this catalogue is 'QUENDALE'."

Among the items mentioned (though not offered for sale here) is the book-length poem *To Circumjack Cencrastus* by Hugh MacDiarmid. On publication in 1930, it received this review in the *Scots Observer*:

> Anti-English sentiment of the most virulent kind abounds, and along with it violent depreciations of British Imperialism . . . culminating in an inexcusable attack on the Royal Family. A pretentious pedantry is another large ingredient. The author revels in all manner of obscure allusions, unintelligible collocations of obsolete or abstruse words. . . . If [he] were concerned with commercial success or popular favour, he could not persist in so extraordinary a medium.

The reviewer was "Pteleon"—better known as Hugh MacDiarmid. Readers are invited to send in other instances of self-reviewing. Priority will be given to unfavorable notices. The well-known case of Anthony Burgess reviewing *Inside Mr. Enderby* by Joseph Kell (aka Anthony Burgess) for the *Yorkshire Post* is ineligible. The same goes for Orlando Figes.

June 18

Our series devoted to documenting dramatic occurrences of the *TLS* in literature has been formally concluded more than once. Some requests to reconsider, however, are too good to resist. Edward Mendelson, literary executor of the estate of W. H. Auden and the author of several books on the poet, asks if we are willing "to reopen this topic long enough to accept an unpublished poem by Auden, written probably in 1930?" It is one of several squibs sent by Auden to Christopher Isherwood. Any regret we feel at exposing Auden's dim view of our predecessors is overwhelmed by satisfaction at being the first to print it:

> You'd best tear up
> The *Times Lit Supp*
> For if you use its files
> As bumf, you'll get piles.

In more affirmative vein, Susan Brandt of Austin, Texas, has sent a passage from Ernest Hemingway's *Under Kilimanjaro*, a hunting memoir issued posthumously in 2005. Who would have marked Papa down as a *TLS* subscriber? On the other hand, why be surprised? Here he is on safari, catching up on back issues:

> At the mess tent Msembi, a member of our religion, asked me what I would like to drink. I did not feel like drinking after having talked about the religion and I told him, "Nothing." He was worried and asked me if I would like snuff. I said I would and when he brought it I put it under my armpit, as a prophet should, and started to read *The Times Literary Supplement*.

David Hawkins of New York believes that *Money in the Bank* by P. G. Wodehouse should not be ignored. Clarissa Cork is an aspiring novelist suffering from a familiar grievance:

> Her publisher's statement had told Mrs Cork that 206 splendid men and women had bought *A Woman in the Wilds*. . . .

> She had had to satisfy herself with the thought that the *Peebles Advertiser* considered the book bright and interesting and the more reserved verdict of *The Times Literary Supplement* that it contained 315 pages.

July 9

Our earliest "-ism" is nudism, to which we are all exposed at the moment of entering the world. For many, this is followed by baptism. Onanism is unlikely to be far away, as well as an acquaintance—brief, we hope—with pauperism, often abetted by idealism. Whether or not you are an adherent of gradualism, you will occasionally encounter heroism (your own, perhaps), egotism, favouritism, and eventually ageism. It'd be a cruel world if there weren't a little sensualism and lyricism along the way.

John Andrews, a writer on *The Economist,* has produced *Book of Isms: From Abolitionism to Zoroastrianism,* with 400 of the things. Many -isms describe a system of thought which people choose to believe in, and most have opposing -isms: capitalism / Marxism; sapphism / phallocentrism; monism / dualism; Bolshevism / Thatcherism. Other -isms refer to forms of behavior which their practitioners might disavow: hooliganism, racism, pessimism. After a while, you long for a little quietism.

In the interests of journalism, we searched Mr. Andrews's book for an -ism we had never heard of, or could not guess the origin of. Our optimism was well founded. There is oligopolism, for example, which, it helps to know, is "a rarely used term for the phenomenon of oligopoly." Catastrophism is the theory that changes in the earth's crust "are the result of cataclysmic events, rather than a gradual process of change" (cataclysm is not an -ism).

Most -isms refer to a particular way of seeing the world. Is there, we wondered, an -ism that obliges its followers to accept more than one point of view? Yes: prism.

July 23

Looking through the recently published volume of George Orwell's correspondence, *A Life in Letters,* we came across this letter to Cyril Connolly, from early 1938:

> I see from the *New Statesman & Nation* list that you have a book coming out sometime this spring. If you can manage to get a copy sent to me I'll review it for the *New English Weekly,* possibly also *Time & Tide.*

Right-thinking literary types today would consider it pretty poor that Orwell was offering to review his chum's book in two separate places. But what comes next is worse:

> I arranged for Warburg to send you a copy of my Spanish book [*Homage to Catalonia*] hoping you may be able to review it. You scratch my back, I'll scratch yours.

Such bargaining would be frowned on now. But how much contact between reviewer and reviewed is tolerated, and how do we in the UK differ from our transatlantic cousins?

A conscientious editor will ask whether the reviewer they have in mind for a book is close to the author. Is he or she mentioned in the index or thanked in the acknowledgments? Is sharing a publisher a disqualification? If in doubt, the editor can ask the putative reviewer: Do you know him/her? Literary London is an overcrowded sphere, like most such communities, but if the reviewer is confident that his or her judgment would not be affected by acquaintance, the commission can go ahead.

In the US, where standards of reporting in general are more rigorous, they do things differently. A prospective reviewer for the *New York Times Book Review* will be asked, as if by the way, "You guys don't hang out together, do you?" Given the importance attached to reviews in the *NYTBR* by the book trade overall, the caution is understandable. Last week, however, we read about situations which made us think that vetting had gone too far. At the *Boston Globe,* the books editor Nicola Lamy fretted over a review by Kate Tuttle of *America and the Pill* by Elaine Tyler May. The women are not friends or colleagues, but according to an article in *Media Matters in America*, Ms. Lamy found out after the review had run that "Tuttle's father had been noted in the acknowledgments of a previous May book." She pushed the panic button, confessed to her editor, and was duly cleared of negligence.

David L. Ulin of the *Los Angeles Times* related the case of the writer "who considered reviewing a book published by Knopf," but was found to have "recently had a novel rejected" by that firm. Ulin stepped in to prevent matters going further. "You have to rely on good faith," he told *Media Matters*. Elizabeth Taylor, literary editor at the *Chicago Tribune*, cited an author who first agreed to review a book, then canceled after the *Tribune* "gave his own book a negative review." She no longer commissions reviews from authors who have books published in the same season.

This seems to us excessive, but the transgressions contained in the Orwell volume continue. A page after his letter to Connolly, we find Orwell (April 18, 1938) thanking his "lifelong friend" Geoffrey Gorer for the "marvellous review. I kept pinching myself to make sure I was awake, but I shall also have to pinch myself if *Time & Tide* print it." Gorer had sent Orwell a copy of his review of *Homage to Catalonia* before sending it to *Time and Tide*. "I'm so glad you liked the book," Orwell concluded. He would be. Hanging out together is sometimes understandable. Sharing a publisher could be unavoidable. But sending your review to the author in advance of publication—that's strictly infra dig.

August 6

Encouraged by our series on self-reviewing (see above, June 4), a reader has directed us to a series that appeared in the *Listener*, journal of the BBC, in 1936, in which leading literary figures of the day were invited to write their own obituaries. Among those who participated in the grisly lark, under the heading "Auto-obituaries," were Rose Macaulay, Bertrand Russell, Edith Sitwell, and H. G. Wells.

Naturally, we are drawn to those who took a stern view of their own past efforts. "He occupied a tumbledown house on the edge of Regent's Park," Wells imagined his future obituarist writing (July 15, 1936), "and his bent, shabby, slovenly and latterly somewhat obese figure was frequently to be seen in the adjacent gardens . . . coughing and talking to himself. 'Someday', he would be heard to say, 'I shall write a book, a real book.'" A few of his works—*Outline of History, Anatomy of Frustration*—were "remarkable" but even those were "now forgotten."

The verdict on Rose Macaulay was no kinder (September 2). Fiction was "never perhaps her strongest suit, for she lacked sustained narrative power and creative imagination." In her final years, she renounced fiction, confining herself to travel books and monographs "on subjects in which she took an interest not shared by the majority. No one could—anyhow no one ever did—call her a great writer." Macaulay lived until 1958, and her best-known novel, *The Towers of Trebizond*, was written two years before her death. For an epitaph, her obituarist (i.e., Macaulay herself) suggested: "An old lady of no great talent, but who managed, on the whole, to put in a pretty good time."

The obituarist serving "the late Miss Edith Sitwell" had a higher opinion of the subject. "Her innovations were many," readers were told, but "never destructive . . . she never violated the laws that governed the old forms." It was wrong to say of Dame Edith, as "sloppy-minded critics" were apt to do, that she was "the poet of childhood." For a simple reason: "she disliked children."

Bertrand Russell's auto-obituary appeared in the August 12 issue of the *Listener*, made up to look as if it was printed in *The Times* of June 1, 1962 (Russell would in fact live until 1970). The philosopher was castigated for "dissipating" his energies in books on sex and education, which "concealed from careless readers the superficiality of the antiquated rationalism which he professed to the end." He was criticized for his pacifist behavior during the First World War, for which he was deprived of his Cambridge lectureship—"very properly"—and sent to prison.

Did any writer pen his or her own obituary without the playfulness instilled by the *Listener*?

October 1

Perambulatory Christmas Books, 4th series. Over the past few years, it has been our custom in the period leading up to Christmas to seek out each week "a neglected book by an established author, purchased from a second-hand bookshop for £5 or less." This time we've changed the rules, intending to look at the presence of foreign writers in London. In each instance, we will relate the visit to a poem or piece of prose. In certain cases this will lead back to the cobwebbed nooks of bookshops.

In May 1904, Guillaume Apollinaire crossed the Channel in pursuit of Annie Playden, an English governess. He stayed with an Albanian friend in the London suburb of Chingford, near Epping Forest. He had first come to woo Annie the previous autumn, staying at 3 Oakley Crescent, off the City Road, not far from the Angel, Islington. The house still stands, though it is known only to devoted Apollinaireans. Last week, we went for the first time to look at the even more obscure Chingford residence, 36 Garfield Road. Would it be a worthwhile monument to the first great avant-garde poet of the twentieth century? According to Leonard Davis of the Chingford Historical Society, a plaque was proposed in 1980 but never materialized.

We regret to say it is just as well. Garfield Road—named after the American president James Garfield, who was assassinated in 1881—is a dismal assortment of small ugly houses, with a huge vacant lot in the center. We found No. 36, modernized out of recognition, with blinds drawn, preventing a peep into Apollinaire's living room. The expedition's sole moment of cheer occurred as we returned to the railway station, where we spotted an oblong Victorian pillar box built into a wall. It was surely used by Apollinaire to post letters to Annie.

His vain courting became the subject of one of his most famous poems, “La Chanson du mal-aimé” (Song of the poorly loved):

> One foggy night in London town
> A hoodlum who resembled so
> My love came marching up to me—
> The look he threw me caused my eyes
> To drop and made me blush with shame.

Annie is also memorialized, kaleidoscopically, in “L’Emigrant de Landor Road.” Of Chingford, however, the poet left nothing, except his unexpected pleasure in watching the golfers on the nearby links.

A single publication is dedicated to Apollinaire’s London adventure: *One Evening of Light Mist in London* by John Adlard, little more than a pamphlet, published by Tragara Press in an edition of 145. We located a copy at the Fortune Green Bookshop, a mysterious operation with a shopfront in West Hampstead, yet which is closed to the public. On request, the proprietor kindly agreed to open up for us, and one evening of light mist in London we made our way there to take possession of the book: mint, numbered 26, a steal at £10.

October 15

Perambulatory Christmas Books, 4th series. We have charted this year’s perambulations to cross paths with those of (mostly) foreign writers in London. The hope is to conjure a charm against the so-called festive fare of many mainstream publishers (*Can’t Be Arsed*, etc.), and perhaps to tunnel into a lost domain. If the charm works, the domain will turn into a bookshop.

In the present instance, the domain is that of the author of *The Lost Domain*, or *The Wanderer*, or *The Lost Estate*—varied attempts at an alternative title for *Le Grand Meaulnes* (1912) by Alain-Fournier, who died in the First World War aged twenty-eight. The only book he published in his lifetime, it has had a deep influence on succeeding generations. John Fowles modeled *The Magus* on *Le Grand Meaulnes.*

In the summer of 1905, the eighteen-year-old Fournier worked as a postal clerk at Sanderson's wallpaper factory near Turnham Green, West London. He lodged with a family called Nightingale at 5 Brandenburg Road, and his letters home are full of complaints about the food. Lunch was a cutlet with a couple of potatoes; high tea at six consisted of bread and marmalade. Craving wine to quicken his palate, he was offered lemonade. "I'm in danger of dying of hunger here," he told his parents, who sent him a dictionary with breadrolls enclosed. Fournier replied: "The rolls, which tasted of dictionary, which weren't cooked and which were no longer fresh, were delicious."

The striking white Sanderson Building, designed by C. F. A. Voysey in 1902–03, still stands in Heathfield Terrace, opposite an older red-brick factory. Brandenburg Road is now Burlington Road. No 5 is in a healthy state, but a plaque to commemorate the Frenchman's stay would further enhance it.

Our old Penguin Modern Classic (sensibly called *Le Grand Meaulnes*) fell out of a rucksack years ago; so we sought one in Skoob Books, the pleasingly overcrowded bookshop close to the *TLS* offices. While searching, we stumbled on the posthumously published *Colombe Blanchet.* This tattered paperback, published by Cherche-Midi (Paris, 1990), presents 143 pages of narrative and 100 of apparatus. Would it contain a hint of the author's English life? Here is a rough rendering of a scene in which some youngsters nervously approach a room in an old house, half expecting to find it occupied by a woman "en déshabillé":

> —There's only a Bible, said Voyle with disappointment.
>
> —And an English Bible, said one of the others. Have you kept on your English since the Ecole Normale?

—My mother was English. I speak it well, said Autissier, a bit put out.

Nothing suggests that Mme Autissier starved her son, so it would be reckless to think she derives from Mrs. Nightingale of Chiswick, whose parsimony has entered literary history. *Colombe Blanchet* is an interesting document for which Skoob charged us £3.

The above item prompted a letter from the BBC broadcaster, Annie Nightingale. It was published in the issue of November 12, 2010.

"Alain-Fournier"

Sir, —I was very interested to read J. C.'s item on the author of *Le Grand Meaulnes,* Alain-Fournier. As J. C. pointed out, the young Henri Fournier lodged with a family named Nightingale in Chiswick in the summer of 1905. These Nightingales, John James and his wife Annie, were my grandparents. Young Henri wrote many letters home describing his experiences in London, and how he was not much enamoured of English grub. Too polite to mention his hunger to his hosts, with whom he got on very well, he sent home for food parcels. J. C. remarks that Mrs Nightingale enters literary history for her parsimony.

Thanks a bunch! I think that's a bit unfair. I don't remember a lot about my grandparents, as they died when I was very young, but their generosity and hospitality were widely known. Alain-Fournier was nineteen at the time of his visit. Teenage boys are always ravenously hungry. Mrs Nightingale then had two young daughters but no experience of the voracious appetite of boys (my father and his brother were born later). Alain-Fournier wrote about my grandfather, "he is exceedingly kind to everybody". J. J. Nightingale was supervising Fournier's work at Sanderson's wallpaper factory, and asked the young man if he would like to lodge with the family. The deal was that Fournier would pay less for his stay, in return for giving my grandfather French lessons. This arrangement seemed to work very well except for the hunger factor.

My grandfather became very close to Henri, who in turn was inspired by him, describing him as "extraordinarily well built, young looking, fair skinned and handsome . . . a poet of the home . . . a poet of the countryside. All Frenchmen seem trivial and petty to me, compared with the blond giant with an eagle's head . . . fair haired and athletic." Such a glowing description almost makes me wonder whether J. J. Nightingale might have partly inspired the character of Augustin in *Le Grand Meaulnes*. It is generally accepted that it was the annual company party and ball to which the Nightingale family invited Henri that provided the raw material for the wedding celebration at the heart of *Le Grand Meaulnes*. An early rave, maybe.

ANNIE NIGHTINGALE, BBC,
Portland Place, London W1.

November 19

Our team of lexicographers continues to labor in the Basement Labyrinth, tortoising towards a new edition of *The TLS Reviewer's Handbook*. Meanwhile, the hares at the *Guardian* have gone and completed theirs. *Guardian Style* by David Marsh and Amelia Hodsdon provides quick solutions to simple problems ("Gambia, the; not Gambia"), as well as grammatical advice, gamely illustrated by howlers from their own papers (the guide also covers the *Observer*). "Avoid constructions such as 'having died, they buried him' . . . or 'Dreary, repetitive and well past the sell-by date, I switched off the new series.'" Known as "danglers," these are among the commonest errors in written English.

Another is the rogue apostrophe. "Don't let anyone tell you that apostrophes don't matter," warns the guide. Has anyone tried to? The poet Michael Rosen wrote to the *Guardian* not long ago to say that "whom" doesn't matter (1), but thankfully *Guardian Style* disagrees. However, there is no guidance on "thankfully," which you have just seen wrongly used (2), nor on the placing of "however" at the start of a sentence (3), nor on the adverb coming before the verb (4). We dispatched a messenger to the Basement Labyrinth with a carefully worded plea. In due course, a reply was forthcoming:

1. To who it may concern: Go figger.
2. Use happily or fortunately. Do not confuse with fortuitously, as football commentators do.
3. *However* is more elegant in a suitable place after the first word, but don't feel obliged.
4. Adverb before verb is permissible if it sounds clumsy placed after.

Guardian Style has an entry under "metaphor" but none under "mixed metaphor." For a riotous illustration of the latter, turn to last Sunday's *Observer*, in which Kirsty Wark, presenter of the BBC arts programme *Newsnight Review*, gave her books of the year:

> Jonathan Franzen's *Freedom* is something of a slow burn where *The Corrections* was like a punch to the stomach, but each is a cat's cradle of family life, and if the measure of a good book is its afterburn, *Freedom* is a great book.

You can't legislate for that. You can, however, avoid printing on the cover of a book dedicated to good prose a horribly crippled ("offensive and outdated"—*Guardian Style*) sentence such as this, by Jon Snow: "If you love words, work with them, or simply toy with them—for me *Guardian Style* is in a class of its own." Or this, by Alex James (whom he?): "The best steer to the freshest style." Or even this, by Iain Banks: "Sense and sensibleness from the newspaper defiantly not owned by rightwing billionaires." Until the new *TLS Reviewer's Handbook* is steered to freshness, *Guardian Style* will fill a gap that is literally crying out to be plugged.

December 17

Racial segregation in Fleet Street: a special report. A friend of ours has received an "Equal Opportunities Monitoring Form" from "Head of Diversity" at the *Guardian*. "We are undertaking a review of our commissioning process and wish to begin capturing census data concerning all of our freelance contributors," Yasir Mirza writes. The exercise is "part of monitoring and evaluating more effectively the diversity of our contributor base." Where once you were judged by your writing, you must now expect genetics to be taken into account.

The first question is about gender: "Male. Female. Prefer not to answer." Our friend ticked the last. There follows a racial interrogation, familiar to citizens of the old South Africa but new to writers for the *Guardian* of King's Place, London. We once overheard a woman, foreign-accented but presumably long resident, trying to explain to a hospital functionary that she was "British." They weren't having it. Like the erstwhile government in Pretoria, like the *Guardian*, they needed to know if she was "Black African," "Black Caribbean," "Dual Asian & White," "Dual Black Caribbean & White," or one of a dozen other categories. She said her race was "human." Madam, you are unreconstructed. "Your ethnic category is a mixture of culture, religion, skin colour, language and the origins of yourself and your family. It is not the same as nationality," says Yasir Mirza. The *Guardian* demands to know about your health as well. "Do you consider yourself to have a disability?" A paralysing aversion to racial categorization doesn't count.

December 24 & 31

Flaubert's *Dictionnaire des idées reçues* is a work better known by repute than in bookish shape. Most modern editions of *Bouvard et Pécuchet* contain selections but the *Dictionnaire* appeared as a discrete volume only in 1913. English versions have styled it *Dictionary of Platitudes, Dictionary of Accepted*

Ideas, Dictionary of Idiocy. A new edition, translated by Gregory Norminton, sticks to a literal rendering: *Dictionary of Received Ideas.*

One of the dictionary's amusing features is the pairing of nouns with specific adjectives. For example, "Wit—always preceded by 'sparkling.'" An assassin is "always cowardly," baldness "always premature," strength "herculean," congratulations "hearty." Champagne should not be drunk but "quaffed."

Our own *Dictionary of Received Phrases* is currently in preparation. In it, you will find, under Wit, "frequently preceded by 'mordant,'" a word seldom seen elsewhere. Another entry has "Scottish education—prized by those rarely in the North." This long-anticipated volume will contain the following entry under Laughed: "In literary criticism, frequently followed by 'out loud'" See also: "Single sitting: I read it in a. . . ." The editors of the *Dictionary of Received Phrases* have asked us to solicit further examples, in particular expressions "often seen in print but seldom heard in speech."

2011

January 14

We have been asked by the editorial board of the *Dictionary of Received Phrases*, now in preparation in the Basement Labyrinth, to thank those who have contributed. An example of an adjective which rarely appears in public without its companion noun is "mordant wit." Its cousin, "coruscating wit," is also a candidate for inclusion. Other expressions which dress up for print purposes are "unvarnished truth" (in speech, truth is usually content to appear plain) and "wry smile." Bedfellows are often strange, communities are close-knit, suburbs are leafy, guarantees cast-iron. While a thing is often hotly denied, it is seldom hotly rebutted, repudiated, or refuted. Why the d-word is hot and r-words are not, is a fiendishly difficult question to answer. Difficulty is frequently fiendish.

The editors of the *Dictionary of Received Phrases* recognize that Flaubert is not their only rival. They also face Myles na gCopaleen, whose "Catechism of Cliché" appeared in the *Irish Times* until his death in 1966. Hugo Brown of Co Wicklow has sent us some entries:

What is the only thing one can wax? Eloquent.
What does pandemonium do? It breaks loose.
If a thing is fraught, with what is it fraught? The gravest consequences.
When things are few, what also are they? Far between.

> In which hood is a person who expects money to fall out of the sky? Second child.

This is tough competition. Myles also asked, at the end of a column, "In what direction should I shut?" and supplied the answer: "Up." We will do the same for the moment.

Our popular quiz game "What Does It Mean?" returns with a citation from *The Novel as Event*, a study of nineteenth-century fiction by Mario Ortiz-Robles, published by University of Michigan Press. In his opening chapter, "What the Novel Does," Mr. Robles, who teaches English at the University of Wisconsin, Madison, writes that

> a performative model of subject formation cannot be thought apart from its implication in regulatory practices operating within discursive regimes that circumscribe the "materiality" of the subject through the citationality of norms.

In case you think we are pulling one cloudy pint from a barrel of otherwise good beer, try this, from a couple of pages further on:

> The foreclosure of the performative in the Victorian novel is thus the condition of possibility of its disciplined re-emergence as the illocutionary hallucination of the performative as a material event of subjectivity that emerges in a discursive nexus that can be generally named "impersonation."

The ability to write sentences impervious to sense deserves proper recognition. We hereby announce the establishment of the Mario Ortiz-Robles Prize for Incomprehensibility.

January 21

Lesser-used languages of Britain and Europe, contd. We asked if there was a contemporary Romany-speaking community in Britain, and if there were poets among it, but have yet to receive a British poem in the Gypsy tongue (Damien Le Bas and others have sent us verse with Romany flavoring). Thanks to the publishers Francis Boutle, however, we now know what it might look like when we do get it. They have just issued *News from the Other World: Poems in Romani* by Iliija Jovanović. Mr. Jovanović, who died recently, was born a Gypsy in Serbia, later served on Romany-affairs bodies, and received literary prizes in Austria. From the section called "Homeless" (Bi Thanesko), we offer some lines of the poem "Who am I?" ("Ko sem me?"). After asking himself if he's Romany, Serb, or Austrian ("Jekh Rom? / Jekh srbino? / Ilil mozda jekh austrijanco?"), the poet emerges with a conundrum:

Kaj tek so lijem
jekh ili aver
lendar te avav,
ikljel o trito andar mande.

The facing-page translation reads: "Whenever I think / that I'm one or the other, / soon the third / sticks out his head."

Boutle has sent us another book, *Old Ways, New Days*, by Rosie Smith, "who still lives a traditional Gypsy lifestyle," and Lindsey Marsh, her cousin. It has many photographs, dating back to the 1920s, and stories of life on the road in London and Kent. In respect of our search, we enjoyed the section "Romani Rokker," which gives "common Gypsy words and expressions." Here are a few: Ark: shut up; Besh: sit; Bori: big (or pregnant); Cams: money; Cushty: fine; Dinlo: stupid; Gavvers: police; Jel aki: get away; Jovell: women; Kenick: nongypsy; Loring: stealing; Luvney: easy girl; Mush: bloke; Needles: gypsies; Poov a gry: put a horse in the field; Rawnie: posh lady; Shiv: knife; Sooti: sleep; Vardo: wagon.

February 4

Communication with the editors of the *Dictionary of Received Phrases* is restricted to a code of short and long knocks on the pipes and ventilators of the heating system in the Basement Labyrinth. Submitting "wry smile," for example, we issued one short knock and two long. The editors' signal of approval is confidential. Here are the latest entries to the Dictionary, modeled on Flaubert's *Dictionnaire des idées reçues.* Not all have received the answering knock from the basement. Preference is shown to phrases that are often seen in print, but seldom heard in speech.

Barmaid	frequently buxom (obs.)
Crime	heinous
Din	infernal
Dinner	slap-up (when one is being treated)
Harvest	frequently bumper
Host	mine
Prophecy	self-fulfilling
Questions	often thorny
Swoop	fell; always one
Tones	dulcet
Wealth	frequently untold.

February 11

The sixth and final volume of *The Essays of Virginia Woolf* covers the years 1933 to 1941. Its subjects range from Walter Sickert to Walter Scott, offering in the latter case a glimpse of gaslit chandeliers blazing over the dinner table at Abbotsford in 1825. An appendix gives Woolf's "wireless broadcasts" and "reflections on a motor car" from the Sussex countryside.

The section that interested us most is "Additional Essays." It contains over forty reviews from the *TLS*, the majority from 1906–08, many of which appear to be reprinted for the first time. In a late diary entry (May 27, 1938), Woolf recorded the retirement of the long-standing editor of the *TLS*, Bruce Richmond, and remembered the pleasure of hearing Leonard call, "You're wanted by the Major Journal!" She would run "to the telephone to take my almost weekly orders. . . . I learned a lot of my craft writing for him: how to compress; how to enliven."

It paints a bright picture, which is dimmed slightly by Stuart N. Clarke, editor of the volume, who says of this apprentice work, "even the most practised reviewer would be hard put to strike sparks of inspiration from the series of trashy novels that Richmond saw fit to set before his tyro reviewer." In fact, Woolf was seldom uninspired. Launching a review of *Occasion's Forelock,* a romance by Violet Simpson set in the House of Commons, the twenty-four-year-old writes: "No one certainly ever took hold of occasion's forelock with greater energy and success than Eustace Gleig in *Occasion's Forelock.*" Most editors would think that sparky enough; a century on, it is an example of how to open a review with a lively sentence (tyros, take note). Likewise, the ending, which is a model of good-natured criticism: "The necessity of marrying the secretary to his chief's daughter brings this good-humoured and loosely constructed book to an end, and no one has any reason to complain."

We are unsure if Mr. Clarke considers *Abbots Verney* by "R. Macaulay" to be trash, but the *TLS* reviewer found it "interesting and indeed remarkable." When it came to a rebuke, she relied on her usual courtesy: "It is undoubtedly a very able and interesting piece of work, and the failures are of the kind that promise success." Was she being playful when she wrote (December 7, 1906), "The author would probably wish us to append a masculine name to the ambiguous initial"? R. Macaulay blossomed into Rose Macaulay.

Over the next few weeks, Woolf reviewed *Disciples* by Mary Crosbie ("always good reading . . . the author's next book will be wholly excellent"), the "admirable" *Memoirs of a Person of Quality*; M. P. Willcocks's *Wingless Victory* ("worth keeping on the shelves, even by the classics"); *The Call of the East* by Charlotte Lorrimer ("the pity is that it is so brief"); *Mam Linda* by Will N. Harben ("an excellent specimen of the American novel"); *The Longest Journey* by E. M. Forster and many other enjoyable books. If they were "trashy," she saw the best in them.

February 18

Rumor has it that the *Dictionary of Received Phrases* has grown so vast that multi-volume publication is the only option. We hear word of appendices devoted to apocrypha, "debatable" phrases, and an essay on method. Our duty is merely to speed suggestions to the Basement Labyrinth, hoping to hear the coded knock which signifies "Approved."

The *Dictionary* will show preference to phrases more common in print than in speech. Take the critics' favorite, "this exhaustive—and occasionally exhausting—account of," etc. (It has already been approved.) Ditto its ally, "despite, or perhaps because of . . .". The following familiars, set out in the manner of Flaubert's *Dictionnaire des idées reçues,* have been submitted but not yet approved:

Attention	frequently rapt
Bystander	usually innocent
Dudgeon	always high
Optimism	advisedly cautious
Reminder	salutary
Thud	often sickening.

From New York, the poet John Ashbery writes to ask, "are you considering French contributions for your palmarès?" Such an appendix is in preparation. Mr. Ashbery tells us that he "used to like pointing out to French friends that the word *allègrement* is used only in French newspapers, in the sentence, "Il porte allègrement ses 80 ans" (He wears his eighty years joyfully)." Mr. Ashbery adds: "Now that I'm an octogenarian myself, this proposition seems even more tenuous."

March 4

Lesser-used languages of the British Isles. David Porter of Clare College, Cambridge, brings news of "a handful of us still using Latin here at the University." He has a colleague who is "a decent neo-Latin poet." Mr. Porter himself has kindly written for us a "short poem inspired by a bit of graffiti from Pompeii":

> **T**remendum admiror nomen tuum non cecidisse
> **L**anguidulo lapsuve doloreve denique quod tot
> **S**criptorum libellos sustineat crepitorum!

Don't overlook the acrostic. Mr. Porter offers his own crib: "I marvel that your awe-inspiring name has not at last fallen in idle error or grief, since it supports so many grumbling writers' books."

March 11

Entries have been flooding in for this year's Mario Ortiz-Robles Prize for Incomprehensibility. Readers will recall Mr. Robles's effort to achieve, in a few sentences, a state of perfect opacity: "a performative model of subject formation cannot be thought apart from its implication in regulatory practices," etc.

The bar is high, but among contenders for the coveted award is Jeremy Redlich, who in an essay called "Reading Skin Signs" in *Performative Body Spaces*, edited by Markus Hallensleben (Rodopi) examines how "bodily borders and bodily identity can be read as fixed and stable only with enormous difficulty." Mr. Redlich proceeds to examine

> how the contours or boundaries of the body cannot be taken for granted as biological givens, but rather how these boundaries are continuously in a process of materialization, subject to the cultural, social and linguistic impressions that mark the bodily boundary, namely skin, as a surface that is coded and decoded like any other text.

Competing with Mr. Redlich in the same collection is Rainer Rumold, who in his essay "Corporeal Topographies of the Image Zone" has this to say about the shape of paintings:

> The function and meaning of verticality and the horizontal becomes the subject of a decisive review of the central space-and-form problem of our normative perceptions. These are constructed via the polarity of the dimensions of length, width and height.

We used to say long and thin or short and broad, but that was before the days of perfect incomprehensibility.

March 18

Is there any subject on which Christopher Hitchens has failed to have his say? He has written books, pamphlets, and articles on matters ranging from Marx to the Marbles, the Kurds to Kissinger, and most recently, and unflinchingly, his experience of cancer. All journalists have opinions, but few express them as eloquently (even egregious opinions) as Hitchens. Gay marriage "demonstrates the spread of conservatism, not radicalism, among gays." Isaiah Berlin was "a skilled ventriloquist for other thinkers." Al Sharpton is "another person who can get away with anything under the rubric of Reverend." Of Francis Fukuyama and the End of History, he wrote, "It is not possible that a solipsistic clown like Fukuyama is history's last word."

Some of Hitchens's opinions have the quality of epigrams. To say "Nobody is more covetous or greedy than those who have far too much" is not only elegant, as good epigrams must be, it also has the flavor of truth, which not all epigrams do. On subjects dear to liberal hearts, one often longs for Hitchens's toney drawl to dispel the feel-good funk. "The more that people claim Obama's mere identity to be a 'breakthrough,'" he said in 2008 of the then-candidate, "the more they demonstrate that they have failed to emancipate themselves from the original categories of identity that acted as a fetter on clear thought." On David Cameron: "People ask, 'What do you think of him?' My answer is: he doesn't make me think."

Without troubling to do the research, you could safely say

that Hitchens has a view on everything. Now you can do the research. Da Capo Press are soon to publish *The Quotable Hitchens*, an A–Z of opinions, edited by Windsor Mann. It has 300 pages, with an average of five subject headings per page. That's opinions on 1,500 subjects. It might have been Winston Churchill who said, "The moment of near despair is quite often the moment that precedes courage . . .", but it was actually Hitchens. He also has opinions about Churchill. "In many of his communications [with Stalin] one gets the distinct sense that he admired the great despot not in spite of his cruelty and absolutism but because of it." Like all sages, he has cryptic moments: "Missing the point is the point"; "Frontiers exist to be conquered." It is the privilege of the gifted epigrammatist to utter sayings which are at once true and untrue. When Hitchens declares that "Irony is for losers," your first thought is: Nice. Your second: Every time? Third: No it isn't.

Hitchens has views on Billy Graham and Graham Greene, Al Gore and Gore Vidal, Men and Mensa, James I and James, Clive, hope and Bob Hope, the Bush family, the Kennedy family, even the Hitchens family. Of Christopher, he says, "By instinct I am a conservative. It's the only thing that stops me from joining them." This time your first thought—he's right—is correct. Of his brother Peter, also a journalist, he says, "He lacks my strange, hypnotic power over women." Again, he could be right. More likely, it's a case of his winning irony.

March 25

In her introduction to *The Methuen Drama Book of Plays by Black British Writers*, Lynette Goddard writes that "black British playwriting is thriving." At the same time, she takes the opportunity to lament "institutional racism in the British theatre sector."

The subject of race in modern Britain is so delicate, so hedged about by hypocrisy and euphemism, so confused, that it has become impossible to talk about it in plain language. In this area, as in many others, we imitate the United States. Questioned once about "racial politics," Saul Bellow replied: "There seems to be such a taboo on open discussion that no habits of discussion have developed, no vocabulary for discussion, no allowance made for intellectual differences, because you are immediately labelled a racist." That was in 1994. It is just as true of Britain today.

A phrase commonly uttered when the subject rears its head is "You can't say that." Can't say it even if you think it. These "taboo" statements needn't be contentious. Most people are familiar with the phrase "black-on-black crime." According to Gary Younge, writing in the *Guardian,* it is among the terms "employed to pathologize a specific community in which every transgression is refracted through an ethnic lens." Add it to the can't-say list. Meanwhile, Mr. Younge quotes with approval a remark of A. Sivananden about "the monumental and endemic racism of this society." Here we refer back to Bellow. If "monumental and endemic racism" describes modern Britain, then language collapses in the face of South African apartheid. Mr. Younge is unwittingly depriving himself of a vocabulary to talk about a prominent issue of the age.

Ms Goddard is the author of articles such as "Staging Black Feminisms" and "In-yer-face Black Womanist Playwriting." She knows about "institutional racism" among theater managers, directors, stage hands, and actors, and is capable of being in yer face about it. As she might be if someone were to suggest that calling a book *Plays by Black British Writers* is itself a segregationist gesture.

April 22

Lesser-used languages of the British Isles. There is one language we have neglected: Old English. Who speaks it now? Just about everyone who speaks English. We do not know how the Anglo-Saxons sounded in the ninth century, but in the recently published *How To Read a Word,* Elizabeth Knowles provides a list of "Old English words still in use today." It includes: ale, bird, black, blood, bread, bride, calf, child, chin, church, clothes, corn, cow, day, death, deer, drink, eat, eye, fat, father, feather, field, five, fox, glass, good, gold, goose, hammer, hand, harvest, hawk, heaven, hell, ivy, jowl, kettle, key, king, lady, man, meat, mouse, murder, nail, name, night, nose, oak, pound, queen, rain, salt, sea, seven, silk, snake, snow, song, sword, teach, ten, thief, thigh, thumb, thunder, tongue, walk, wife, woman, worm, year, youth.

All human life is there. The list has more nouns than verbs, and no pronouns, articles or prepositions, making sentence construction difficult. Nevertheless, we have had a go at creating some Old English drama out of Ms. Knowles's lexicon:

> Black night. Hammer-hand thief. Pound? Ten. Walk, lady.
> Lambs laugh. Fox eyes five. Blood chin. Eat.
> Day: harvest, bread. Night: glass, drink ale, song, woman,
> heaven. Morning: hell.
> Fat goose. Sword. Feathers. Meat.

Ms. Knowles reminds us that Latin, being the medium of the Church, was influential on the language even then, and our earlier researches have established that Latin itself is still spoken (see above, March 4). Sheila Barksdale has sent us a witty example of a Latin import in a haiku written at Burton Court, Herefordshire, which she finds "a wonderfully peaceful place." One morning, however, "I was inspired to write this":

> ancient Roman camp
> waking to rooks' hic haec hoc
> on a fallow field

June 10

English Heritage blue plaques have been installed on buildings all over London to honor writers including the great American poet-critics, T. S. Eliot and Ezra Pound. Another great poet-critic, William Empson, an English one to boot, and a representative of Anglo-Oriental amity, has none. For many years, Empson lived in a house at the corner of Rosslyn Hill and Hampstead Hill Gardens, NW3, where he and his wife entertained London's literati. Pass by, and you practically hear the walls cry out for a blue plaque.

A plaque to honor Empson has now been installed on a building in Marchmont Street, Bloomsbury. It happens to be blue, but it was not placed there by English Heritage; rather, by the admirable Marchmont Street Association, which exists "to raise awareness of the rich history of the Marchmont area." While living at No. 65, Empson completed *Seven Types of Ambiguity* (1930); later on, at No. 71, he wrote the works contained in his first collection, *Poems*, as well as the criticism in *Some Versions of Pastoral* (both 1935).

Ricci de Freitas of the Association told the assembled watchers that the plaque was sponsored by a Japanese student of Empson, Miki Fukayama. The recent tsunami prevented her from attending, but Empson's sons Jacob and Mogador were there to perform the unveiling, as were several Empson grandchildren and great-grandchildren. Mr. de Freitas noted other past Marchmont luminaries, Emlyn Williams and John Barbirolli among them. He was delighted to see in the crowd the poet and former poetry editor of Faber and Faber, Christopher Reid. "Did Faber publish Empson?", Mr. de Freitas asked. Mr. Reid brightly said they did while his predecessor T. S. Eliot was in charge, but, less brightly, that somehow they had lost him.

Also among the watchers was Nicholas Murray, whose recent book *Real Bloomsbury* offers details of Empson in his Marchmont Street room. The rent was 28 shillings per week and it was rather squalid. But, Empson wrote to I. A. Richards, "I have a taste for squalor." The Mayor of Camden, Abdul Quadir, in full mayoral regalia, offered some friendly words, before Jacob Empson read from his father's "Homage to the British Museum." At that point, a lengthy file of French tourists passed by on the opposite pavement, each pulling a little trolley. Some paused as Jacob declaimed: "Let us stand here and admit that we have no road." Taxi drivers appeared to agree. One or two Marchmontians with evidently a deeper attachment to squalor than to Empson joined the entourage;

> Let us offer our pinch of dust all to this God,
> And grant his reign over the entire building.

Robed customers emerging from the New Bloomsbury Halal Food Store, which occupies the ground floor of No. 65, cast indulgent glances in our direction. An Empson great-grandchild began to cry. Mr. de Freitas, having been advised that two representatives of the *TLS* were in the audience, requested that they make themselves visible. One pointed out that the *TLS* has published more posthumous Empson material than any other journal. A fair Empson granddaughter dispensed wine. Professor Warwick Gould reminisced about the great man, while onlookers flashed cameras. With at least seven types of ethnicity in evidence, it was a unique and curiously joyful London occasion.

July 8

There was a time in the early 1950s when, upon arrival in the *TLS* office of a book about cannibalism or Voodoo, the editor would drop it in an envelope and say, "This is one for Paddy." Patrick Leigh Fermor, who died last month at the age of ninety-six, is now best known for his connection to Greece and his youthful trek across Central Europe in the direction of Constantinople (as he insisted on calling it). But in his first book, *The Traveller's Tree*, an account of a journey by schooner through the Caribbean islands published in 1950, he was in pursuit of "the whole phenomenon of Afro-American religion." Before long, the *TLS* was commissioning the former mountain guerrilla fighter and Intelligence Corps Liaison Officer to write on related matters. He could open a review of a book on Haiti in 1953 by telling readers that "The bibliography of Voodoo—

or Voudoun, as some purists insist, with little basis, on spelling it—mounts impressively." A discussion of cannibalism in the correspondence columns of the *TLS* was just the sort of thing to elicit a contribution from Fermor: "Apropos of the recent letters about the ethical and culinary aspects of cannibalism, may I quote from a book I wrote years ago. . . ."

There followed a list of the gustatory advantages of various folk, according to the palates of the Caribs who "invaded the Caribbean chain, eating all the male Arawaks they could lay hands on and marrying their widows." The book he wished to quote from was, of course, *The Traveller's Tree* (it was by now 1980), which included this pre-Columbian version of a restaurant review: "French people were considered delicious, and by far the best of the Europeans, and next came the English. The Dutch were dull and rather tasteless, while the Spanish were so stringy and full of gristle as to be practically uneatable."

In later years, Paddy—as he was known to friend, reader, and stranger alike—wrote for this paper on various topics, including Crete, scene of his wartime adventure. In the common run of Grub Street, there are many people one could call on to evaluate an anthology of nonsense—but *Poiemate me Zographies se Mikra Paidia*, which Paddy reviewed in 1977, was nonsense in modern Greek. In December 1979, he contributed a clamorous, ringing poem on the subject of Christmas:

What franker frankincense, frankly, can rank in scents
 with fawn-born dawning?
Weak we in Christmas week, lifetime a shrieking streak—
 lend length and strengthen!
Poultice the harm away, charm the short solstice day!
Send strength and lengthen!

A Visit to Patrick Leigh Fermor (1915–2011)

We have received this "personal reminiscence" from a correspondent:

In 2005, I was commissioned by a newspaper to write a profile of Patrick Leigh Fermor. A preliminary meeting took place at the West London home of Magouche Fielding, widow of Xan, PLF's comrade-in-arms, but my editor insisted that no piece about Fermor could appear without a first-hand account of the house which he designed and helped build in the mid-1960s in Mani, at the southernmost tip of the Peloponnese. So it was that, after an overnight stay in Athens and a five-hour drive to the village of Kardamyli, I rang Paddy from a seaside pension.

"Good Lord. You're here already!" he exclaimed, though all proper warning had been issued. "Look here. Come to supper *straight away*. It'll be a rotten supper. But come to supper *straight away*." Desiring nothing more than an ouzo with equal part water (no ice), followed by a soft pillow, I had the presence of mind to resist. Paddy was understanding. "Look here. Come to lunch tomorrow. It'll be a *much better* lunch." Suppers and lunches, it transpired, were prepared by different cooks.

At about one the following day I set off for the two-kilometre walk from Kardamyli, with directions from a villager. "As the road bends to the left, you take the footpath to the right. Go through the olive grove, and arrive at Mr. Fermor's door." What could be simpler? There was indeed a bend in the road and a footpath to the right. But there was also another, closer to the bend, up ahead. Then another. After involuntary exploration of hitherto uncharted olive groves and what seemed a sizeable stretch of the Mediterranean coast, I squelched into Paddy's house from the shore, to find him seated on the sofa reading the *TLS*.

"Good Lord. I think you're the only creature, apart from a goat, who has come in that way. We *must* have a drink straight away." The last was among his favorite phrases.

Lunch lasted some six hours. (Lemon chicken, with litres of retsina or red Lamia.) Songs in various languages were sung, including a rendering of "It's a Long Way to Tipperary" in Hindustani. Lost lines of poems were sought in books on the surrounding shelves. An anecdote about my lately deceased father and his claim to have seen salmon leaping in a narrow Perthshire stream, confirmed after his death, threw Paddy into a search for the perfect epithet: "The corroborating salmon. The justifying salmon. The proving salmon."

Well into the evening, I prepared to leave. "Look here. Come to lunch on Sunday" (this was Friday). I said I would be on my way back to Athens. He was startled. "Good Lord. You're leaving already! Then come to supper tomorrow." I did so, after an all-day hike in the Taygetos mountains which rear up behind the house that Paddy built, as the Gulf of Messenia opens before it. This time, I arrived punctually, to be admitted by the allegedly rotten cook (in fact, supper was very good). She directed me to Paddy's study in a separate building in the garden. I knocked before entering, to find him at his desk, alone in Mani on a late March evening, dressed in Jermyn Street shirt, pullover and grey flannels, reading a Loeb Horace. Towers of manuscripts could not obscure him. Among them, perhaps, was a draft of the third and concluding part of his epic walk from the Hook of Holland to Constantinople—the first, though not the last, heroic adventure of Patrick Leigh Fermor.

August 19 & 26

The cover of *Inside Jokes: Using humor to reverse-engineer the mind* (MIT Press) shows photographs of all three of its authors. Matthew M. Hurley and Reginald B. Adams are chuckling merrily, possibly at one of the jokes in their own book—"Yesterday my computer beat me at chess. But it was no match for me at kick-boxing"—but the third, Daniel C. Dennett, is gazing glumly at the sky. Perhaps he's just read that subtitle again. Or maybe he hasn't heard the one about the dumb blonde who spent an hour looking at a can of orange juice because it said "concentrate." Or about the newspaper ad that said, "Illiterate?

Write now for free advice." Or the man who was walking down the street with a banana in his ear. A passer-by stopped him. "Did you know you have a banana in your ear?" "Speak up! I have a banana in my ear!"

It's a laugh, or so you think until *Inside Jokes* goes into reverse-engineer mode:

> We must resist the temptation to divide the emotional and cognitive components and model them separately, engineering the cognitive aspect by creating an agent that can create data consistency in its knowledge representation and then engineering the emotional aspect by creating an agent that can get a good feeling from hearing jokes and engaging in socially mediated enjoyment.

Be serious. Or if you can't be, try reverse-engineering this:

> An Asian man walks into a US currency exchange with 2,000 yen and receives $77. Next day, he enters with another 2,000, but gets only $66. Why so little? "Fluctuations," says the teller. The Asian storms out, but not before shouting, "And fluc you Amelicans, too!"

The authors, who have been longlisted for the Mario Ortiz-Robles Prize for Incomprehensibility, say, "This joke nicely illustrates how our spurious automatic filling-in during spreading activation can contribute to a falsehood in a mental space." In a better humor, they say things like this:

> A six-year-old and a four-year-old decide to start swearing. "When we go down for breakfast," the older one says, "you say hell and I'll say ass." Downstairs, Mom asks the younger what he'd like for breakfast.
>
> "Hell, I think I'll just have cornflakes."
>
> Mom whacks his head and sends him back upstairs, to the horror of his brother. "And what do you want for breakfast?", she says when he is downstairs. He starts to cry. "You can bet your ass it won't be cornflakes."

As for the story that Dennett was asked while staying with some animal-loving Brits, "Would you like to see our daughter's beautiful pussy?"—one, we don't believe it; two, we've heard it too often. It's an "urban legend" joke. Now we know why he is staring at the sky. He's trying to think of better gags.

Tell him this one:

> A young country priest is accosted by a prostitute on his way through town. "How about a quickie for £20?", she asks. The priest hurries on. He encounters another woman. "£20 for a quickie, father?" Bewildered, he heads back to the country. There he meets a nun.
>
> "Pardon me, sister, but what's a quickie?"
>
> "£20," she says. "Same as in town."

The best piece of engineering in *Inside Jokes* is the oldest one: It's how you tell them.

September 9

From time to time, as part of the effort to cut out the second Babycham before dinner, we fall to compiling lists. Readers with long memories might recall our attempt to find a book for each letter of the alphabet: *"A"* by Louis Zukofsky; *From A to B and Back Again*, Andy Warhol; *C*, Peter Reading; *The Ascent of F6*, Auden and Isherwood; *G*, John Berger; *H*, Robert Graves . . . and so on down to *Z* by Vassilis Vassilikos, via *The L-Shaped Room*, pausing only to *Dial M for Murder*.

The other evening, we picked up *The Two Faces of January* by Patricia Highsmith, which made us think of the recent novel *February* by Lisa Moore, and then (chuckling at our own ingenuity) *The Long March* by William Styron. We have yet to read *The Enchanted April* by Elizabeth von Arnim and *The Darling Buds of May* by H. E. Bates. *Juneteenth* is the unfinished second novel by Ralph Ellison. *July's People* is by Nadine Gordimer. Allan Massie wrote *Augustus*, Elizabeth Bowen *The Last*

September, Tom Clancy *The Hunt for Red October*. With a wintry shiver, we open Flaubert's *November*. *The Dean's December* rounds off the year.

Soon we'll get round to plays on the days of the week (someone must have done *Never on a Sunday*). Then what? How about film titles with numbers from one to ten, starting with *The Wild One*. Oh yes, a single Babycham's the limit from now on.

September 23

Our effort to cut out the second Babycham before dinner appears to have struck a chord in many readers (NB, September 9). After compiling a list of novels with the months of the year in the titles, we pledged to apply ourselves, if resolve should weaken at an inviting wink from the sparkling fawn on the Babycham bottle, to film titles with numbers one to ten.

No need. Jeffrey Susla from Woodstock, Connecticut, has done the work for us. His list goes like this: *One Fine Day*; *Two for the Road*; *Three Days of the Condor*; *The Four Feathers*; *Five Fingers of Death*; *With Six You Get Eggroll*; *Seven Brides for Seven Brothers*; *Eight Men Out*; *Nine Months*; *10 Things I Hate About You*.

Another reader goes one better, "spicing the game" by giving us a list of films with literary links. The first and ninth cheat slightly: *Twenty One Days* (1940) made from John Galsworthy's play, *The First and the Last*, scripted by Graham Greene; *Two for the Road* (1967), screenplay by Frederic Raphael; *Three Comrades* (1938), screenplay by F. Scott Fitzgerald; *The Four Feathers* (1939), from the novel by A. E. W. Mason; *Five Finger Exercise* (1962) from the play by Peter Shaffer; *The Inn of the Sixth Happiness* (1958), from the novel *The Small Woman: Gladys Aylward* by Alan Burgess; *The Door with Seven Locks* (1940) from the novel by Edgar Wallace; *Dinner at Eight* (1933) from the play by George S. Kaufman; *The Thirty-Nine Steps* (1935) from the novel by John Buchan. *Ten Little Indians* (1945) from the novel by Agatha Christie (later retitled *And Then There Were None*).

This leaves us free to concentrate on plays featuring the days of the week. A single preprandial Babycham tastes all the better when you have something to think about while drinking it.

October 14

Since word leaked that *The TLS Reviewer's Handbook* is at a late stage of production in the Basement Labyrinth, other publications have rushed to take advantage. *Vanity Fair* is said to disallow the use of "pen" as a verb (does anyone allow it?), as well as words such as "opined" or "quipped" to mean "said."

John Rentoul, a political writer on the *Independent on Sunday*, has now come up with *The Banned List: A Manifesto Against Jargon and Cliché*, which ends with an A–Z of forbidden terms. Readers of our *Dictionary of Received Phrases* will be familiar with some; writers who pause for an instant before they pen a sentence will find it hard to disagree with any. We offer here one or more examples from each letter of Mr. Rentoul's alphabet.

Affordable housing. Blue-sky thinking. Bottom line. Comes with the territory. Critique (as a verb). Does what it says on the tin. Edgy. Eatery. Elephant in the room. First priority. Fit for purpose (not). Game changer. Get over it. Hard-working families. Hearts and minds. In the mix. Interface. Issues. Joined-up government/thinking. Key, as in "key to." Level playing field. Learning curve. Makeover. Moral compass. Move on. No-brainer. Outside the box (thinking). Panacea. Plethora. Perfect storm. Quantum leap. Robust. Rocket science. Sea change. Stakeholders. Talismanic. Tough love. Vibrant (referring to non-white areas). Wake-up call. Whisper it. Who knew? You couldn't make it up. Zero-sum game.

An invitation has gone to Mr. Rentoul to join the editorial team in the Basement Labyrinth, on a live-in contract.

October 21

Ion Trewin, the administrator of the Man Booker Prize, has defended this year's judges, who have favored "readability" as a criterion of excellence, and dismissed the views of "so-called literary critics." Some interpret readable as lowbrow, but Mr. Trewin is not having it. "No one wants something with literary quality which is unreadable," he says. "That would be daft."

We are probably daft ourselves, but nevertheless wonder how a piece of writing can have "literary quality" yet be unreadable at the same time. The matter is apparently subjective. Many people will tell you that *Mrs. Dalloway* and *Absalom, Absalom!* are unreadable—and they couldn't care a fig for the quality. They are entitled to their views. But you wouldn't ask them to judge the Booker Prize.

Andrew Kidd, a literary agent, has had similar thoughts. Last week, he outlined a plan to set up a rival: the Literature Prize. "We feel a space has opened up for a new prize in the UK that celebrates excellence and is judged by experts in the field of literature," Mr. Kidd says. The inference is clear. The chair of this year's Booker judging panel is a former head of MI5. One of the judges is a Labour MP, with no literary track record. Another recent chair was a retired Conservative politician. Would you have gone to them for advice before publishing *The Waste Land*?

Mr. Kidd set out his plans in the *Guardian*. "It was inevitable that we would be accused of elitism," he wrote. "I'd like to think it's the opposite." We felt daft again. The Literature Prize is to honor the best but is opposed to the elite? Mr. Kidd also says that his prize is "not about exclusion." Here we draw the line. When the inevitable invitation arrives, asking us to chair the judging panel, we will insist on excluding novels without literary quality, even though admired by Mr. Trewin. "The public deserves a prize that says to them: 'for what it's worth, this is what a panel of experts feel were the best novels, published this year,'" Mr. Kidd writes. We were, for what it's worth, even more confused. The only thing of which we are certain is that Mr. Trewin is enjoying all the publicity that Mr. Kidd has given the Man Booker Prize.

October 28

Richard Bradford's *Lucky Him: The life of Kingsley Amis* (2001) was described as "an original and stimulating book" by Martin Amis. Mr. Bradford has now published *Martin Amis: The biography.* It portrays the son as "a cabinet of contrasts: tortured, eloquently aloof, kind, obsessive, loved by women."

Our mind ever on higher things, we consulted the index under *Times Literary Supplement.* Mr. Amis began working for the paper in 1972, shortly after finishing his first novel, *The Rachel Papers.* His initiatory tasks included the writing of a review of William Empson's edition of Coleridge's poems. The piece elicited an irritated response from Empson, who corrected some errors and tried to guess at "what was drifting around in the almost human brain of the reviewer". The youthful reviewer picked himself up and wrote a manly reply: "Apologies are due. . . ."

Exciting stuff. Unfortunately, it scarcely detains Mr. Bradford. His book contains several mentions of the *TLS,* most related to the subject's "ravenous libido" rather than the texture of his criticism. Amis met his present wife, Isabel Fonseca, "through the *TLS,*" Bradford writes: "olive skinned, fine boned, with piercing dark eyes and hair soulfully black . . . she had become a magnet for men." In the late 1980s, Ms. Fonseca oversaw what are now the Commentary pages of the *TLS.* She is remembered fondly.

At the moment of the fateful meeting, Amis was still married to Antonia Phillips, "outstandingly beautiful," who, it so happens, also worked at the *TLS* at the time of their first encounter. She oversaw art reviews, and wrote on the subject herself. She too is remembered fondly. Before his attachment to Ms. Phillips, Amis stepped out with Mary Furness, who—by now you hardly need telling—"worked at the *TLS*."

> She was beautiful, but carelessly so; if she was aware of the effect her mere physical presence had upon men then she showed no conscious recognition of this knowledge. She was dark-haired, with a magnificently sharp facial bone structure, and slightly taller than Martin. He was smitten.

What a place to work! (Ms. Furness, by the way, is remembered fondly.) Mr. Bradford makes plain the joy of sub-editing in another reference: "The *TLS*, whose list of part-time female staff would come to resemble an antechamber for Martin's love life."

As for the Empson controversy, you may read Amis's original review (unsigned) in the *TLS* of December 15, 1972. "With endearing *Boys' Own* eagerness, Professor Empson follows up what would have happened if the Mariner . . ." etc. Empson's objections and the reviewer's rejoinder are in the issue of January 12, 1973.

November 11

Perambulatory Christmas Books, 5th series: the "Back to Basics" tour. That rough crucifix we fashioned out of old Penguins must be working. The vampiric virus of Christmas "humor" books with titles of the *Do Ants Have Arseholes?* variety appears to be shrinking in its coffin. There are fewer than ever this year.

Still, our work goes on. The number of second-hand bookshops on Charing Cross Road has dwindled in recent years, but three good ones remain, almost side by side on a stretch near Leicester Square: Any Amount of Books (to which we shall return), Henry Pordes, and Quinto. The last is, in fact, two shops: a posh antiquarian affair upstairs (trading as Francis Edwards), with Quinto in the basement. Here, the stock is changed regularly, and most items are under £5. It was to the lower depths that we gravitated on a wet November afternoon.

No modern literary journal has attracted as much opprobrium as *Encounter.* The title need only be uttered or written for the inevitable pendant phrase to follow: "funded by the CIA." The sponsoring body was, in fact, the Congress for Cultural Freedom (CCF) and early issues state the connection explicitly on the contents page, with the happy assurance that "The views expressed in *Encounter* are to be attributed to the writers, not the sponsors." France had the CCF-funded *Preuves,* under the leadership of Raymond Aron. If the editorial view took an anti-communist squint, it was hardly surprising in post-war Europe, with Stalin's corpse barely cold. We bought six issues at Quinto, ranging from 1953 to 1961.

The inclination to impute wicked motives to *Encounter* has always struck us as an inverted form of radical chic. It was a beautifully produced magazine, especially in its earliest incarnation. It employed the world's best writers. Was Albert Camus a CIA stooge, for giving British readers in the inaugural issue (October, 1953) a glimpse into Roman ruins in northern Algeria? His essay was published in English for the first time, as were his notebooks, posthumously, in 1961: "At the cinema the little woman from Oran weeps at the hero's misfortunes. Her husband begs her to stop. Look, she says, in the middle of the tears, let me make the most of it."

Encounter was not even right-wing. In 1954, Leslie Fiedler wrote a lengthy denunciation of Joseph McCarthy. Christopher Isherwood spoke admiringly of the "German writer and revolutionary," Ernst Toller. Richard Wright welcomed the emerging African independent nations. Dwight Macdonald, once a leading light at the left-wing New York journal *Partisan Review,* became an associate in the mid-1950s. If it was part of a CIA plot to set the world to rights, it sounds like an admirable one. The interest of these old issues—£1.50 each, in fine condition—is exceptional. The brainwashing has so far been rather pleasant.

IN A POKY ROOM in the Irish Cultural Centre in Hammersmith last month, Eddie Linden sat and worried. Friends arrived, many speaking with Irish accents, and congratulated him. He looked increasingly worried. A representative of this paper gave a speech, during which he held up copies of Mr. Linden's magazine, *Aquarius*, and a cartoon in which Mr. Linden was seen confessing his sins at the Pearly Gates—and asking the Almighty if He would like to buy a copy of *Aquarius*. The friends chuckled. Mr. Linden looked more worried than ever. Anthony Rudolf read a poem about Mr. Linden, which went down well with the listeners. Nothing, however, could un-worry the man at the center of the assembly, which had gathered to celebrate the publication of his new book of poems, *A Thorn in the Flesh* (Hearing Eye, £7.50). If titles could worry, that's what this one would be doing.

At last, the crowd could contain its impatience no longer. "Gie us 'City of Razors,'" someone cried. This is Mr. Linden's tour de force. If you haven't heard him recite it, you don't know how poems read aloud can sound. He recites from memory, eyes closed, a hand clasped to his forehead. The subject is gang violence in his native city, Glasgow:

A woman roars from an upper window
"They're at it again, Maggie!
Five stitches in our Tommie's face, Lizzie!
Eddie's in the Royal wi' a sword in his stomach
and the razor's floating in the River Clyde."

Applause was momentous. Worry subsided. Friends queued to have copies of the new book signed. And the Almighty took a copy of *Aquarius*.

November 25

Where are the poets of the war? After a recent despatch on this long-running topic, we received an email from Lieutenant Colonel Delius Singer RAMC, Medical Officer of the Black

Watch, serving in "Forward Operating Base Shawqat, Helmand Province," Afghanistan. "I receive my *TLS* after a delay," Lt Col Singer wrote. He was responding to our request for poems from the war in Afghanistan, and he attached a grisly verse—"written after a bad day"—to prove that "something is being produced."

How does the *TLS* reach Helmand Valley? Would Lt Col Singer tell us what he likes or dislikes about the paper? Do his fellow soldiers borrow it? What other reading matter is around? A reply came, with unnecessary apologies for the delay. "Access to the internet has been difficult of late." We can do no better than quote it in full:

> In answer to your enquiries: I do get the *TLS* in Helmand by postal subscription. It makes its way via the main base at Camp Bastion and then is delivered forward by helicopter to our location. After a thorough read by me, it is passed on, usually by hand. Occasionally, if an essay or article will be of particular interest to someone elsewhere, I repackage and give it to a convoy or individual heading that way. As a result some copies are remarkably well travelled and some have even seen action.
>
> I for my part read nearly all of each issue but particularly any reviews on the fine arts, classics or natural history. Regular favourites are any Freelance featuring Hugo Williams and NB—not least the seasonal £5 book search which no matter where I am always conjures up the comforting smell of old books and takes me off to Cecil Court or some such missed corner.
>
> As for general reading, for young soldiers it is usually books written on the back of previous tours by other soldiers. For young officers, the Flashman novels of George MacDonald Fraser are a perennial favourite. Also being read at the moment are *The Iliad,* [Doris Lessing's] *Diary of a Good Neighbour, Lucky Jim,* Sherlock Holmes, Conrad's *Nos-*

tromo and *Rebels* by Fearghal McGarry. I am reading Xenophon's *Anabasis*. So there is a good mix of the traditional and contemporary being consumed.

Lt Col Singer attached two more poems, one of which, "Transmitted Live," describes a unique feature of contemporary warfare. "Computer plane," he explains, "is what the insurgents call our drones."

It is on task.
We never know his name,
But he has been
Positively Identified
Walking in the sun we watch him
On screen, on line, follow his final trajectory
The walking dead transmitted live.
Above, sightless and soundless our proxy circles
A technical kill haunting the poppy fields
Far beyond comprehension—simply a computer plane.
He hears nothing, strolls on in sandals
Felt perhaps, only a sudden breeze
The herald of our cutting edge.

December 9

A Visit to Christopher Logue (1926–2011)

Christopher Logue, who has died aged eighty-five, had a relationship with the *TLS* spanning more than half a century. His poems began to appear in the paper in the mid-1950s when he was based in Paris, part of a crowd that included the novelist Alexander Trocchi, the future Grove Press editor Richard Seaver, and Austryn Wainhouse, a youthful but enduring translator of the works of the Marquis de Sade. Together, they oversaw the magazine *Merlin* and its publishing imprint Collection Merlin, which gave the world *Watt* and *Molloy* by Samuel Beckett, Genet in English, and Logue's debut *Wand and Quadrant* (1953).

From that moment, Logue, a lost boy without further education, with a military prison record and difficulties with girls, was found. In addition to placing poems in the *TLS* and elsewhere, he began doing something quite new: reading them aloud. Logue's poetry was "public"—and dramatic—from the start. "Poetry and the spoken performance of it were never separated in my mind," he said. In 1959, he recorded *Red Bird,* with verses by Pablo Neruda, in which Logue's projectile, la-di-da voice and Neruda's dewy lyricism skid along on the surface of jazz arrangements. The Beats in San Francisco were doing something similar, but Logue declined to be either beat, blue, or boxed-in. In 1962, he issued an unusual booklet, *Patrocleia,* which caught the attention of a *TLS* reviewer:

> Modern poetry is more intellectually fashionable than Homer just now. So although a taste for the two is so rarely combined as to seem almost incongruous, a modern poet's version such as Logue's, which is vigorous, unscholarly, sometimes brilliant, occasionally cheap, never dull, may be greeted with a sympathetic curiosity.

Logue would have relished the compliments—even "occasionally cheap"—with the big haw-haw-haw laugh that friends knew well. He greeted bad reviews of his work the same way, liable to say of some hatchet job: "Absolutely RIGHT!" Another laugh. Next project.

Which might have been: writing a musical (*The Lily-White Boys*), a play for the Royal Court (*Antigone*), a screenplay for Ken Russell (*Savage Messiah*), acting in *The Devils* by the same director (as Cardinal Richelieu), designing poster poems ("LAST NIGHT IN NOTTING HILL / I SAW BLAKE PASSING BY / WHO SAW EZEKIEL / AIRBORNE IN PECKHAM RYE"), or sorting out Pseuds Corner for *Private Eye.* The major work was to be his Homer, published under the general title

War Music. It is poetry drummed out to the tempo of a contest, a wrestling match if not a bloody battle. A friend of ours who visited Logue at his home in South London describes the 5-metre-long flow chart nailed to the wall of his study:

> A phrase from Pope's translation of the Iliad sat next to quote from a *New Yorker* article about the Gulf War: "a million footprints, / Empty now". He used to accumulate quotidian matter until something shaped itself into verse. "This is actually in Homer", Logue would say, next to a reference to Book V, Line 289 (Diomedes prepares to kill Pandarus in battle); "this I invented." He was keen to emphasize the shapeliness of his metrics. "A basic iambic pentameter throughout, from which one may deviate. It's a tremendously versatile line."

Logue's battle scenes are prefaced with stage directions and injunctions: "Cut to the fleet"; "Look West"; "Now hear this";

> Panotis' chariot yawed and tipped him
> Back off the plate by Little Ajax' feet.
> Neither had room to strike, and so the Greek
> Knocked his head back with a forearm smash,
> And in the space his swaying made, close lopped.
> Blood dulled both sides of the leafy blade.
> Fate caught Panotis' body; death his head.

In 1957, Logue upbraided T. S. Eliot in the Letters column of the *TLS*, on the now common charge of anti-Semitism, provoking Eliot to respond: "Your correspondent Mr. Christopher Logue quotes as evidence of my Fascist sympathies part of a sentence from my Commentary in the *Criterion* of February 1928. Permit me to give this sentence in its full context. . . ."

It would have provided the born mischief-maker with pleasure, but the thing that really counted was poetry—for which he had a capacious memory—and the squabble did not affect his high opinion of Eliot. Logue's Homer is likely to endure as one of the great long poems of the twentieth century. When *Patrocleia* appeared in 1962, Henry Miller wrote to Lawrence Durrell: "Just stumbled on Chris Logue's extraordinary rendition of Book 16 of the *Iliad*. I can't get over it. If only Homer were anywhere near as good."

IT'S THE PRIZE SEASON, and we are deep in daily conference over the longlist for the Jean-Paul Sartre Prize for Prize Refusal. Readers will recall how Sartre turned down the Nobel in 1964. John Berger was awarded the Refusal in 1972 when he gave half his Booker Prize money to the Black Panthers. Other Refusal recipients include Hari Kunzru, who refused the John Llewellyn Rhys Prize in 2003, upset that it was funded by the *Mail on Sunday*. Amitav Ghosh said no to the Commonwealth Writers Prize. With the Prize for Prize Refusal, you can refuse a prize and still get a prize.

Last week, the judges of the Saltire Scottish Book of the Year honored Alasdair Gray's magnificent volume, *A Life in Pictures*, despite the author having said he did not want the prize. "I was given the Saltire award years ago for my novel *Lanark*," Gray explained. "While I was glad of it, I said I didn't want any more awards." The judges refused to accept his refusal, and sent him £5,000 by post. "My wife had been furious that I'd refused because from time to time we do need money," Gray said. He refused to reject their refusal of his refusal. Our Sartre Prize certificate is on its way to Glasgow by *pneumatique*.

December 16

Now that you have established yourself as a writer, how much money will you need to live on? Can you hope for some Arts Council help? Will your advance cover the two or three years it takes to write a book? Can you expect lucrative freelance work on the side? The answers, so far as they concern the average scribe-in the-street, are: 1) It had better be not much. 2) Pull the other one. 3) Hardly. 4) No. If the recessionary mould that has set in all over Grub Street has escaped your notice, you are either a) very lucky, or b) posing.

In 1946, the literary journal *Horizon* asked some contemporary authors to answer similar questions. The Arts Council did not exist, but socialism was in the air and *Horizon* phrased the second question thus: "Do you think the State should do more for writers?"

The disparity in the amounts given in answer to question one ("How much money will you need to live on?") is striking. Elizabeth Bowen needed "£3,500 a year net," whereas Alex Comfort, with a wife and child, made do with £500. Stephen Spender thought "a married writer, if he makes his wife his cook, needs £700. . . . If he does not wish his wife to be a domestic slave he needs £1,000 a year." C. Day Lewis wished for a private income of about £300 to supplement earnings. He was one of the few to suggest "a second occupation," which would bring the writer "into contact with other people."

In 1946, an ordinary decent wage would be about £8 a week. You would not expect George Orwell to go far above the mean. He cited "£10 a week after payment of income tax [as] minimum for a married man, and perhaps £6 a week for an unmarried man." Julian Maclaren Ross, a writer who was often of empty pockets, asked for "£20 a week, not including rent," which would have paid for a lot of drinks at the Wheatsheaf. "Whether I get it or not is another matter." The saddest reply came from the art critic Robin Ironside. "Because I am too poor, I have never been to Greece; with £15 a week, I believe I could contrive to do so." Rose Macaulay raised the possibility of "good-natured parents."

Dylan Thomas was not alone in feeling that the State should cater for artists' material needs (the Soviet Union had such arrangements). Orwell opined that "if we are to have full Socialism, then clearly the writer must be State-supported." Until then, "the only thing the State could usefully do is to divert more of the public money into buying books for the public libraries." Bowen supported the idea of pensions for writers "who have worked hard."

One of those answering the questions was the man who posed them, Cyril Connolly, the editor of *Horizon*. "If he is to enjoy leisure and privacy, marry, buy books, travel and entertain his friends, a writer needs upwards of £5 a day net. If he is prepared to die young of syphilis for the sake of an adjective he can make do on under." As for taxpayers' money, "The State's attitude towards the artist should be to provide luxe, calme et volupté." Why stop there? "Big business could do much more for writers. Even the general public can send fruit and eggs."

SINCE THE JEAN-PAUL SARTRE Prize for Prize Refusal was endowed with the money from the Frenchman's refused Nobel, writers have proved willing to go to immense lengths to acquire it. No sooner had the judges settled on this year's winner—Alasdair Gray, for his initial refusal of the Saltire Scottish Book of the Year award—than Alice Oswald announced her refusal to be included in the shortlist for the T. S. Eliot Prize for poetry. Her withdrawal was followed by that of the Australian poet John Kinsella. Both cited an ethical objection to the sponsor, the investment company Aurum, which manages hedge funds. The reminder that Eliot worked for Lloyd's Bank could not placate them. Few doubt that they had a Sartre Prize for Prize Refusal in their sights.

If they thought it was that easy, they were wrong. This year's Refusal is in Glasgow—no one refuses a Sartre Refusal—and Kinsella and Oswald will have to wait until next year before learning if they have been considered for what everyone is calling "the Big One." If left high and dry, without the Eliot or the Sartre, they may console themselves with the philosophy of our founder and first winner—"Hell is other people's prizes"—delivered with a diagonal wink when we handed over the coveted certificate.

2012

February 17

February 14 will henceforth be known as Saint Jeanette's Day. Fresh from having issued a 250-page public shaming of her adoptive mother, Jeanette Winterson is "optimistic about love again":

> love in every shape and size and disguise. Known love, new love, love's ghosts, love's hopes. . . . Love is an ecosystem. You can't neglect it, exploit it, pollute it, and wonder what happened to the birds and the bees.

With money "gone"—"it was an illusion"—there is an opportunity to "re-think love."

Once a child preacher in Accrington, Lancashire, Jeanette has never ceased quoting from the Book of Jeanette. No other contemporary writer would get away with it—imagine Julian Barnes instructing us to "re-think love"—but for some reason she does. The *Guardian* gave up its front page on February 14, for Jeanette to say, "hug those who love us—and give some hugs to those who don't get loved enough." And to say it again: "Love your loved ones. Love the stranger."

There was something for every member of the flock. If "love is an ecosystem" has you re-thinking just that bit too much, try "There are so many different kinds of love," or "Love is an alternative currency." Or, indeed, "Children need so much love."

Teenagers were not forgotten. "They need to see that love can change and deepen." Think about it, then re-think about it. Money is an illusion, but "love isn't a commodity."

"We all had a fantasy that love could take care of itself." We did, didn't we all? Now let's make the planet "a place we can call home." Love your loved ones. (Saint Jeanette didn't re-think that one through.) The piece will remain on the website until April 1, when the *Guardian* will take it down.

March 16

We are sad to announce that the Mario Ortiz-Robles Prize for Incomprehensibility is losing its sponsor. We thank Mr. Robles for founding the prize. He is leaving to pursue clear prose.

While we await news from the Basement Labyrinth of a new patron, submissions are being considered for this year's shortlist. One that has a strong chance of making it is *Exotic Spaces in German Modernism* by Jennifer Anna Gosetti-Ferencei—or, to be precise, the entry concerning the book in the OUP (US) catalogue.

> In an examination of the concept of the exotic and of spatial experience in their cultural, subjective, and philosophical contingencies, Gosetti-Ferencei shows that exotic spaces may contest and reconfigure the relationship between the familiar and the foreign, the self and the other. Exotic spaces may serve not only to affirm the subject in a symbolic conquering of territory, as emphasized in post-colonial interpretations, or project the fantasy of escapism to a lost paradise, as Utopian readings suggest, but condition moral, aesthetic, or imaginative transformation.

If 288pp of further explication is tempting, it can be yours for $110. If you can supply us with a paraphrase, you may find that your application for a lifelong unpaid internship in the Basement Labyrinth has been successful.

April 13

In *Vengeance*, the new novel by Benjamin Black, death stalks the east coast of Ireland. "The Delahayes and Clancys have been rivals for generations. When a second death occurs, Quirke begins to realize that terrible secrets lie buried within these entangled families . . . nothing is quite as it seems."

They said it. On the spine we find the author's name—Benjamin Black—and the title. On the front cover, we read a qualified version of the author's name, "John Banville writing as Benjamin Black," followed by the title. The copyright page tells us that "The right of Benjamin Black to be identified as the author of this work has been asserted by him," etc., whereas the biographical note tells us that "John Banville lives in Dublin." The back cover of the bound proof (*Vengeance* is released in June) announces an exciting project: "Lead promotional plan in place to build Benjamin Black fan-base to new levels." Nothing is as it seems. The Benjamin Black fan base may or may not be bolstered by the bio note's reminder that "John Banville's novels have won numerous awards, including the Man Booker Prize in 2005." It adds: "*Vengeance* is the fifth novel in his Quirke Dublin series." His? Whose?

The assumption of a new identity used to be a bit of masked-ball fun for a prolific writer. Barbara Vine is the author of seven crime novels, considerably fewer than those of her colleague Ruth Rendell. As Rendell's success grew, her publishers couldn't resist bestowing some of it on Vine: "Barbara Vine is Ruth Rendell, the bestselling crime novelist." Julian Barnes once wrote seedy thrillers as Dan Kavanagh. Word soon got out and Barnes fans bought the Kavanagh books—there were four—just to see how high-mindedness looked when brought down low. Were Dr. Barnes to swallow the infernal potion one foul night and turn into Mr. Kavanagh yet again, you may be sure the publishers would be quick to broadcast his secret.

Is it no longer possible to be just an ordinary alter ego? When Romain Gary died in 1980, France lost not one but two

Goncourt winners. The rules forbid presenting the award to the same author twice, so Gary, who had won the Goncourt in 1956 with *Les Racines du ciel*, became Emile Ajar, and won it again with *La Vie devant soi* (1975). No one put "Romain Gary writing as . . ." across the cover of Ajar's books. Gary revealed the secret only in his suicide note. Ajar's false identity was the real thing.

April 20

The *TLS* has hit the screen again. Not the big screen this time. Our last outing in moviedom was as an eye-catching extra in the film *Iris*. Then, the *TLS* was a folded treasure idling around the Oxford house of Iris Murdoch and John Bayley. Our latest role was just last week, in an episode of the BBC1 drama *EastEnders*, in which all conversation seems to begin and end as shouting, with a brief interval for screaming in between. In the unlikely event of a victor ever emerging, the series will come to an end.

Cut to an Albert Square living room on April 12. During a lull in the bawling, Michael Moon is seated in an armchair, reading a magazine. He is interrupted in this un*EastEnder*-ish activity by his fiancée, Janine, who presents him with a typed copy of their pre-nuptial agreement. Michael places the magazine on his lap while he speaks. The camera hovers at his shoulder. He has been reading . . . the *TLS*! Now, though, he must engage with Janine. Our contribution to the drama is over.

We may not have said anything, but our appearance was pregnant with meaning. Michael Moon is described to us by one keen watcher as both "an aesthete" and "a psychopath." One of those explains why he is reading the *TLS*. The paper was open at a review of a book about Pope Benedict. The reviewer was our Religion editor Rupert Shortt. To semiologists among you, all is becoming clear: Michael wants the world to believe he is concerned with matters of the soul. He is . . . but not as he would have us think.

The Pynchonesque attention to detail on the part of the

script writers does not end there. Some months ago, the refined Mr. Moon was seen reading a different journal: the *London Review of Books*. No, we are not about to say that this demonstrates his essential wickedness. Yes, we are pleased to take it as proof that even psychopaths can change.

May 11

As far as we know, the Queen's Diamond Jubilee does not include a celebratory reading list. If it did, what would it contain? The Royal reputation for bookishness has seldom burned brightly, and Her Majesty's subjects are said to be going through hard times, so the safe course would be to issue a list of English classics. *Hard Times* would be a start; *A Tale of Two Cities* might be risky, depicting as it does "a revolutionary Paris, running red with blood," in the words of the new Penguin English Library edition.

One option would be to seek recommendations from eminent persons. When the call comes from the Palace, we will not hesitate to nominate *In the Year of Jubilee* by George Gissing. The story is set in 1887, the year of Queen Victoria's Golden Jubilee (the novel was published seven years later). It largely concerns a group of women—would-be writer Nancy Lord and the French sisters, all from Camberwell—and their sometimes surprisingly unVictorian antics. During the festivities, Nancy meets a man on the street, with whom she goes to a restaurant to drink champagne. "She was fascinated by his rough vigour." There is an unwanted pregnancy. Beatrice French, a business woman, keeps a bachelor flat in Brixton, produces cigarettes and claret for visiting friends, and makes flirty jokes about "sleeping single." As for Jubilee Day itself, Gissing's description would surely fit our own forthcoming event:

> Along the main thoroughfares of mid London, wheel-traffic was now suspended; between the houses moved a double current of humanity, this way and that. But for an occasional

> bellow, or for a song uplifted by strident voices, or a cheer at some glaring symbol that pleased the passers, there was little noise; only . . . the low, unvarying sound that suggested some huge beast purring to itself in stupid contentment.

Should the Palace accept our recommendation, Her Majesty will wish to read the novel in advance. But how shall we procure a copy for her? Apart from reissues of *New Grub Street* and *The Odd Women,* Penguin has ignored Gissing. He wrote some twenty other novels, most obscure to all but a few: *The Crown of Life, The Whirlpool, Will Warburton, Thyrza, Born in Exile, Eve's Ransom*; each is highly readable but none is easy to find. We haven't mentioned his Dickensian seam: *The Nether World, The Unclassed,* and others.

The neglect is baffling. The relaunched Penguin English Library includes worthy works such as *Doctor Thorne* by Trollope and Frances Burney's *Evelina,* but nothing by the man of whom Orwell said, "England has produced very few better novelists." If you can find *In the Year of Jubilee* in the year of Jubilee, pleasure is guaranteed.

June 1

Winterson Wonderland, contd. Reviewing Jeanette Winterson's memoir *Why Be Happy When You Could Be Normal?* in the *New York Review of Books* (May 24), Joyce Carol Oates praises the author's artistic engagement. Winterson, she says, "is a fierce and eloquent supporter of the literary arts, having lived through Thatcher's England as a university student at Oxford."

Is that Thatcher's England in which tanks rolled on to campuses, soldiers rounded up the intelligentsia, and bonfires were made out of books beloved by Jeanette Winterson? Or Thatcher's England where a working-class girl from Accrington could go to Oxford and receive not just a free education but a generous maintenance grant as well? Thatcher's England was followed by John Major's England, in which university access was unprecedentedly expanded. This was followed by Blair's England—at last, the people's party in power!—where free education for the likes of Ms. Winterson (and the likes of us) was abolished. It is necessary to be fierce and eloquent about something, however. Ms. Oates offers this passage from *Why Be Happy When You Could Be Normal?*:

> So when people say that poetry is a luxury, or an option, or for the educated middle classes, or that it shouldn't be read in school because it's irrelevant, or any of the strange and stupid things that are said about poetry . . . I suspect that the people doing the saying have had things pretty easy.

Few things are stranger than this. Many folk feel poetry is not for them, but we can't recall ever hearing it described as a luxury, or "an option"—except by someone indulging the luxury of coming over all embattled. People don't speak like that. The poetry police does exist: its membership is made up almost entirely of poets, seeking to police the "bad" poetry of others. Those who say "strange and stupid things" about poetry tend to be critics. We would be happy if, in a normal world, people cared enough about language to detect their own bad faith and justify ferocity. As Joseph Brodsky once said, censorship is good for writers: it gives them something to push against. Ms. Winterson might have benefited from that. But not even in Thatcher's England were they vetting the versifiers.

August 10

A Visit to Gore Vidal (1925–2012)

Everyone seems to be writing reminiscences about encounters with Gore Vidal, who has died aged eighty-six, so we asked a friend of ours to provide one. Here it is:

> On a Friday in March 2008, I found myself ascending the Hollywood Hills, to be admitted to a house that could have

served as backdrop to one of the more Gothic episodes of *Columbo*. Mini-staircases connected proliferating rooms; plaster arches stretched between functionless beams; a wrought-iron gate guarded the living room. Vidal had left La Rondinaia, his fabled villa on the Amalfi coast a few years before, no longer able to negotiate the steep cliff paths. He was on the telephone when I arrived—I was there on commission from a newspaper—and continued talking for about ten minutes while I stood nearby.

Vidal was wearing a mauve fleecy baseball jacket with the number 93 on the sleeve, and jogging pants held up by braces. On the table beside him was a magenta cocktail, with a mysterious foundation; possibly vodka. We succeeded in concocting some small talk—his house was "the typical abode of a Hollywood hack writer for television in 1950s," as he himself had once been—and soon the Filipino butler Nobero arrived to say, "Lunch is served, Mr. Vidal." Getting up, Vidal tapped his knee: "Pure titanium." He required help with all his movements. Around the dining table were six chairs with metallic back-rests moulded into the shape of goats' heads at the crest. "I bought these in Rome twenty years ago. The dealer saw my interest and immediately started, Oh . . . ancient-this, cinquecento-that. . . . I said, No they're not. They're the chairs from the movie *Ben-Hur*. I wrote it."

Lunch consisted of soufflé, endive and avocado salad (Vidal: "I invented this salad"), then raspberries and cream. Nobero was on hand with wine. When the dishes were cleared away and I produced my tape recorder, Vidal reverted to his pre-lunch taciturnity. "What was Tom Driberg's title?" he would ask, apropos of nothing. Or: "How is Nicky Haslam?" I was little help with these inquiries. Having cleared the table, Nobero reappeared with a bottle of cognac. "Mother's milk," Vidal called it—no allusion intended, apparently, to his detested mother (see his memoir *Palimpsest*), who, to compound the irony, spent her life "in pursuit of the perfect martini."

Literary gambits were deflected with set-piece imitations of Princess Margaret or Truman Capote. When I tried to join in, mentioning the latter's infatuation with Colette and his extravagant claim to have carried "everywhere" a set of glass paperweights she gave him, Vidal snapped: "He never met her! Everything he said was a lie."

In between questions about the provenance of his bright first novel, *Williwaw*, and the courage needed to publish *The City and the Pillar* in 1948—admittedly, they sound boring when put like that—Vidal fell asleep. I let him doze for about fifteen minutes, meanwhile taking notes. "Dreams," he said, when he came to. "If I don't remember my dreams, who will? I dream in great detail." Once, he dreamed of Henry James in a tomb, "wearing a red waistcoat. There was dust all around. He took my hand, then everything disappeared."

Hoping to lead up to the influence of Sir Walter Scott on Vidal's *Narratives of Empire* series, by far his best work in my view, I asked if any particular author had been inspirational. "Noooooooo." Later, however, when he invited me to root around upstairs in his study-cum-bedroom, I saw next to a shelf of editions of works by Vidal himself, a complete Walter Scott. By the time I descended, his denial had been forgotten. "I love Scott. He was the one who got me started on the historical novel."

The telephone rang. "Will you get that?" I made a move, but Nobero had reached the kitchen extension first. It was Peter Bogdanovich, director of *The Last Picture Show* and other films. He and Vidal were working towards a production of an unperformed play by Tennessee Williams, and he was on his way over. By then, having ditched thoughts of an in-depth interview, I was beginning to feel at home. Vidal's assistant, who had admitted me six hours earlier, was summoned, bringing welcome youth to the assembly. His first novel was soon to be published. His presence kindled godfatherly warmth in Vidal. Bogdanovich arrived, and turned out to be genial and amusing.

Somehow the talk turned to the *TLS*, and Vidal—a second bottle of cognac had by now been opened—had got it into his head that I was the editor. "You'd better keep in with him," he told Bogdanovich. "He runs the *TLS*." It didn't seem worth correcting. "Gore, weren't some of your pieces in *United States* first published there?" asked the director, referring to the recently published *Collected Essays*. "Oh at least a dozen," came the touchingly proud reply. The brandy glass was drained and held forth. Nobero had gone off-duty, so I obliged. "Mother's milk."

August 17 & 24

The International Writers' Conference took place over five days at the McEwan Hall, Edinburgh University, in August 1962. "Nothing was properly discussed," Stephen Spender wrote in his report in *Encounter*, "but some interesting things were said." This is commonly the case. The more unsettled the times, the more embattled the participants, the more interesting the things said will be. "There was a great deal about sex, homosexuality and drugs," an anonymous *TLS* leader writer stated; "too much for most." He or she delighted nevertheless in a "highly provocative week."

Spender described a discussion on "Scottish Writing Today" in which Scots literary elders huddled self-protectively around a carafe "filled with neat whisky. The genie of this Aladdin's lamp gradually took over." Despite the influence of the genie over Edinburgh's poets, the day belonged to a heroin-addicted Glaswegian Beat writer, Alexander Trocchi. The work of his adversaries, Hugh MacDiarmid chief among them, was "turgid, petty, provincial, stale cold porridge, Bible-clasping nonsense," Trocchi said. "Of what is interesting in the last ten years in Scottish writing, I myself have written it all."

This was bold, since few had heard of Trocchi. His sole novel to date, *Young Adam*, came out the year before. Some pornographic yarns had appeared pseudonymously in Paris, but his mastercrime, *Cain's Book*, had yet to be published in Britain.

It was at Edinburgh in 1962 that Norman Mailer described William Burroughs (also present) as "the only American novelist living today who may conceivably be possessed by genius." Mary McCarthy concurred, and wrote an influential review of *Naked Lunch* in the launch issue of the *New York Review of Books* the following year. Henry Miller seemed to onlookers to be putting literature into action, when he said: "Whenever we see a pretty woman we want to go to bed with her. Let's stop talking about it—let's just do it." At the end of the week, McCarthy said: "If I were to describe in a novel the conference which we have been attending, I would have to tone it down to make it sound credible."

The fiftieth anniversary of the event will be marked at this year's Edinburgh International Book Festival, a successful commercial show run on the grounds that the author has a book to promote, the organizers want a famous face, so—let's just do it. A good time will be had by all, but no one will come away feeling that events would need to be toned down to sound credible. No one will demonstrate "the future," as Burroughs did in the McEwan Hall, by giving how-to lessons in cut-up and fold-in techniques. To him, the strategies of *Naked Lunch* were already old hat, even though that novel, like *Cain's Book* and *Tropic of Cancer*, had yet to appear in Britain. One of the conference organizers, John Calder, published all three in due course.

For five days, Calder and his co-organizer Jim Haynes had situated the avant-garde in Scotland. Questions for debate at this year's Festival might include: Is censorship good for writers? Is an avant-garde still possible, when everything is permitted and nothing causes scandal, barring careless use of racist or sexist language? Does today's cutting edge lie not so much in what we read as in the technologies used to read it? Cut up these sentences and see if they turn into something more interesting.

To look back at the Writers' Conference is to invite the melancholy thought that few remain to talk about it. MacDiarmid and Trocchi cross claymores in the clouds, with Mailer and McCarthy looking on. Both organizers are still here, however. Jim Haynes, who lives in Paris, visits the Festival every year. We reached him in Edinburgh this week, and in the spirit of Joe Brainard's *I Remember*, asked him for a dozen "I remembers" about the event. Mr. Haynes said, "Let's just do it," and we picked up a pencil.

> "I remember seeing a long queue outside the McEwan Hall on the first day and thinking, this is going to be a success.
>
> "I remember two young women at the end of the queue who asked me if it was true that Lawrence Durrell and Henry Miller were going to be there.
>
> "I remember taking them by the hand and leading them into the Students' Union and seating them between Durrell and Miller.
>
> "I remember Mailer being angry with the translator of *Dr. Zhivago,* who had made a pass at Sonia Orwell at a party in the New Town, and throwing the guy down a flight of stairs.
>
> "I remember how the translator, because he was so drunk, bounced up and down and walked back upstairs and the party continued as if nothing had happened.
>
> "I remember having dinner in a Greek restaurant with Sonia and John Calder, and Sonia getting upset with something John said and hitting him over the head with a bottle of wine and knocking him out.
>
> "I remember thinking Oh my God she's killed John.
>
> "I remember Kushwant Singh saying that homosexuals couldn't experience real love, and Stephen Spender mumbling under his breath that they could experience it doubly.
>
> "I remember the Scottish literature day, and John asking

what wine should be served, and I said serve them the wine of the country.

"I remember that the MacDiarmid–Trocchi encounter was everything people say it was: wild, outrageous, deeply felt on both sides.

"I remember the police coming to 161 Rose Street where Burroughs was staying and finding some white powder.

"I remember them thinking it was talcum powder, and leaving."

Jim Haynes opened the Paperback Bookshop, near George Square, in 1959.

September 28

Mention French grammar in educated company and it is certain that within a minute the topic will have turned to the subjunctive, to which the French are as passionately attached as they are to brioche and good manners in children. The second reflex assertion will be that mastery of the subjunctive is as difficult to attain as that of a Chopin *étude*. Neither assumption is quite correct—many French do love their grammar (and the children are generally well behaved) but some native speakers regard use of "le subjonctif" in ordinary speech as "un peu littéraire." Even so, they tend to know it when they see it.

But what about its dowdier-sounding English cousin? Is it in use at all, beyond the common "were" for "was," coming after "if." "If I were you, I'd buy it . . ."; "If I were to go, might you follow?" As with French, certain types feel that the subjunctive renders speech a wee bit posh, and as with French it can be avoided, thus: "If it was up to me, I'd buy it"; "If I go, will you follow?"

In fact, the subjunctive is common in English, though speakers may be unaware they are using it. "I wish I knew when I did"—*voilà*. Confusion threatens whenever "may" or "might" intrudes, they being interchangeable in some situations, though not others. In the case of the subjunctive "May the best team win," only "may" will do. "Might the best team win?" is and can only be a question. Count the subjunctives in the following conversation:

A: "Come what may, arrive at noon for lunch, lest you be hungry later."
B: "Is it necessary that I be there?"
A: "Suffice to say, I might insist."
B: "Perish the thought."
C: "Far be it from me to interfere, but were I not to come, might it help?"
A: "Heaven forbid."

These matters are discussed in a pleasant book, *Grammar for Grown-ups* by Katherine Fry and Rowena Kirton, together with delights such as attributive, predicative, and postpositive adjectives, and the distinction between obsolescent / obsolete; oral / verbal; loath / loathe; luxuriant / luxurious; marinade / marinate. Let the authors not be too harshly judged for the clunking "This book hopefully shows that good grammar is more important . . ." on the first page. Long live the subjunctive. (That's one, too.)

October 5

When traveling, Drummond Moir copies the wording of signs in hotels: "To call a broad from France, first dial 00." "Please leave your values at the front desk." "French widow in every room." He has seen an advertisement for Dickens's fifth novel, "Barney, by Rudge," read in a newspaper that "Bishops Agree Sex Abuse Rules," and enjoyed a government report that promised, "There can be no scared cows." A notice in his car park assures drivers: "Illegally parked cars will be fine." All find their way into *Just My Typo.*

Among the most enjoyable is the metatypo, such as the deferential erratum from the *Dublin Journal*: "In our last issue: for

His Grace the Duchess of Dorset, read Her Grace, the Duke of Dorset." Punctuation is all, as station sign-writers know: "Passengers must stay with their luggage at all times or they will be taken away and destroyed." Who will argue with the slogan of the well-known insurance firm: "Prudential—were there to help you"?

Did Fox News really broadcast the bulletin, "Obama Bin Laden is dead"? Did an anti-immigration group carry a sign that said "Respect Are Country: Read English"? And while it is delightful to think of the church choir congregating for evening sinning practice, we do wonder. Never mind. As an 1864 edition of the Bible suggested, "Rejoice and be exceedingly clad!"

October 12

Perambulatory Christmas Books, 6th series. By now, you are familiar with our purpose: to pay tribute to the thriving second-hand book trade of London and environs (we have also written about shops in Edinburgh, Paris, Berkeley and beyond), and to offer festive reading suggestions as alternatives to *My Shit Life So Far.*

We don't visit the same shops on each tour of duty. Last year, we skipped Fosters, on Chiswick High Road, because it seemed a bit pricey. Is it still there? Last week, we strode out west and felt a pang of autumn pleasure on seeing the white-painted, villagey bow window, above which the sign says "Books." Inside, there are tons of the things, ranged long, piled high. A few commoners foraged in the outdoor barrows and, knowing our place, we joined them. We lighted on an oddity: *Declaration*, published by MacGibbon & Kee in 1957, in which John Osborne, John Wain, Kenneth Tynan, and others "outline their roles in our society." The word "commitment" hung in the air, though it sounded better across the Channel. France had Existentialism and Juliette Gréco; Britain had Angry Young Men and Alma Cogan. It was one year after the Soviet invasion of Hungary, which broke some people's faith, but not others':

> I am convinced that . . . there is a new man about to be born, who has never been twisted by drudgery; a man whose pride as a man will not be measured by his capacity to shoulder work and responsibilities which he detests, which are too small for what he could be.

Doris Lessing—the words are hers—still believed that collectivism could abolish inequality and boring work. Colin Wilson, whose book *The Outsider* had been published in 1956, was at the opposite pole. Like Lessing, he abhorred drudgery. "We live in an age [when] workers clock-in and discuss the football results or last night's television programme." For him, the medicine man was not Marx, but Nietzsche; not Lenin, Kierkegaard. "Heroism is individualism." The filmmaker Lindsay Anderson compared Britain to a nanny state—an early application of that concept. "Nanny lights the fire and sits herself down with yesterday's *Daily Express*; but she keeps half an eye on us too, as we bring out our trophies from abroad, the books we have managed to get past customs."

The editor of *Declaration* was the twenty-four-year-old Tom Maschler, who began by thumbing his nose at the *TLS*. A leader writer on the paper had taken a perplexed view of "complicatedly motivated aggressive hysteria . . . the typical mood of many of our cleverest youngest writers." Fifty-five years on, even Mr. Maschler might see what the author was getting at. As for the "new man" envisaged by Lessing, he turns out to be more interested than ever in football and television. Even so, it is easier to be an Outsider today than it was then. No ideology is required; only the civil philosophy of live and let live. For this enjoyable curiosity, with a cover by Eduardo Paolozzi, we paid £2.

November 16

Spare a thought for the foreigner grappling with English spelling and pronunciation. The tough demanded the dough. She coughed up, as she ought to have done. "I was quite right," she would later write to the wheelwright. "It was a rite of passage, but he looked thoroughly rough." Her daughter's laughter sounded fraught. The dame, always called madame, had good blood. As she liked to read, books were read. She was born in Leicester and attended Magdalen, but preferred life in Kirkcudbright or Milngavie. Her niece was brought to Borough Market by Mr. Brougham.

That's the easy bit. When class enters, things get worse. The haberdasher from Hereford who says "hurricanes hardly ever happen here" inhabits a different England from the 'aberdasher from 'Ampshire who says, "They don't 'ardly never 'appen 'ere neither." It is no use issuing an hortatory, "In English the aspirate 'h' is pronounced," because within an hour, honestly, your honor will be hors de combat. If you refer to an historic hotel, why not an hotel with an history? If you discuss the ants in your pants with your aunts at a dance, using the same *a* all through, you are probably Scottish or Irish, in which case you are spared the class—not *closs*—anxiety.

Some of these matters are discussed in *Choose the Right Word,* an "easy-to-use" guide to "better English." We have improved our English by learning not to address strangers as "mate"—"many find it objectionable"; we have also learned not to say "the hoi polloi" (the "hoi" is the *the*), that flotsam floats, while jetsam is on shore. We know the difference between discreet and discrete, but have never learned (learnt?) when to say burned and when burnt, hanged or hung. We will continue to say air hostess—*Choose the Right Word* suggests the ugly "steward"—except when we mean hair 'ostess.

2013

January 11

About once a year, there is a mini-debate about the timidity of book reviewing. It has been going on for some time. "Sweet, bland commendations fall everywhere upon the scene; a universal, if somewhat lobotomized, accommodation reigns." That was Elizabeth Hardwick, in 1959. More recently, a writer in the online journal *Slate* suggested that the blogging, tweeting free-for-all that sometimes passes for criticism fosters too much "niceness," not necessarily a nice quality.

To halt the saccharine spread, the not-so nice sharpened their tools and carved out the Hatchet Job of the Year. The first award went to Adam Mars-Jones, for a review of Michael Cunningham's book *By Nightfall*, and the shortlist for the second has been announced. There are eight nominations, including Richard Evans's review of A. N. Wilson's *Hitler* ("It's hard to think why a publishing house that once had a respected history list agreed to produce this travesty"; *New Statesman*), Claire Harman on *Silver: A Return to Treasure Island* by Andrew Motion ("at every turn the former Poet Laureate clogs the works with verbiage"; *Evening Standard*), Allan Massie on Craig Raine's novel *The Divine Comedy* ("some of the writing is very bad"; *Scotsman*), Camilla Long on Rachel Cusk's story of her marriage break-up, *Aftermath* ("quite simply, bizarre . . . acres of poetic whimsy and vague literary blah"; *Sunday Times*) and Ron Charles on Martin Amis's "ham-fisted" *Lionel Asbo* (*Washington Post*).

The favorite is likely to be the review by Zoe Heller of Salman Rushdie's memoir *Joseph Anton*, which appeared in the *New York Review of Books* last month. One commentator had already relished it as "a hatchet job among hatchet jobs"; another welcomed the "most pointedly brutal review" of 2012.

Brutality is never nice. Enjoying a healthy demolition as much as anyone, however, we reached for Ms. Heller's piece with a certain shameful anticipation—only to discover that it is thoughtful and well-written, not in the least brutal; on a par with the excellent review of Rushdie's book in the *TLS* by Eric Ormsby. Hatchet-job prizes are good fun (not so much for Rushdie, Cusk, and others) but it would be unfortunate if critics felt they were being urged to draw blood, to show off their "sharp" edge. The reviewer's chief responsibility is to the potential purchaser of the book, who, unlike the remunerated reviewer, is asked to pay hard-earned cash for the product. The most difficult task for a reviewer is to remain true in writing to the feelings experienced while reading, to convey them in elegant, entertaining prose. It's tougher than being brutal.

January 25

Martin Luther King, Jr Day is a federal holiday in the United States, allotted the third Monday of the month of January. This year it fell on January 21, which happened also to be the day set aside for the public swearing in of President Obama for his second term. Quite a day. As if there weren't enough on January 21's plate, it was the inaugural George Orwell Day.

We know this because we read it in the newspapers. They knew about Orwell Day because they received a press release from Penguin Books. But what now? Usually, on a Day set aside for an important personage, something happens. People have a holiday or eat haggis. On Orwell Day, we could have visited the writer's grave at All Saints, Sutton Courtenay, in Oxfordshire, or raised a glass in the Moon Under Water to "one of Britain's most influential writers" (the press release), or staged a protest against the omniscient CCTV cameras under whose gaze we live our daily lives. A Day when the governing classes of "England, My England" agreed to use the English language in clear and thoughtful ways would be welcome. But all that happened on Orwell Day was that Penguin released some titles—*Nineteen Eighty-four, Animal Farm, Homage to Catalonia*—with attractive dust jackets.

The knowledge that Orwell Day was conceived in partnership with the Orwell Estate doesn't help us. Why this year? Orwell died on January 21, 1950, making it sixty-three years since his death. If they had waited a few months, they could have launched Orwell Day on June 15, 2013, the 110th anniversary of his birth. A round figure, at least.

This set us wondering how you go about inaugurating a Day. Just by saying so? January 25 is Burns Night, when people who read little Burns celebrate the immortal memory. But Burns was the Bard. April 23 is the birthday of the writer whom Scots think of as the other Bard, but it is not, so far, his Day. Could it be, if someone just decided to turn it into one? Norman MacCaig died seventeen years ago, on January 23, 1996. Perhaps it's time for MacCaig Day? He was one of Scotland's eminent modern poets, and ought to be better known in the provincial South. On January 20, 1974, the poet (and *TLS* old boy) Edmund Blunden died. That'll be forty years next year. Give him a Day! The more we think about it, the more we like the thought. Choose your saint. Preferably when you have something to promote. A Day only lasts twenty-four hours.

February 1

A Visit to Rimbaud and Verlaine at Home

We have written before about the rooming house at 8 Royal College Street (formerly Great College Street), Camden, in which Arthur Rimbaud and Paul Verlaine lived between May and July 1873. You might have seen us loitering on the pavement outside, invoking the spirits within: "wrestling," as Rimbaud put it, or fencing with knives wrapped in towels, until one or the other scored a body-hit. The door remained locked, however; our hands had not overlapped with Verlaine's on the banister, nor our shoulders bumped against the jambs that Rimbaud's once did. When the opportunity turned up, therefore, we seized it.

The invitation came from the poet and publisher Anthony Rudolf; also present were the novelist and *flâneur* Iain Sinclair and the poet Deryn Rees-Jones. Michael Corby, who now owns the house, immediately relished Sinclair's surprise at seeing portraits of Mrs. Thatcher and Winston Churchill in the symbolists' hallway. Mr. Corby is an outspoken member of the UK Independence Party (UKIP), but is proud of his quondam Continental lodgers. He led us to the top floor.

No one is sure which room the poets rented. In his excellent biography, *Rimbaud*, Graham Robb says only that it was "on an upper floor." Evidence for this exists in a letter in which Verlaine describes climbing the stairs. Mr. Corby is convinced that the small uppermost room is the one, "because it would have been the cheapest." Sinclair, almost bumping his head on the undulating ceiling, was inclined to agree. "The vibe is right."

Rudolf stood by his conviction that it was the front first-floor room. Before Verlaine recorded climbing the stairs (our fingers have now overlapped), he had been to market to buy a fish for supper, and some oil to cook it in. "I was approaching the house," he later told Ernest Delahaye indignantly, "when I saw Rimbaud observing me through the open window. For no good reason, he started to snigger." Could a man on the street observe a sniggerer at the small upper window, clearly enough to take offence? It seems more likely that the laughing provocateur would have been on the first or second story. "I climbed the stairs anyway and went in," Verlaine continued. Rimbaud greeted him: "Have you any idea how ridiculous you look with your bottle of oil in one hand and your fish in the other?" There then followed the famous quarrel. Verlaine slapped Rimbaud on the face with the fish, because, as he put it to Delahaye, "I assure you, I did not look ridiculous."

Our party descended to the second floor, trading Rimbaud–Verlaine anecdotes on the way, then to the first. Was it here that parts of *Une Saison en enfer* and *Les Illuminations* were composed? Where the lads got drunk, where Verlaine howled with guilt at abandoning his wife and child, then "kissed and embraced . . . a heaven, a dark heaven" (Rimbaud)? As Mr. Corby delivered an enjoyable tirade against the poets' British Museum library colleague Karl Marx, we took note of an original folding door. When opened, it connects to a smaller room. Might they have been able to afford the two? It is always assumed that they were broke, but Verlaine's "patient mother" sent money to London, according to biographers, and he may have had savings.

We thanked Mr. Corby and departed happy, if still undecided about the location. The image of the connecting door would not leave us, however, and later on we read again Rimbaud's prose poem "Vagabonds," which most likely refers to the Camden period:

> Pitiful brother! What atrocious vigils I owe to him! I did not have a fervent grasp of this undertaking. I responded by laughing at this satanic scholar, and made for the window. . . . [Then] I stretched out on a straw mattress. And, each night, almost as soon as I was asleep, the poor brother would get up, mouth rotted, eyes torn out, and pull me into the room. . . .

Remark not only the window—the first floor casements offer fine views of the street—but Rimbaud's straw mattress ("une paillasse") in another room. The pitiful Verlaine was able to enter without a key, then pull his neighbor into his room. A connecting folding door would make this operation feasible.

Before we left, Mr. Corby had ushered us all into the ground floor living room, where the poets' landlady, Mrs. Smith, might have dwelt. On his mantelpiece, he keeps a giant ornamental fish, representative of the creature at the heart of the drama. Now that we appear to have solved the Riddle of the Room, we must set about determining what species of fish hit Rimbaud's face.

February 22

To prove that the habit of literary correspondence is not dead, Frederic Raphael, a kenspeckle figure hereabouts, and Joseph Epstein embarked on an exchange of emails throughout the year 2009. The result, gathered together as *Distant Intimacy: A Friendship in the Age of the Internet*, stretches to over 300 pages, signed off from the US, "Best, Joe," and from England and France, "Tout à toi, Freddie." If you like this, from Joe to Freddie, chances are you will like *Distant Intimacy*: "Miranda Seymour fades for me into that blur of English biographer women: Hilary, Hermione, Claire, and the rest—One Fat Englishwoman, as I like, collectively, to think of them." Freddie singles out Claire Tomalin for alleged crimes committed against him, as well as other literary ladies. One was married to a former editor of the *TLS* (John Gross), author of a "dull, skimpy and smug autobiography." Tout à toi, indeed.

Neither correspondent seems to have much time for other writers. What Epstein says of Beckett—"high on the list of the world's most overrated"—holds true of "Mailer, Updike, Roth," destined to be sunk by the relentless "bonking" which "gives their scribbling its drama." Gore Vidal, still living when the exchanges begin, is "best likened to a car with a dead engine whose horn nonetheless keeps sounding off" (Joe). Disliked for most things, Vidal "put affectations of pedantry between himself and the profane crowd," but Freddie catches him using faulty Latin. Harold Pinter, "may he rest only half in peace" (Joe), is the author of "pukey little poems."

There is a certain fascination in witnessing finely tuned sensibilities exhibiting their wounds. Even the *TLS*, generally well spoken of, fails to please every time. Joe to Freddie: "When the annual *TLS* issue on Scotland arrives, I feel as if I have a week off. A Scottish editor at the *TLS*, fellow named"—here we are obliged to draw a discreet veil—"once asked me if he had edited me 'too Calvinistically.' When I asked him to clarify, he said, 'You know, taken too many amusing things out of the piece,' which in fact he had done." There was a place for Calvin as editor of *Distant Intimacy.*

April 19

Attentive readers will be aware of our interest in the London residence of Arthur Rimbaud. We have observed that he spent more time in the English capital than in the French one. We have also noticed that on two occasions, the summer of 1873 and the spring and summer of 1874, Rimbaud's stay coincided with that of Vincent Van Gogh.

While Rimbaud the Londoner has gained official status, Van Gogh's shade walks among us more or less unremarked. This is partly because he created no notable works in the city, but also because he was not a perambulator, as Rimbaud was. We know that he wore a top hat ("you cannot be in London without one"), went boating on the Thames and visited Dulwich Picture Gallery. While living at 73 Hackford Road, Stockwell, SW9, he fell in love with the landlady's daughter, Eugenie. "I now have a bedroom such as I always longed for, without a sloping ceiling and without blue wallpaper with green fringes. I lodge with some charming people. . . ." Eugenie Loyer rejected Vincent's approaches. When his behavior became eccentric, he was asked to move out.

Last week, in newly created Van Gogh Walk, late Isabel Street, just yards from Hackford Road, we found ourselves surrounded by children playing hide and seek in the shelter of recently erected art installations, taking aim at a basketball hoop, roller-skating in and out of decorative plant beds embellished with inscriptions from Van Gogh's letters: "If one loves nature one finds beauty everywhere," etc. The chair in which we sat alluded to Van Gogh's wood and wicker chair. The semicircular crescent beds host plants which, if allowed to blossom, will show blue and yellow flowers in homage to his palette. A tree-trunk sculpture, intended to evoke the painting "Undergrowth with Walking Couple," with footholds for climbing, was earning the appreciation of infant art lovers.

Van Gogh and Rimbaud had almost identical lifespans (1853–90 and 1854–91, respectively). Had they met at the British Museum, for example, they would have found much to talk about (both spoke French and English). Van Gogh was on the point of abandoning business to dedicate his life to art, just when Rimbaud was deserting art for business. By 1874, Rimbaud's wrist bore the scars of a crime passionnel; Van Gogh's ear would one day be sacrificed for love.

The walk in its Isabel Street incarnation was said by one of our new acquaintances to have been "bad." He didn't mean bad in the bad-is-good sense. "Cos of that estate," he said, gesturing backwards with a hide-and-seek look. Asked what he knew about the man in whose honor the no-go area had become go-go-go, he replied, in the same not-unfriendly way, "Ar'ist." His female companion, more romantically inclined, volunteered the detached ear. A dashing cyclist with a mohawk haircut, all of eight years old, paused to give his own unequivocal view: "Excellent."

April 26

At Bonhams, New Bond Street, the second part of the extraordinary *Roy Davids Collection, Poetical Manuscripts and Portraits of Poets,* comes up for sale. There are revelations even in the handwriting: wildman Dylan Thomas had small, neat lettering; Muriel Spark, so particular in many ways, wrote in a wayward scrawl; Tennyson's hand is schoolboyish, William Morris's coiled in barbed wire; Robert Lowell mixes upper and lowercase block letters in a single word.

There are many Scottish poets in this catalogue, under the letter M: MacCaig, MacDiarmid, MacLean, Muir. The single manuscript we covet, however, is "Lines, in Praise of the Royal Marriage" by William McGonagall, an unpublished work of five quatrains. The marriage was between George, Duke of York, and Princess Victoria Mary, or "May."

McGonagall has been saddled with the label "world's worst poet," but detractors seldom take the trouble to read him with attention. His verse is memorable; it is enjoyable; it is distinctive. You will travel a long way before meeting someone able to identify the work of Alfred Austin, the contemporary Poet Laureate, but reel out some lines by the Bard of Dundee—"Ye lovers of the picturesque, if ye wish to drown your grief, / Take my advice, and visit the ancient town of Crieff"—and the rhythm is as good as a signature. McGonagall's name is the only one that many Scots could offer if asked to identify a national poet, after Burns.

His unique trait as a poet is to lack the least trace of the poetic. His verses would broadcast the news, at a time when some listeners at public recitals were illiterate. Although mocked by the public, his feelings were reflective of the common people. Think of his poem on the unveiling of the Black Watch Memorial at Aberfeldy: "As they gaze upon the beautiful Black Watch monument, / I hope they will think of the brave soldiers and feel content." When did the event take place?

'Twas in the year of 1887, and on Saturday the 12th of
November
Which the people of Aberfeldy and elsewhere will
remember.

They certainly will now. In "The Ancient Town of Leith," the poetry of reportage is taken to a higher plane: "And as for the Docks, they are magnificent to see, / They comprise five docks, two piers, 1,141 yards long respectively." Parodists always fail to catch the essence of McGonagall, which resides in his sincerity; imitations pale when set beside the real thing,

The poem up for auction (£2,000–3,000) is not one of his best but, like everything he did, it is unmistakably his:

May their hearts always be full of glee.
And be kind to each other and ne'er disagree,

And may the Demon discontent never mar their happiness.
And may God be their Comforter in times of distress.

Note the characteristic traits of good will and restraint of feeling, which those who mock McGonagall consistently overlook, and sometimes lack.

May 3

We were dismayed—too feeble a word—to find our name missing from the list of the world's leading thinkers published by *Prospect.* There are sixty-five of them. Could not a place have been found in the foothills of the mighty peak for the author of *Wise Man Say*? The world's 65th leading thinker is "Jean Pisani-Ferry, economist," of whom we confess to knowing nothing. We do know of No. 64, Robert Silvers, editor of the *New York Review of Books,* but while our admiration for his journalistic know-how is without limit, we are unable to pass on a single one of his thoughts. He doesn't think at all (in public); as an editor, he arranges the thoughts of others. "J. C., aphorist and perambulator" would have looked splendid at No. 64. Or at 63, where, alas, we are usurped by Jessica Tuchman Mathews; Carmen Reinhart and Ngozi Okonjo-Iweala are 59th equal. Confessions of ignorance are apt to become tiresome.

Zadie Smith (35) and Hilary Mantel (33) are more elevated thinkers, according to *Prospect* ranking. How would you characterize their thought? Our guess is that you haven't a clue—as you would have, for example, about the thought of a novelist such as George Orwell or Jean-Paul Sartre. Going yet higher, we find Nate Silver, a statistician, and Asghar Farhadi, a filmmaker. Ali Allawi, "Iraq's minister of trade, finance and defence," occupies fourth spot in the list of the world's great thinkers. Second is Ashraf Ghani, president of Afghanistan, who had "a stint at the World Bank." All were voted for by *Prospect* readers.

The world's premier thinker is Richard Dawkins, founder of the Dawkins Award, given to "notable individuals in recognition of their work in promoting atheism around the world." We are happy not to be thought notably worthy of this honor. The list may be viewed on the magazine's website. It shows readers' comments, a helpful guide to how people think in the digital democracy. Here is one:

> Why voters chooses Richard Dawkins that I did not understand in my opinion he is pompous writer want publicity so always wrote loud rattling. He did not wrote anything in his entire life some thing original. He life long writing is carbon copy of Darwin.

Give that reader a vote, and he would surely cast it in favor of the author of *Wise Man Say.*

May 17

Grammar wars are breaking out all over. Readers may recall the Battle of the Apostrophe, sparked by a Devon council's threat to obliterate the little signifier from possessive street names. Beck's Square and Blundell's Avenue in Tiverton were in danger of becoming, poorer by far, Becks and Blundells. A fortnight ago, something called the Bad Grammar Award was given to a group of academics who had put their names to an open letter to the Education Secretary Michael Gove—on the subject of grammar. Mr. Gove wants more emphasis on nuts-and-bolts grammar in schools than has been the case in recent years. The 100 academics maintain that forcing young children to take spelling, punctuation, and other tests "will put pressure on teachers to rely on rote learning without understanding." They add: "Little account is taken of children's potential interests and capacities, or that young children need to relate abstract ideas to their experience, lives and activity."

That sentence would not pass a grammatical test, whether set by Mr. Gove or most decent teachers. Nor would the following win points for elegance in style and eloquence in expression—the proper criteria for judging prose, with or without prescriptive grammar:

> The proposed curriculum consists of endless lists of spellings, facts and rules. This mountain of data will not develop children's ability to think, including problem-solving, critical understanding and creativity. Much of it demands too much too young.

The writer and excitable anti-prescriptivist Michael Rosen joined in with an article based on the premiss that "there is not one correct form of Standard English." The problem with the value judgement "correct," Mr. Rosen said, "is that it suggests that all other ways of speaking or writing are incorrect. This consigns the majority to being in error. Gove might be happy with that way of viewing humanity, but I'm not."

In the twinkling of a conjunction, a linguistic debate has become a question of human rights, and the grammar war is intertwined with the class war. We have little doubt that Mr. Gove is as aware as Mr. Rosen is that there are many different ways of speaking English coherently and expressively. (Both were educated at Oxford.) The antagonists differ only over the belief that a basic standard of verbal and written expression will help children to make their way in the world beyond the local community. An idiolect may be functional there, but perhaps not elsewhere. Mr. Rosen is possessed of admirable zeal, but he is apt to give the impression that an acquisition of English grammar disables people for life.

Good grammar is an aid to eloquence, though not the only one. Avoidance of hackneyed phrases—"mountain of data"; "too much too young"—also contributes, as does attention to vernacular rhythm. The most desirable attribute of all, surely, is versatility of phrasing and tone, allied to an extensive vocabulary, so that the speaker may vary the register according to where he is or what he wishes to say. It used to be acceptable to speak one way in the street and another in the classroom. Did it cease to be so only when the adoption of Received Pronunciation, or "BBC English," became a political matter?

The bad temper of the Grammar Wars leads to everybody calling everybody else a fool. The charge is implicit in Mr. Rosen's outbursts. The judges of the Bad Grammar Award call the 100 signatories fools. English adult learners of foreign languages feel like fools when unable to grasp the difference between a verb and a noun, an adjective and an adverb. "No one taught us," they wail. The insistence that inculcation of such simple skills is crippling to personal expression is one of the more puzzling, not to say foolish, beliefs of our time.

May 24

The magazine *Poetry* (Chicago) asked a number of versifiers to list "A few don'ts," to mark the centenary of Ezra Pound's famous injunctions, put down in the March 1913 issue of the journal: "Use no superfluous word, no adjective, which does not reveal something"; "Don't use such an expression as 'dim lands of peace.' It dulls the image," etc.

Today's don'ters tend to be more elliptical: "Don't betray the people you right about," says Reginald Dwayne Betts, perhaps punningly. "Work in a place where no one knows what an iamb is." "Don't be the poet who, ensconced in your tenure track, dismisses the man on the corner selling his work—he could be Whitman." You don't say. Jill Alexander Essbaum picks up the sepulchral tone: "All sorrow is sacred. . . . Don't speak when a poem is speaking to you. . . . Honor thy father and mother." Sina Queyras implores us to "Understand that terror is pleasure," before going all sage like the others: "Not the prayer, the moment before the prayer." William Logan adopts a different tone, no more helpful: "Don't be any form's bitch. . . . Don't think you're special."

It is left to a critic, Marjorie Perloff, to return to Poundian common sense. She issues five don'ts (Logan has twenty-seven; Betts twenty-one). Here are four, pared down:

Don't underestimate the importance of a sense of humor, of irony. Satire, parody, mock-epic are hardly "inferior" forms of poetry.
Don't play the victim card.
Don't forget that all poems are written with an eye (and ear) to earlier poetry and that to write poetry at all one must first read a lot of the stuff.
Don't take yourself so seriously.

Don't bet on it. (That's one of ours.)

June 7

The first mention of vodka in English was made by a Scotsman, Captain Cochrane, who drank the liquid serpent while in Russia in 1820. He called it "vodka (whiskey)," a sketchy comparison, at best. Any respectable Caledonian will insist that whiskey drinking is far too important an activity to involve the complementary consumption of food. Vodka drinking, on the other hand, is too important to be undertaken without it.

English vodka drinkers have never got the hang of this crucial detail. The new *Dedalus Book of Vodka* by Geoffrey Elborn contains an extract from *Angel Pavement* (1930) by J. B. Priestley, "the first appearance of vodka in English fiction," in which Mr. Golspie, a shady businessman, induces Miss Matfield, a proper typist, to down a glass or two. Miss Matfield thrills to the "incendiary bomb" which "had burst in her throat and sent white fire racing down every channel of her body." It is delightful, but it lacks an essential ingredient: the pickle.

We asked the writer Zinovy Zinik for the correct approach. "The ritual of consuming vodka is a special kind of yoga, with its own system of breathing," he told us. "Or rather, there are two systems. According to the first, you breathe in deeply, gulp down an entire glassful and then, still holding your breath, take a bite of something salty (pickled cucumber or salted herring). Then you let the air out of your lungs.

"The second system is the opposite: you breathe out, emptying your lungs, gulp down a glass and take a bite of the pickle while holding your breath. No one has so far proved which of the systems is more efficient. With the third glass, the drinker achieves a state of bliss, true paradise. The sensation does not last long, however, and all the glasses that follow are attempts to regain the paradise-of-the-third-glass lost."

July 19

Our constituents will be aware that as the year's end approaches, we customarily don hobnailed boots and tramp the streets in search of "a neglected work by a known author," or something of the sort, for the edification of more sedentary readers. We avoid firm definitions, but "neglected" would probably exclude any book that has had a publisher in the present century.

It was with surprise, then, that we saw John Williams's novel *Stoner* referred to on the educated website The Literary Saloon as "largely overlooked." *Stoner* was published just last year by Vintage Classics, the paperback arm of Random House UK. If you like American design, you may purchase the New York Review Books edition (2006). *Stoner* is available in current French, Spanish, and Italian editions. If you prefer, you may have it as an audiobook.

The overlooked *Stoner* came to the Saloon's attention by way of the *Daily Telegraph*, where on July 13 John Sutherland referred to it as a "Lazarus miracle." On publication in 1965, Mr. Sutherland wrote, *Stoner* "came, it was read, it was forgotten." Actually, no: it came, it was read, it went into paperback, it crossed the Atlantic, it was issued in London by Allen Lane in 1973, and reviewed favorably in the *TLS*. In the first decade of the present century, it was published in translation in Europe; it was reissued in the US in 1966, 1972, 1987 and 2006.

Mr. Sutherland was prompted to write about *Stoner* after hearing Ian McEwan talk about it on BBC Radio 4. Asked for a summer reading tip, Mr. McEwan, who is also published by

Stoner's latest publisher, Vintage, suggested it as "the beach book for 2013." A week or so later, Mr. McEwan's friend Julian Barnes chose *Stoner* as his holiday reading in the *Observer*: a novel "by a forgotten American . . . that deserves to be rediscovered." *Stoner* has been rediscovered by Nick Hornby ("brilliant, beautiful, inexorably sad, wise, and elegant"), Geoff Dyer ("beautiful and moving, as sweeping, intimate and mysterious as life itself"), Bret Easton Ellis ("almost perfect"). The actor Tom Hanks has rediscovered *Stoner*: "one of the most fascinating things that you've ever come across." Colum McCann rediscovered it again and again, having "bought at least fifty copies, using it as a gift for friends. . . . It is universally adored by writers and readers alike."

Mr. Barnes joked that the author of *Stoner* could be confused with the guitarist of the same name, but omitted to mention another novelist called John Williams, usually distinguished by the use of the middle initial A. He is the author of *The Angry Ones* (1960), *Night Song* (1961), and *The Man Who Cried I Am* (1967). Born in 1925, John A. Williams really is in need of the Lazarus miracle.

August 9

When decimal coinage replaced the old pounds, shillings and pence in February 1971, the former Monty Python star Michael Palin made a solemn entry in his diary: "a small portion of our language dies forever." There may be people reading this who do not know what a threepenny bit refers to, or a tanner, a bob or two, a florin, a dollar or a half-dollar (in UK currency). The farthing, the shilling, and the guinea have just about survived.

Palin's diary entries are included in *A London Year*, published by Frances Lincoln. He resented decimalization "less than the all-figure telephone numbers which dealt a blow to local feeling in London and made it practically impossible to remember phone numbers". His own area code, for Kentish Town, was GULliver, which after 1966 changed to 485 (GUL 2929 became

485 2929). Some of the old name codes reflected the areas they served directly—BAYswater for Bayswater, for example—while others were indirect: ABBey (Westminster); BALham (Tooting); CHErrywood (South Wimbledon). HOGarth for Shepherds Bush referred to the artist's residence nearby—Chiswick, more accurately, but Chiswick was CHIswick.

Many of the codes were literary, GUL among them. In pre-numerical days, BYRon sent calls through to people in South Harrow, DICkens to Highbury, FLAxman to Chelsea. Logic lurks in these groupings of capital letters. It is no doubt ignorance that leaves us scratching our head over IVAnhoe in Buckhurst Hill. The Paddington exchange was AMBassador, because of the prevalence of embassies in the area. Enfield was KEAts (he went to school there). The presence of hop merchants in Southwark meant that the exchange was not SOU, reserved for Southall, but HOP. HAM went to Hampstead, while Hammersmith was RIVerside. Bloomsbury was MUSeum. Someone must know why Wimbledon was LIBerty, Finchley VIRginia and North Wembley DRUmmond.

August 16 & 23

Crowds continue to gather outside the cavernous entrance to the Basement Labyrinth, as rumors spreads that the new edition of *The TLS Reviewer's Handbook* is imminent. It will contain an appendix, "The Etiquette of Making a Pitch." A "pitch" is a suggestion from a freelance writer to an editor—let's call the editor Jonathon—concerning an article or a book. Rule No. 1 in "The Etiquette of Making a Pitch" is don't say "pitch." It marks you out as an *ingénu* who wishes to appear as an initiate. Rule No. 2: Don't address Jonathon as Jonathon. For reasons unclear, it is hard for some people to use Mr., Mrs., or Ms. (or Sir or Madam) when dealing with strangers. Rule No. 3: Do not say "Hi" or "Hope you had a good weekend" or "Hope you are having a good day." Your hopes will be to no avail. Rule No.

4 covers the others and is therefore the most important of all: If in doubt, fall back on common courtesy.

Here are three examples, all genuine, of How Not To Approach Jonathon. The first could be used at "pitch" workshops throughout the land:

> Hi Jonathon
>
> Love your work and was wondering if you could consider a review of my work for *TLS*
>
> if you don't ask you don't get
>
> thanks Jonathon
>
> Joe

> Thank you for considering my review of the new novel, "The Fisher Kings," for publication in your zine/blog. My submission is withdrawn published elsewhere.

> Dear Jonathon,
>
> I write for a literary blog called —, the irreverent web presence of an independent bookstore. I think some of our posts might be of interest to you. For example, there's Library Night, featuring my dorky New Zealand childhood, a lamb deboning machine, and a three-wheeled motorcycle. We'd love it you followed us on Twitter. Please feel free to forward this to all the book nerds in your life. Have a smashing week,
>
> Tracey.

Orders for the new *Reviewer's Handbook* are now being taken.

August 30

Literary telephone numbers: the Gallic dimension (see NB, August 9). Michel Delarche writes to say that in Paris at the end of the 1970s, "some older people still used the three-letter, four-digit codes" when called on to give their telephone numbers. Monsieur Delarche's first number started with 343, corresponding to DIDerot. "Since the telephone exchanges in Paris had been named after the streets where they were located," he goes on, "Paris was replete with literary phone numbers: BALzac, BOIleau, BOSsuet, BUFfon, CHEnier, FLOrian, GUTenberg, LAMartine, MIRabeau, RENan, SEVigne—and last but not least VOLtaire."

September 6

Visit to Seamus Heaney (1939–2013)

Seamus Heaney's contributions to the *TLS* began in 1965, the year his life as a writer began in earnest. The first was "Lint Water," which appeared in our pages on August 5, 1965, three months before the appearance of his debut collection: not *Death of a Naturalist*, as you might assume, but *Eleven Poems*, a twenty-page booklet published by Queen's University, Belfast. Heaney, who has died aged seventy-four, was accessible and bountiful in his good will and good humor. A friend of ours offered to recall a day spent in Dublin with the poet. We present his report here.

> No sooner had I arrived at the house on the Sandymount Strand, than Seamus whisked me off in his not-so-shabby Mercedes (Classic FM on the dial) to see the Martello Tower at Sandycove, which features in the opening scene of *Ulysses*. "This is it. The same sea that sprayed old 'stately plump' as he stood here in his yellow dressing gown lathering his chops." In *Ulysses*, Seamus said, "the English language opens like a pack of cards in the hands of a magician." From the tower, we proceeded to a restaurant in central Dublin. Drivers in cars that rolled alongside at traffic lights recognized him, as did the staff in the restaurant. It was an effect of what he called, deploying to full effect his big cuddly-toy smile, "the N-word"—the Nobel Prize, awarded to him in 1995. We had finished lunch and were preparing to leave,

when the waiter appeared with two well-stocked tumblers of Bushmills, compliments of the house. Seamus thanked him graciously, but the voltage of his smile dropped. We had already done justice to a bottle or more of good wine. He had to steer the Merc back to the Strand. I had to steer him towards a taped conversation once we got there. He looked at me; I looked at him. With regret, the contents of the two glasses were tipped into a handy plant pot. We hoped it wouldn't waft a "heavy, nauseating fall-out" when the waiter came to collect the dishes.

Back home, his wife Marie—pronounced "marry"—settled us in the country farmhouse-style kitchen, while a pot of corned-beef soup burbled happily on the hob. Did she charge us with taking care of its welfare? Seamus talked of literary relations between Scots and Northern Irish, of the books in his childhood farmhouse at Mossbawn, County Derry, "just a dictionary, an algebra, and one or two others," of the tart profile by his schoolfellow and quondam friend Seamus Deane that appeared in the *New Yorker* in 2000. Deane described the young Heaney as "calm and sly," which hurt, he said. To Deane, he was "always 'well in' with those in power." For a moment in the kitchen, Heaney was in the school blazer and flannels of St Columb's College again. "Well, fair enough. I was head prefect."

Is there a faint smell of burning in the air? The great good talker carried on—talk that no Bushmills could have improved: poetry and song fragments, church reference decorated with Latin phrase, Derry place names—all wrapped up in the G-word: gratitude, his life's ruling principle. In the middle of a quotation from Kavanagh or MacCaig, Marie burst into the kitchen. "My corned-beef soup!" Her tone and his countenance—always ruddy, now more so—suggested it wasn't the first time. "There goes supper."

In a later communication to do with the article which lay behind our rendezvous, Heaney responded patiently to requests for details, and added a few of his own. A postscript read: "One day we'll have the whiskey." Not a word about the soup.

October 4

Picking up a glossy Penguin edition of Graham Greene's novel *Brighton Rock* in a friend's house the other day, we read on the cover that it is "Now a Major Motion Picture." Is it? Was it "major" even in 2010 when the film in question appeared, with Helen Mirren in the role of Ida (not to be confused with the Boulting brothers' 1947 version)? We have a vague memory of its release, thanks to the disproportionate amount of publicity movies attract when a household name is in the cast. One of five films Ms. Mirren made that year, it disappeared almost immediately, on the back of weary reviews.

What is a major film? *Casablanca*, maybe; *City Lights*; *High Noon*; *Vertigo*; *8½*; *The Battle of Algiers*; *Les 400 Coups*; *The Bill Douglas Trilogy*. Throw in something by Bergman. Everyone has their own ideas and their own list. We successfully avoided the latest screen version of *Brighton Rock*. The cover image on the unhappy Penguin of Sam Riley, who played Pinkie, compounded by an inane foreword by the screenwriter Rowan Joffe, put us off rereading the novel. We have never heard anyone mention the film in conversation, even to say they disliked it. What's the "major" bit?

A new edition of William Faulkner's novel *As I Lay Dying* has just been issued, with a picture of the actor (and director) James Franco on the cover, and the same legend, "Now a Major Motion Picture." It drew criticism from pro-Faulknerians and anti-Francoites, and the familiar philistine response: "If this causes a single kid in high school to pick up Faulkner's novel, then the film will have done its job."

As I Lay Dying is, in fact, officially a minor motion picture. The *Huffington Post* reported this week that "James Franco's adaptation of *As I Lay Dying* was scheduled for a Sept 27 theatrical debut. Days before the film was set to arrive in theaters, however, it was announced that it will not be shown on the big screen." The distributor, Millennium Films, plans to release Franco's *As I Lay Dying* on October 22, on iTunes.

At the end of August, a brick-sized copy of *Salinger*, edited by David Shields and Shane Salerno, arrived, bearing a self-directed compliment on the cover: "The Official Book of the Acclaimed Documentary Film." That'll be the acclaimed film that had yet to be released when the book came out? The acclaimed film that was panned when it appeared last month? If Salerno and Shields cause one kid in high school . . . then who cares what fictions they come up with?

November 8

Algeria's most famous writer, and Africa's first Nobel Prize-winner, would have celebrated his one hundredth birthday on November 7, had he lived. Albert Camus was not a French writer. He identified entirely with the country of his birth and upbringing; with the exception of his late novel *La Chute*, all his major writings are set there.

Everyone is talking about Camus, so we took the opportunity to visit the archives, to see how long the *TLS* has been talking about him, and what has been said.

Not surprisingly, given the fact that Paris was under occupation in 1942, the *TLS* overlooked the publication of *L'Etranger* by Gallimard that year. Often thought of as Camus's first book, it was in fact his third: two collections of essays, *L'Envers et L'endroit* and *Noces*, both issued by a small Algerian press, preceded it. The author was already well known when the *TLS* reviewer of *The Outsider*, in Stuart Gilbert's translation (June 22, 1946), wrote: "A considerable amount of critical discussion of M. Camus's short novel, or of the ideas and philosophy which can be attributed to it, has preceded its publication in this country."

The paper made up for having missed Camus's first novel in the original by reviewing his second, *La Peste*, at the time of publication, and in glowing terms. "While the latest books of M. Sartre and of Mlle de Beauvoir have added nothing of importance to their earlier work, *La Peste* stands out, beyond any discussion, as of capital importance to the development of M. Camus" (August 2,1947).

The reviewer, at the time anonymous, was Gabriel Marcel, a writer born within the lifetime of Rimbaud and sometimes called the first French existentialist. Translations of this "work of art," he said, were bound to appear soon. *The Plague* duly arrived in 1948, in what our reviewer, Anthony Powell, called "an excellent translation" (Stuart Gilbert, again). A review of Camus's first play, *Caligula*, the same year proves that the adoration was not unquestioned: "On stage, Camus's gorgeous claptrap might be relieved by telling theatrical strokes. But the play as a whole does not add up."

There was nothing to discuss in 1949, but in 1950 the paper took account of another aspect of Camus's activity, journalism: "It was through the clandestine press of the Resistance that the silence of the Occupation was first broken. Among the most prominent of the various newspapers that then passed in circulation was *Combat*, whose voice was often that of Camus." Much space was given to *Actuelles*: 1944–48. *L'Homme révolté* (*The Rebel*) was noticed, in both French and English editions, in 1953. By then, the author, who had lived through poverty, survived tuberculosis, and been active in war, had just turned forty.

INTERLUDE

The Murdoch Shilling

All through my years at the *TLS*, I put up with people making remarks—not always good-humored ones—about "taking the Murdoch shilling" or "working for the dirty digger." Some refused to write for a Murdoch-owned paper. In the mid 1980s, Alasdair Gray urged me to approach the novelist and short story writer James Kelman who was, Alasdair said, eager for work as a reviewer.

I duly did so. My relationship with Kelman was distant but real enough. In the summer of 1979, when appreciation of his fiction was still at local level, I had rung him at home in Glasgow to ask if he had a short story he could let me read for possible inclusion in the *New Edinburgh Review*, of which I was then the editor. He said he would rummage around and see, but admitted he had all but given up sending out short stories, having become frustrated by rejections and—worse, from his point of view—alterations by interfering editors to his punctuation and preferred ways of configuring dialogue.

I assured him that he wouldn't encounter any such problem with us, and "Keep moving & no questions" appeared in the Winter 1979 issue of the *NER*. A little later, the fledgling publisher Polygon—formerly Edinburgh University Student Publications Board, base of the *New Edinburgh Review*—persuaded Kelman to excavate more of his work from the drawer, and issued a book of stories under the alluring title *Not not while the Giro.* I was pleased to see that the book included what might be regarded as his comeback, "Keep moving & no questions." A novel followed, then another. But a review for a Murdoch-owned paper? "I couldn't do that," Kelman said, and replaced the receiver.

Seen from my own sheltered position, the *TLS* as a "Murdoch paper" never appeared to be in danger of imminent closure, as people sometimes liked to predict it was. If the worst came to the worst, surely, he would sell it off by itself to—it was pleasant to imagine—a bountiful proprietor with stately premises in a Bloomsbury square. The word was, however, that he appreciated the touch of class it brought to his stable, which was in other places lacking it.

A rare occasion when it was necessary to submit to the specter of domineering proprietorship arose when Lindsay Duguid commissioned a review by Alan Rusbridger of a new biography of Murdoch by William Shawcross. Rusbridger was employed by the *Guardian* but had not yet become its editor, and occasionally he reviewed for us.

The result was predictable. Like most people on the paper he worked for, Rusbridger disapproved of the subject's professional conduct in certain areas, and of his general cultural outlook in almost all of them. The review contained no allegations of a more serious sort, however. If some well-substantiated revelation of unlawful behavior had been brought to light and deserved to be made public, the editor of the *TLS* might have had to convene a meeting of his staff and to offer them, one by one, the opportunity to refuse the Murdoch shilling.

But no. While the book had the appearance of endeavoring to remain impartial, the review would only end up sounding like the latest cry in what was by now the routine clamor of anti-Murdoch complaint. If published, its main distinction would be that an attack on Rupert Murdoch had been given space in one of the papers he owned.

The editor of the *TLS* at the time was Ferdinand Mount. He read the review, then telephoned Rusbridger and said, with that suggestion of reasonable good humor that was seldom far away in his dealings with others, something like, "Alan, am I correct in assuming that you are not eager to see the *TLS* closed down?" Rusbridger was correspondingly reasonable, accepted a kill fee, and the piece was set aside.

Many years later, in 2006, by which time I was a columnist with a weekly space to fill, word reached me that a thriller by a well-known *Guardian* staff writer had been sent by the paper's fiction editor to the crime novelist Michael Dibdin for review. The novel was published under a pseudonym and Dibdin was in the know, but he had trashed it so comprehensively that Rusbridger, now editor-in-chief of the *Guardian*, intervened and instructed the books department not to run the piece.

Was there a little item here for NB? I contacted a friend on the books pages at the *Guardian*, to check what I knew so far. He sounded uneasy, and before the story could move along an email arrived from Rusbridger.

> Jim: I gather you've been asking about the non-running of Dibdin's review. If you are planning to write something I hope you can acknowledge that there are few entirely innocent pots and kettles in such matters. I can speak of personal experience: the *TLS* commissioned me to write a review of a book concerning one R. Murdoch. On receiving my copy the editor rang me and told me he was sure I would "quite understand" that the *TLS* couldn't possibly run it. He paid me a modest kill fee. The difference with me and Dibdin was that—until now—I never blabbed about it.
>
> Times change, and I am perfectly happy for you to include this little story were you minded to write about the *Guardian*.

This in itself was so elegant and "reasonable" that there was no question of doing anything other than ditching the item.

NB

2014–2017

2014

January 17

A pressing matter has been brought to our attention by the team in the Basement Labyrinth, as they comb final proof sheets for rogue commas in preparation for the new edition of *The TLS Reviewer's Handbook*. They have sent up the following sample sentences, with the familiar request: "Quid faciam?"

> If a novelist spends on average two years on a book, how much money does she need in order to live comfortably? The cost of living might oblige her to share living space. Each writer is expected to solve the problem in her own way.

We have been pondering the issue of the non-gender-specific pronoun since reading a piece about interviews on the *New Yorker* website. The author, Hannah Rosefield, quoted a contemporary novelist on the subject of the interview form: "A writer's life is in his work, and that is the place to find him." His work? Him? Ms. Rosefield offered no resistance to the conservative usage, but responded in kind when making her own generalizations. Speaking of a recently published collection of interviews, she remarked: "Too often the profiles read as if the writer is sitting alone . . . in her glamorous apartment." Switching her attention to live interviews before an audience, she observed: "What people really want to know is what it is that the writer does that enables her to transform ordinary words . . . into art." Her apartment? Her art?

In Ms. Rosefield's first statement, a definite and an indefinite article would have served as well: "A writer's life is in the work, and that is the place to find it." In the second, "his or her glamorous apartment" would not have offended the ear. Ms. Rosefield's solitary "her" has a political purpose; worse, from a literary point of view, it is confusing. She begins her discussion with Henry James being interviewed in 1904; she dates the birth of the modern interview to E. M. Forster's mild grilling by the *Paris Review* in 1953, and ends by citing an imaginary interview with J. P. Eckermann by Gore Vidal. Roland Barthes is quoted along the way. Ms. Rosefield would like to see inside Peter Carey's house. We learn that Haruki Murakami gets up at 4 am. None of these guys sits alone in her glamorous apartment or explains what enables her to transform ordinary words into art.

What to do? As always, we advise consulting the *Handbook* (if you can find a copy). "Best practice: avoid. When sound permits, use 'he or she'; sometimes, 'they' is suitable; when avoidance is impossible and sound or other factors prohibit 'he or she,' resort to tradition."

May 9

Questions were raised some years ago about the fate of royalties from Hitler's biography *Mein Kampf.* The author made no arrangements for the management of his estate, perhaps failing to foresee that the book would sell in large numbers for years to come. There are many editions of *Mein Kampf* in circulation, including the "Special Banned Edition," the "Unexpurgated edition (profusely illustrated)" and the "Stalag edition." All are subject to European copyright restriction, which protects ownership of an author's work for seventy years after death. The royalties generated by *Mein Kampf* since 1945, not to mention publishers' profits, amount to a considerable fortune.

The question of who benefits is complicated and the trail is pitted by legal wrangling. The US government seized the copyright to *Mein Kampf* during the war, but in 1979 it was sold to the publisher Houghton Mifflin. It is estimated that they sell about 15,000 copies of the book every year—a respectable backlist figure for any book. In Britain, where the latest edition was published by Pimlico, a division of Random House (1992; reprinted 1993, 1994, 1998, 2001, 2002, 2004, 2005, 2007, 2011), the rights are handled by Curtis Brown. In both cases, efforts have been made to donate profits to charity. In 2001, however, the London-based German Welfare Council ended an arrangement which had existed with Curtis Brown since 1976, by handing back a substantial sum.

Because Hitler was a resident of Munich at the time of his death, the immediate recipient for much of the royalty revenue is the Bavarian finance ministry. The book is banned in Germany, but that doesn't stop the euros rolling in, from India, Turkey, and other countries where it is a big seller. Again, the federal government has tried to direct the millions towards worthy causes, only to encounter the same difficulty of finding charities willing to accept them. The ban doesn't deter underground traders. One German language edition is published by an outfit calling itself Elite Minds Inc.

At the end of 2015, *Mein Kampf* comes out of copyright. When that happens, anyone will be able to produce an edition, with whichever cover insignia they choose. In the German context, while the end of copyright settles the awkward matter of financial distribution, it is likely to make suppression more difficult.

To surmount this problem, according to Timothy W. Ryback, author of *Hitler's Private Library*, the state of Bavaria allocated €500,000 to the Munich-based Institute for Contemporary History, with the aim of producing a "critical edition" of *Mein Kampf*. The idea was to set the 800-page work in historical context, outlining Hitler's sources and motives. The appearance of such an edition would lift the book out of its forbidden status, relished by latter-day Nazis. According to Mr. Ryback, however, writing on the website of *The European,* Jewish groups have joined certain German intellectuals in opposing the scheme. In what Mr. Ryback calls "an unfortunate about-face," the Bavarian state has decided not to fund it, after all. The elite minds are leaving *Mein Kampf* to Elite Minds Inc.

June 6

The *TLS* in modern literature, second series. Hugh Keyte writes from South London to alert us to *The First Lady Chatterley* by D. H. Lawrence, published in the US in 1944 and latterly by Penguin. Who would have guessed that Constance Chatterley was a reader of the *TLS*—even if her subscription had lapsed by the time Lawrence finished the third and final version? Here she is, musing on life's gentler pleasures:

> But at the same time, she was sad. . . . She would always want to read Swinburne again sometime: she would always want to play a bit of Mozart to herself . . . see a Russian ballet . . . and she would always like to be able to glance at *The Times Literary Supplement* to see if there might be some thrilling book.

Some twenty pages further on, we find her husband in pontifical mood: "Oh, property is at the root of all religion. Even *The Times Literary Supplement* says that the ownership of property has become a religious question." In which issue was that view given? Clifford Chatterley does not specify.

The First Lady Chatterley is thought by some to be superior to the third. Mr. Keyte observes that it has "none of the third version's embarrassing stuff about John Thomas," although it does have "the all-time ripest piece of Lawrentian erotic claptrap: 'But for the penis we should never know the loveliness of Sirius or the categorical difference between a pomegranate and an india-rubber ball.'"

July 4

Midsummer Perambulations. Soho played host to London's Gay Pride festival last Saturday, and the Charing Cross Road bookshops joined in the fun, with window displays showing camp classics such as *Desire in the Shadows* and *Daddy's Boy*. Once inside the perambulator's favorite emporium, Any Amount of Books, we reflected on the transient nature of taboo. Not much chance now of Ronald Firbank's *Prancing Nigger* making it into the window—yours for £2 in a neat Penguin Classic, embracing two other Firbank titles—or *The "Nigger" of the Narcissus*. We could have bought an attractive Livre de Poche called *Dix Petits Nègres*, but the original of Agatha Christie's tale has long since been recast as *Ten Little Indians*.

And perhaps rightly so. No word carries such woeful baggage in English today; no decent person would use it thoughtlessly in conversation, even in familiar company. Newspapers that cheerfully play host to once-unutterable obscenities refuse to print it, resorting instead to prim asterisks or the wincing "n-word." Teachers shrink from it. Students in US colleges are issued trauma warnings before being confronted with *Huckleberry Finn* or *The Sound and the Fury*, two of American literature's greatest works. Even Hemingway and Fitzgerald are dubious (see, if you dare, *The Sun Also Rises*). In Britain recently, a BBC presenter was ousted from his post after playing the old song "The Sun Has Got His Hat On," which happens to contain the word.

But here comes the problem. Some African Americans use it frequently, and certain black authors exploit its shock value. No one would seriously suggest censoring the title of Dick Gregory's autobiography—just that word and nothing else—or changing Ed Bullins's play *The Electronic Nigger* to *The Electronic N-word*, or Gil Scott-Heron's *The Nigger Factory* to *The Indian Factory*. Why single out Agatha Christie? We are assured that the fact that the author is African American makes the difference. But if there are things A can say which B cannot, what is the equality we put so much store by worth? Who owns the English language? Don't we have equal rights in linguistic matters?

At Any Amount, we put aside the Firbank and the French Christie, and lighted on a copy of Carl Van Vechten's novel of the Harlem Renaissance, *Nigger Heaven* (1926), an engaging story of a young black writer, Byron Kasson, and a librarian, Mary Love. There are many fine passages, such as this one, in which Byron observes the Harlem populace going to work:

> From all the side-streets, up the avenues, they marched: Negro workmen and workingwomen, all leaving the walled, black city temporarily to labour in an alien world. Some were bowed and old and walked slowly and with pain. Others were young and sinewy and chattered as they marched rapidly forward. The thought struck him that it was like a symbolic procession, the procession of an oppressed people. Thus the Jews went out into the desert to build pyramids for the Pharaohs.

Even in the 1920s, Van Vechten's title attracted trouble. His father, generally supportive, advised against it. The book has suffered ever since because of it. But people such as Langston Hughes knew him well enough to see that his intentions were not cheap. It is thanks to Van Vechten that the James Weldon Johnson Collection of African Americana was established at Yale. His photographic archive of black writers and singers is unequalled. For a US first edition—battered and bruised but with a good clean text—we paid £2.

August 1

How is English spoke? How should she be? We know that English footballers can no longer spoke her proper, ruining the country's World Cup chances as a consequence. You might think the BBC hires new radio presenters on condition of having poor enunciation. On a minor perambulation the other day to the charming Bloomsbury book dealer Collinge & Clark, we found the ideal guide: *English As She Is Spoke*, a phrasebook first issued in Paris under a different title in 1855. Numerous editions of Pedro Carolino's little helpmate since then have steered foreigners through thickets of communication. No need to go hungry in the morning, for example:

> John bring us some thing for to breakfast.
> Yes, Sir; there is some sousages. Will you than I bring the ham?
> Yes, bring-him. We will cup a steak.

The English have always been healthy eaters. Among the food you will find on the typical table—"Quadruped's beasts"—are Shi ass, Roebuck, Dragon, Lioness and Dormouse. If he survives the carving, John will prove useful when the time comes to go out:

> John, make haste, lighted the fire and dress-me.
> Give me my shirt.
> There is it sir.
> Is it no hot.
> Bring me my silk stocking's.
> Its are make holes.

The communicative visitor, presumed to be a gentleman, may wish to return home with an example of native woodwork. Confronted by a carpenter who asks, "Which hightness want you its?", he should answer clearly, "I want almost, four feet six thumbs wide's, over seven of long." With the gardener he will need to know if "The artichoks grow its?" Expect the reply: "I have a particular care of its."

Carolino's English is idiomatic, certainly, and none more so than his chapter on that subject, "Idiotisms." While dining on the cup steak sliced from the chap's ham, our visitor might entertain guests with tales of "building castles in Espagnish"; or else advice: "A horse baared don't look him the tooth"; or just something to get them thinking outside their own idiotism:

"The stone as roll not heap up not foam. . . . With a tongue one go to Roma." How can the hosts not love him?

In the preface to the 1967 edition of *English As She Is Spoke* that we plucked from the outdoor barrows, Leslie Shepard notes that "There is a strange excitement in incoherent yet dramatic gibberish. . . . the inescapable suggestion of deeper significance lurking behind the frantic complexities." At Collinge & Clark, the owner was dispatching a very expensive book, but took time off to marvel at that strange significance, charging us £3 for it.

THE *TLS* IN LITERATURE: a final round-up. It has been diverting to find ourselves cropping up in poems and novels, in London, New York, or in the African bush with Hemingway. In Jilly Cooper's *Harriet* (1976), the heroine, not alone among the Cooperingian sorority, has a "muddled feeling . . . of the importance of intellectual things." She hopes in an unspecified future to write books herself, and daydreams of "being reviewed one dizzy day in *The Times Literary Supplement*. 'Miss Harriet Poole in her first novel shows sensitivity and remarkable maturity.'"

Dizzy-making, indeed. Dizzy in a different sense is Penelope Fitzgerald's fantasy in her first novel, *The Golden Child* (1977), of a lecture at the Sorbonne by Dr Tite-Live Rochegrosse-Bergson—"arrant nonsense"—being "eagerly taken down by the two journalists. A serious résumé would evidently appear in *The Times Literary Supplement*." Is it the kind of thing we do? We hadn't noticed. You might say the same of *The File on Death*, a crime novel by Kenneth Giles (1973), in which a local vicar makes money by shooting and stuffing birds, which he then sells by advertising in the *Observer*. "Like that fellow who sells women through *The Times Literary Supplement*."

That's quite enough to puzzle over for a while.

August 8

How many First World War books can the nation bear? Our history editor estimates that the numbers arrived in this office reach treble figures. We have seen at least five books with the title *The Great War*, and more than one each of *1914* and *1913*. Some have allusive or ironic titles: *To End All Wars* or *Over by Christmas*. Others are pitiful: *A Broken World, Harry's War*. The horror is meant to be felt in *Trench, Ring of Steel, Attrition*. Nurses are given their due in *Veiled Warriors* and *Dorothea's War*, while *Into Touch* records the story of rugby internationals who perished. *First World War Curiosities* and *Cockney War Stories* have a lighter touch. There is a ton of the stuff.

As there was, apparently, at the very start. On turning to the *TLS* of August 6, 1914, with the war just a day old, we find on the front page a list of "Books of Importance on the European Crisis." They include *Germany and England, The Whirlpool of Europe, Servia and the Servians* [sic], *The Men Around the Kaiser* and a score of others. Indeed, the first *TLS* to reach readers under "the present situation" amounts to a special number on the war's origins. One review tackles the new topic of aerial bombardment: it was not going to be possible "to forbid or restrict the warlike use of aircraft." An article on cartography offers maps prepared by *The Times*, "to supply the public with the means of following every development of the great war." Note the use of the now common term, only a few days into the conflict.

The next week's *TLS* continued the theme, with a reminder that, as always, life went on; "A hint to the holiday-maker: get out your cycle and spend your time exploring some of the beauty spots of the homeland." The same issue offers what is likely to be the first Great War poem to have appeared in any journal: "Thou Careless, Awake!" by the Poet Laureate, Robert Bridges. "Stand, England, for honour, / And God guard the Right!" Such sentiments rang from every corner in August 1914.

Over the succeeding weeks, the paper published many poems related to "the situation," mostly abysmal to modern ears. "Happy England" by Walter de la Mare grimly suggested that "Her peace that long hath lulled asleep / May now exact the sleep of death." In the issue of September 10, Thomas Hardy maintained the stirring tone in "Men Who March Away," with, however, a note of poignancy, if not ambiguity—another first, perhaps, in the annals of the poetry of the Great War:

In our heart of hearts believing
　　Victory crowns the just,
　　And that braggarts must
　　Surely bite the dust,
March we to the field ungrieving . . .

"Is it a purblind prank, O think you?" Hardy asked on behalf of the infantrymen, answering immediately, "Nay." The war was just a month old, but his "Men who march away" were not coming back.

August 22 & 29

A novel is a novel is a novel. A translation is a translation. Your translation of our novel might be faithful, smooth, perhaps better written than the original; it is not, though, the same book. That seems obvious, but is apparently not so to everyone. In the *Guardian* last week, Jean Findlay wrote about C. K. Scott Moncrieff's English rendering of *À la Recherche du temps perdu.* It was the first of three attempts. In 1981, Terence Kilmartin published a revised version of Scott Moncrieff; more recently there has appeared a translation by several hands. All have their champions, but "if you want to read the Proust that Proust saw published," said Ms. Findlay, "then you must read the Scott Moncrieff translation." An even better way to read the Proust that Proust saw published would be to read the Proust that Proust wrote.

In the latest issue of the *Atlantic*, Nathaniel Rich reviews the new novel by Haruki Murakami, *Colorless Tsukuru Tazaki and His Years of Pilgrimage*, taking as his theme "the riddle that is Murakami's prose." Ah, Mr. Rich reads Japanese, we thought; how impressive. Then he told us that Murakami "learned to speak English by reading American crime novels." Ah, Murakami has started writing in English; how impressive.

As either would be, were it the case, but neither is. Murakami writes in Japanese. Mr. Rich reads him in English translation. This does not prevent him asserting that "no great writer writes as many bad sentences as Murakami does." His crimes include "awkward construction," of which Mr. Rich gives an example: "Just as he appreciated Sara's appearance, he also enjoyed the way she dressed." It doesn't seem too bad to us, but the question is: constructed by whom? How do you make the connection between the English phraseology and the Japanese text? We couldn't do so. We admire those who can. Mr. Rich is not among them.

Murakami is also guilty of "cliché addiction." It would be interesting to know the status of cliché in Japanese prose, given that it is a more complex affair in English than is generally supposed. Mr. Rich isn't equipped to tell us, but he knows a good English cliché when he sees one: "He really hustled on the field. . . . He wasn't good at buckling down. . . . He always looked people straight in the eye." Who wrote these "ugly sentences"? Not Murakami. In the course of a 2,000-word article, Mr. Rich mentions Barry Manilow, Elvis Presley, Stephen King, and other pop-culture icons (talking of clichés), but not once does he mention Philip Gabriel, the translator of *Colorless Tsukuru Tazaki and His Years of Pilgrimage.*

September 5

As the referendum on Scottish independence approaches, our thoughts turn to ways in which Scotland will remain separate from the rest of the United Kingdom, no matter what happens on September 18. The church, the legal, banking, and educational systems, will retain their distinctive features. There is, however, another unique area, seldom mentioned: grammar.

We don't mean couthie phrases of the "Lang may yer lum reek," "Haud yer wheesht" variety, but syntactical construction.

This came to mind as we read James Wood's essay in the *New Yorker* of August 25 on the novelist and short story writer James Kelman. Kelman is not so much a Scot as a citizen of the Republic of Glasgow, a provenance reflected in his writing on almost every page. Quoting generously, Mr. Wood sets a new record for the use of what we will considerately call "the f-word" in a *New Yorker* article (and that's saying something). Sharp as he is, however, he failed to make plain to American readers Kelman's distinctive use of "but." Let's recast that: Sharp as he is but, he failed to make plain. . . . On the Glaswegian tongue, "but" functions as "though" or "however" and often comes at the end of a sentence. Or it functions just as "but"—placed at the end but. Let's eavesdrop on two friends, Big Tam and Wee Shug, at the bar of a Glasgow pub:

> Tam: "Ah'm daft aboot thon *New Yorker*."
> Shug: "Ah like it an aw. There's a loat a swerrin' in it but."
> Tam: "Stoap buyin' it well."
> Shug: "Ah'd miss James Wood but."

Mr. Wood concocted some fancy theories about Kelman's "but," without quite getting it right. He omitted any mention of the deployment of "well" at the end of a sentence—the place where you might expect to find "then."

> Tam: "Change owr tae the *LRB* well."
> Shug: "It's no the same but."
> Tam: "Stoap greetin' well."

At which point, Big Tam rolls his copy of the *TLS* into a baton and prods Wee Shug's arm. He does this repeatedly. Shug says, "Gonnae no do that," which is nothing if not another example of independence by other means. Tam intimates his intention to "Shoot the craw," not before reminding Shug of their weekly book group meeting, at which the volume under discussion is

Not not while the Giro by James Kelman. Tam proudly says he read it in one sitting.

"Gaun yersel big man," Shug says in deadpan congratulation. About the book group, he has a confession to make: "Ah'll no can go." The Glaswegian grammatical perfection of those sentences does nothing to reduce Big Tam's exasperation. "Yir huvin me oan. Yir the main speaker but."

"Get anither yin well."

Could Mr. Wood be persuaded to step in?

September 19

Here we go again: who or whom? That or which? Less or fewer? Don't protest, "It doesn't affect you and I," because it does. To blithely split or not to split an infinitive? Hopefully, you never use hopefully to mean "I hope." Thankfully, you know when "fortunately" is the right choice. You are aware what fulsome and fortuitous actually mean. You know to use actually as little as actually possible. These are usages up with which no reader of *The TLS Reviewer's Handbook* need put.

Language mavens—those exotic birds only ever mentioned in articles about usage—are said to abhor transgressions of the rules. They are also known as prescriptivists or purists, according to Steven Pinker in his new book, *The Sense of Style: The Thinking Person's Guide to Writing in the 21st Century*, as well as "language police, usage nannies, grammar Nazis." The other brigade—language changes, so relaxez-vous—are called descriptivists. But who are these grammar Nazis who insist that only the original meaning of a word is the correct one, or that English grammar should follow Latin? Is there a single sane person alive who believes that modern speakers ought to sound like John Dryden? Our hunch is that progressives set up straw purists in order to knock them down.

In general, however, Mr. Pinker offers sensible, not to say self-evident, reasons why you should endeavor to write as clearly and elegantly as you can. Doing so "ensures that writers will get their message across"; it "earns trust." We warmed to Mr. Pinker when he added a third reason, less often stated; good literary style "adds beauty to the world." If your prose clunks at the wheels and rocks on its axle rods, who'd want to travel in your car? After he has had a chance to read his own book, Mr. Pinker will never again use a phrase like "linguistic bubbe meises" or write a sentence such as "With an allergy to abstraction and a phobia of cliché, Wilkerson trains a magnifying glass on the historical blob called 'the Great Migration' and reveals the humanity of the people who compose it." Prescriptivists and Descriptivists alike are holding their heads in their hands.

Mr. Pinker devotes a section to the curious modern anxiety besetting the uses of who and whom. It is easy to tease *whom* advocates—think of the song retitled "Whom do you love?"—and quite a few people do. He quotes the American writer Calvin Trillin: "Whom is a word that was invented to make everyone sound like a butler." Mr. Trillin, who was educated at Yale, knows how to sound like a butler whenever he wants to, and when not to when he doesn't. So does Mr. Pinker (Harvard). So does our own Michael Rosen (Wadham College, Oxford), who once ran a campaign to commit *whom* to the linguistic flames. They can all use *who* when *whom* would be strictly correct, because they have knowledge. Why Mr. Rosen should wish to deprive his young charges of the advantages he enjoys is a mystery.

"No one needs to be reminded that ain't is frowned upon," says Mr. Pinker, deploying another straw purism. No it ain't. Any versatile language user knows it ain't necessarily so. It is there to create an effect. But if ain't and who are all you've got—if you don't know your less from your fewer, your effect from affect—then affectless is what you are likely to be. Is it your fault? Or the fault of those nice boys from Harvard, Yale, and Oxford? If you yourself can't explain why you languish in the communicative underclass, don't worry. They'll do it for you.

October 10

The *TLS* in Literature. It's over, as we have more than once said. To put it another way: We can't go on. We'll go on.

John Blazina writes from Toronto to alert us to—how come no one mentioned this before?—an "abhorrent" occurrence in Barbara Pym's novel *No Fond Return of Love.* Dulcie's cleaning woman, Miss Lord, arrives, having just had lunch. Dulcie inquires as to the menu:

> "Egg on welsh and a Russian cream."
>
> "It sounds . . . "—Dulcie hesitated for a word—"delicious. . . . What exactly is Russian cream?"
>
> "It's a kind of mousse with a sponge base and jelly on the top", said Miss Lord. "The jelly can be red, yellow or orange." She finished her coffee. "Were you going to throw these flowers away? Unsightly aren't they." She bundled up some slimy-stalked zinnias and dahlias in *The Times Literary Supplement* and went out to the dustbin with them.

Barbara Pym, you will recall, languished in the doldrums for sixteen parched years, until the *TLS,* in co-operation with Philip Larkin and David Cecil, resuscitated her career in 1977. *No Fond Return of Love* (1961) was the last of her novels to be published before the drought. There is no resentment in our stating that. We mention it only to spare you the thought that the issue in question was the one that rescued her.

October 17

Is the anglophone reading public's reluctance to tackle works in translation a recent phenomenon? Not long ago, or so it seems, every student's bag bulged with Sartre and Camus, Dostoevsky and Tolstoy, Kafka and Mann. How could Ivy Compton-Burnett or Angus Wilson—no disrespect to either—compete?

Patrick Modiano, who has been awarded the Nobel Prize for Literature, is the author of two dozen mostly short novels, linked to thriller and mystery genres, with modernist tints. His work has been translated into some thirty languages. English is one of them—a handful of novels have appeared here or in the US—but you would never know it from a perusal of even the better bookshops. On our perambulations, we have never seen a single English Modiano. The day after the Nobel announcement, we made our way to the splendid new Foyles shop in Charing Cross Road. As feared, there was no trace of the Nobel Prize-winner on the otherwise all-embracing shelves of fiction in English. At the desk, we were told that one book is available, in print-on-demand form. We declined the offer to order it. Had many people been asking for his work? Yes, they had.

Deciding to take our chances, we made our way up to the French department. Between Michelet and Molière, however, there was just an empty space. At Inquiries, a gentleman with an English accent that must have enchanted many a foreign visitor asked, "Which language does he write in, sir?" We did not omit to mention that he had won the Nobel Prize the day before. Paper and pen were offered. "Write down the name, please, sir."

Mildly *décontenancé*, we set out for the European Bookshop in Warwick Street, where we were faced with an abundance of Modiano. We contented ourselves with two: *Rue des boutiques obscures*, which won the Prix Goncourt in 1978, and *Quartier perdu*. Fifty pages into the latter, we are captivated. One taste gives the flavor of the whole: the narrator, Jean Dekker, writes *policiers* under the name of Ambrose Guise. Dekker was born in Boulogne-Billancourt, outside Paris, in 1945. That rang a bell—probably because we read at the front of the book a moment before that Modiano was born in Boulogne-Billancourt, in 1945. Dekker was partly brought up in London and regards English as his first language. Modiano was brought up in Belgium and spoke Flemish. Dekker's mother was a dancing girl; Modiano's was an actress.

Meanwhile, the mysteries of Dekker / Guise's life unfold with pleasing irregularity. Any moment now, there will be a scene in which a man enters a London bookshop in search of a novel by Ambrose Guise. He will be asked to "write down the name, please, sir." It's that sort of story.

October 24

When a colleague approached the other day with an open book, uttering sage maxims, we thought that advance copies of the Happy Holidays edition of *Wise Man Say,* our ever-expanding collection of sense and sapience, had arrived ahead of schedule. "All great artists draw from the same resource: the human heart." We couldn't have put it better. In fact, no one could put it better. "Cooking is like writing poetry: be careful in the choice of your ingredients and respectful of how they work together." It's us! Surely it's us. "A person's speech is a mirror to his or her soul." Who else would be capable of it?

But no. For its Happy Holidays treat, our patient public must wait a little longer. Taking commercial advantage of the delay, Virago have rushed to fill the gap with *Rainbow in the Cloud: The Wit and Wisdom of Maya Angelou,* from which the above are taken. Leaving you hungry for more. "One must be open to what life has to bring. I have learned that a friend may be waiting behind a stranger's smile." How true, how true. "A conversation between friends can sound as melodic as a scripted song."

And with that deep-fathomed sense of mystery that causes even the author of *Wise Man Say* to pause in wonder: "Always be concerned when a naked man offers you his shirt; a person can't love you if he or she can't love him- or herself." There are several reasons not to accept a shirt from a naked man, but none better than this. As Ms. Angelou, who died earlier this year, said: "I realized I was not a writer who teaches, but a teacher who writes."

Not to be outdone, we offer the following: Those who cannot wait for the Happy Holidays edition of *Wise Man Say* may purchase *Rainbow in the Cloud* for £12.99.

October 31

In a recent article in the *Guardian*, the critic Terry Eagleton was allowed to play the game that has appealed to us all at some stage: what would you do if you were king for a day? Many of King Terry' s edicts were sensible. On-the-spot fines would be issued "to people who say 'refute' when they mean 'deny' and 'fortuitous' when they mean 'fortunate.'" People who tell you "that they literally exploded with laughter will be literally exploded. Those who talk about life as a journey will have their travels rapidly terminated."

Terence the First might be too merciful a monarch. Why only a beating-up for people who bump into you on the street while texting? As king, he would abolish prisons, but compensate by proposing a graver punishment for serious offenders: having their mobile phones taken away.

We were enjoying this and dreaming of some social improvements of our own—how about issuing licences to shoot lights-jumping cyclists on sight?—when we arrived at the end of the piece. "Finally, a well-known English literary journal would be asked to state publicly why it has done a hatchet job on every book of mine it has reviewed for the past forty years."

We know which journal the king is talking about—this one—because he named it in a book of interviews published some years ago. The publisher was Verso, also responsible for Mr. Eagleton's *Saints and Scholars*, which the literary journal in question called "Ingenious, erudite and entertaining." Some hatchet job. Is a new edition of *Figures of Dissent* (2003) on the way? If so, the publishers may want to quote the opening remark of a review in that English journal: "Terry Eagleton has turned into a brilliant book reviewer." Of his memoir, *The Gatekeeper* ("scintillating"), it was said in the *TLS* that King Terry looked back "not so much in anger as in wonder—and with enviable wit—at the forces that have shaped him."

Mr. Eagleton is a prolific writer—five books between 2002–04, for example. Even he, sulking on his throne, might feel a grudging gratitude towards the journal for keeping up with his production. There has been some disapproval of glib Marxist theoretical criticism along the way, but even here the plebeian cat knew how to look upon an anti-capitalist king. Of *Literary Theory* (1996), the *TLS* said, in retrospect, that it was "probably the most influential volume of literary criticism [of] the past thirty years."

Reviewers of books in these pages are free to say what they please, so long as they write elegantly and within the bounds of decency. Even royalty is subject to the law. The description of Mr. Eagleton as a "brilliant" reviewer is good enough for us, because reviewing books is what he does for the *TLS*.

December 5

The rise and fall of literary reputations, contd. Consider the ascent of Edith Sitwell. Something in the air, circa 1925, made the reading public eager for a profusion of lines such as these:

> In the lateness of the season, I with the golden feet
> That had walked in the field of Death, now walk again
> The dark fields where the sowers scatter grain
> Like tears, or the constellations that weep . . .

There is no end to them—eighty lines in this poem, "Eurydice," alone. She also turned her hand to humorous rhymes, situated somewhere between the Keats of "There was a naughty boy" and Walter de la Mare: "Lily O'Grady, / Silly and shady, / In the deep shade is a lazy lady." For a twenty-year period from 1918, when her first collection *Clowns' Houses* appeared, Sitwell published almost a book a year—mainly poetry, but also biography: *Elizabeth I*, *Alexander Pope*, *English Eccentrics*.

In wartime, Macmillan indulged a Sitwellian whim and accepted for publication *A Poet's Notebook*, a thick sheaf of quotations with a few of her own jottings tagged on. "In these notes we see Poetry and her necessities as they are seen by the eyes of the poet." The proportions are 90 per cent citation, 10 per cent Sitwell. Under "On Poetry of the Greatest Kind," we find Karl Barth: "The theme of the Gospel . . . proclaims Eternity as an event." Before you can figure out what it means, the eyes of the poet fall upon you: "Is not this true of the greatest poetry?" Next, a quotation from Wagner: "Music would seem to reveal the most secret sense of scene, action, event, environment." Sitwell: "Is not this also true of Poetry?" Music is a favorite point of reference. Orlando Gibbons said, "Rhythm is melody stripped of its pitch." Sitwell said, "This should be remembered." Of the lady lazy and shady, there is no trace.

During or after the war, her voice lost its own rhythm. The great flow of books from the 1920s and 30s slowed to a trickle (she was made Dame Edith in 1954). The reading public found itself receptive to the more austere voice of F. R. Leavis: "the Sitwells belong to the history of publicity rather than of poetry." The voice did not need to add: "This should be remembered."

The fiftieth anniversary of Sitwell's death falls on December 9. The year before she died she wrote to the *TLS* about William Burroughs's novel *Naked Lunch*, reviewed in the issue of November 14, 1963: "I do not wish to spend the rest of my life with my nose nailed to other people's lavatories. I prefer Chanel Number 5." She had been sought out by Allen Ginsberg on a visit to London not long before, which may seem surprising at first. On reflection, however, they were well suited: flamboyant, hieratic, unself-doubting. Our copy of *A Poet's Notebook* cost £2.50 from the bountiful basement at Quinto, Charing Cross Road.

P. D. JAMES—also known as Phyllis or Baroness James of Holland Park—who has died aged ninety-four, was a regular contributor to the *TLS* for over twenty-five years, on topics ranging from the latest *Inspector Morse* mystery to *Notes on Nursing*. She was an editor's dream: easy to contact (she picked up the phone, in the days when we phoned), biddable, unfussy—"*The Great Train Robbery*? Oh, that might be interesting"—

and trusted to turn in the specified number of words, in her case around 1,500, on a typescript requiring few interventions. Curious now to think that when a pair of books on Jack the Ripper arrived in the post, a chin was scratched and then a voice heard to wonder: "Could this be one for Phyllis?"

That particular review appeared in April 1975. "The continuing fascination with the Whitechapel murders is difficult to explain," she wrote. "There have been more prolific and more ingenious murderers. . . . Nor do the crimes offer any great psychological interest." One of the books under review, *The Complete Jack the Ripper* by Donald Rumbelow, introduced readers to the term "Ripperologist"—a "somewhat repellent word," wrote Baroness James (she entered the House of Lords in 1991). She led readers delicately through the grim details, ending on a note that reminded us that the reviewer of *The Complete Jack the Ripper* could also be called on to write about *The Faber Book of Church and Clergy*:

> Is it too much to hope that these books will see the end of the great Ripper saga and that the mad butcher and his victims may be left to silence or to the judgment and mercy in which their generation, more easily perhaps than ours, found it possible to believe.

December 12

Christmas in the Basement Labyrinth is traditionally marked by interns requesting cancellation of holiday leave. Some have even asked that pay be withheld, a touching request that becomes all the more so when you remember that they do not receive any. The confusion can be put down to the joy of fulfilling work. Prizes, prizes, prizes. There was a shocked silence when the winner of the All the Prizes Prize was announced at the annual labyrinth party. In previous years, the APP has been reserved for Amos Oz, and he seemed likely to carry it off again (five honors in 2014 alone). But no. It was us! Apparently, we have won so many of our own prizes—including the Incomprehensibility, though we keep that quiet—that the All the Prizes Prize is the only one left. After much comradely pushing and genial persuading, we advanced to the podium.

Meanwhile, it has been pointed out (again) that of the world's great aphorists, only three are regularly credited with aphorisms they did not utter: Oscar Wilde, Mark Twain, and us. It will not surprise readers to learn that our name often appears under "To be vain is a mark of humility rather than pride" (in fact, Swift wrote it) but when we read that we are supposed to have said, "Some circumstantial evidence is very strong, as when you find a trout in the milk" (in reality, H. D. Thoreau), we know a scholarly edition of *Wise Man Say* is called for.

2015

February 6

The *TLS* in literature: third series. It is surprising that no one has alerted us to the central role played by the *TLS* in Philip Roth's early story "The Kind of Person I Am," from the *New Yorker* of November 28, 1958. At a cocktail party "in the neighborhood of the University of Chicago," the narrator—he is called "Philip Roth"—starts a conversation with "an intelligent-looking young woman," who looks at him "as she might have gazed at the cover of a volume the title of which was unknown to her." When they talk, she checks him out by guessing the kind of magazines he reads. *Partisan Review*? Yes, he does.

> "And the *Reporter*," she said. "You read that?"
> "Yes."
> "And the London *Times Literary Supplement*?"
> "Yes."
> "Subscriber to *that*, aren't you?"
> "No!" I said triumphantly. "I buy it at the bookstore."
> "Of course!" she said. "That way you have to *carry* it home. With the cover page out."

Unwilling to be categorized, Roth throws out all the copies of the *Reporter* and *Partisan* he can find. He resolves to "cut out buying" the *TLS*. After an experiment with this new self, however, he realizes that it is no better than the old one. He picks up the phone to call a repairman about his broken hi-fi set. "But then I thought, Why not be the kind of person who drops by the shop to talk it over on the way to the bookstore to buy *The Times Literary Supplement*? I could carry it home with the cover out."

February 13

This year marks the centenary of the birth of Thomas Merton (1915–68). A Trappist monk and latterly a priest, under the name of Father Louis, Merton was also a prolific writer of poetry. He is occasionally confused with another American monk-poet, William Everson, who joined the Dominican Order in 1951 and became Brother Antoninus. Born in 1912, Everson was associated with the San Francisco Renaissance, a Beat-affiliated movement of the 1950s.

It is surprising how many others from the same sphere—largely known for vagabondage, promiscuity, and drug use—were spiritually motivated. The West Coast poet Gary Snyder studied for years in the Shokoku-ji Temple in northern Kyoto, acting as assistant to a Zen master. His friend and former school fellow Philip Whalen, also identified with the Beats, was Abbot of the Hartford Street Zen Center in San Francisco. Merton, like Snyder, was published by New Directions, a house noted for "alternative" poetry. Everson's publisher was the even more hip Black Sparrow. Are there other priest- or monk-poets with an avant-garde mission?

Britain has produced few in that line, though you might think of Gerard Manley Hopkins and the late Peter Levi, both of whom combined poetry with the Jesuit priesthood. In recent times, instead of the monk, Britain produced the "Catholic novelist." The best-known, Graham Greene, Evelyn Waugh, and Muriel Spark, happen to be three of the major figures in post-war fiction.

Merton's autobiography, *The Seven Storey Mountain* (1948), is reissued by SPCK. The cover sports remarks by Greene and

Waugh. The first calls it "an autobiography with a pattern and meaning valid for all of us"; Waugh describes it as a book "of permanent interest in the history of religious experience." Novelists and poets don't talk like that anymore.

July 24

Emboldened by the continuing discussion of Proust in the *TLS* in recent months, we took the opportunity during a recent sojourn in Normandy to visit his mythic resort, Balbec. In reality, Balbec is Cabourg, roughly equidistant from Caen to the West and Deauville to the East. Proust went there for the sea air between 1907 and 1914, staying at the Grand Hôtel. Balbec is the setting for many of the most congenial sections of *À l'Ombre des jeunes filles en fleurs*, volume two of *À la Recherche du temps perdu*. On first arriving at the Grand Hôtel, Proust took his maiden voyage by elevator:

> The manager came forward and pressed a button, and a person whose acquaintance I had not yet made, called "lift", . . . came rushing down towards me with the agility of a squirrel, tamed, active, caged. Then, sliding upwards again along a steel pillar, he bore me aloft in his train towards the dome of this temple of Mammon.

Last week, we stood in the lobby of the same temple and gazed at the elevator—in the same place, though renovated and without the attentions of either manager or boy called "lift." On the town side of the hotel, there is a crescent driveway before the entrance, where once horse-drawn carriages deposited their occupants, and now gleaming Mercedes and Lexus cars—small tanks, in fact—do the same. At the back are the "sands bathed in light as far as the first bastions of the sea." The promenade along which Proust longed to walk on his first night at the Grand now bears his name. On the beach stood a bandstand, from which, in his bedroom, he heard the sounds of violins, mingling with the waves, "humming like a swarm of bees that had strayed over the water."

The bandstand is no longer there, and the dining room in which he ate was beyond our unProustian budget. A restaurant attached to the hotel on the sandy side offered something doubtless beneath the notice of the Narrator but dear to us: *moules-frites à la crème*, accompanied by cider. The Casino, in which readers encounter the Baron de Charlus, still stands.

Cabourg is notable for its gothic, labyrinthine villas, each built in individual style, radiating in a semi-circle from the hotel—"an unreal city," Proust's biographer George Painter called it. Visitors find them spectacular; Proust less so. The painter Elstir's studio stood "on one of the newest avenues of Balbec, in which his villa was perhaps the most sumptuously ugly of all." We noted one called "Baalbek," referring to the ancient city which might have been part of Proust's inspiration; in addition, he wished to invoke a Norman-Viking sound, varying the hereabouts common "Dalbec." The "bec"—a stream—is familiar in place names throughout the region, as we learn from the lecture given by the pedantic Brichot during a trip in the Little Train in a later volume. We would have liked to board that train, but while there is a railway station in Balbec, there is none at Cabourg.

Few references to *À la Recherche* intrude into the present-day streets of Cabourg—no Café Albertine, no Coiffure de Charlus—but we bought some madeleines from a pâtisserie and dipped them in a plastic mug of the tea we had brought in a flask. The tea had acquired a stewed flavor, and the madeleines were rather pasty, but no less evocative for that.

November 27

Carol, directed by Todd Haynes and starring Cate Blanchett, may or may not be a stimulating film, but it is based on one of the dullest of Patricia Highsmith's twenty-two novels. At its best, Highsmith's intrigue derives from the guilty thoughts of an innocent person, or the clear conscience of a guilty one. There is no crime in *Carol*; just a repetitious story of two women in love.

Originally called *The Price of Salt* (1952), *Carol* was Highsmith's second book. That she herself knew the mode was not for her is suggested by the fact that she published it under the name Claire Morgan. Forgotten for decades, *Carol* is currently being acclaimed as a classic. "It soon chalked up a million copies," Jill Dawson wrote in the *Guardian* in May, referring to the Bantam paperback of 1953—an implausible figure, now repeated whenever the novel is mentioned. You will find it on Wikipedia, for example (source: "Dawson, Jill, *Guardian*, May 13, 2015"). Ms. Dawson's own source is likely to be Highsmith, who claimed in the afterword to the 1991 reissue of *Carol*—the first to use her real name—that the 1953 edition sold "nearly a million." That's already a reduction. A Bantam paperback from 1969 estimates "over half a million copies in print."

Million-selling or even half-million-selling books were as rare then as they are now. The initial print run for one of the biggest books of 1952, *The Old Man and the Sea*, was 50,000 copies and we may assume that Steinbeck's *East of Eden* had a similar production, though both books sold many times that figure as their reputations grew. That year's Mickey Spillane (*Kiss Me Deadly*) might have sold half a million.

There are now several editions of *Carol* to choose from, including one issued by Norton under the original title. On the cover, we read: "The novel that inspired *Lolita*"—a contentious claim and one that would have baffled Vladimir Nabokov. Where did it come from? In Volume Two of Brian Boyd's comprehensive biography of Nabokov (*The American Years*), there is a mention of Carroll, Lewis, but none of *Carol*, or of Highsmith, Patricia. The source is likely to be an article by Terry Castle, Professor of Humanities at Stanford, published in the *New Republic* in 2003. "I have long had a theory that Nabokov knew *The Price of Salt,* and modelled the climactic cross-country car chase in *Lolita* on Therese and Carol's frenzied bid for freedom."

You can have theories about whatever you choose, but this one hasn't got much going for it: Nabokov began writing *Lolita* in 1949; by the time *The Price of Salt* appeared, his novel was largely complete. It is likely he never heard of "Claire Morgan," before or after. We have a theory that Ms. Castle doesn't know *Lolita*'s publication history: in a second piece on the subject (*Slate,* May 23, 2006), she gives the date of the first edition as 1958, three years late.

You can say anything you like about Highsmith these days, as long as it fits the project. Phyllis Nagy, who wrote the screenplay of *Carol,* told the *Guardian* that Highsmith found *Plein Soleil*—the 1960 French adaptation of *The Talented Mr. Ripley*—"ridiculous," even though it is well established that its star, Alain Delon, was her favorite Ripley. As for the film of *Carol,* Nagy is confident that Highsmith "would have finally thought we've got something."

We have another theory: it's safer, on the whole, to stay at home and read *The Cry of the Owl, The Tremor of Forgery, This Sweet Sickness, Deep Water,* or any of the Ripleys.

2016

January 8

The 2016 Perambulatory Tour kicked off in Lyme Regis, on the south coast, at the border of the counties of Dorset and Devon. It was a bank holiday; the promenade was thick with aimless tourists; spray from the Channel soaked the Cobb and all who dared walk there; hardy swimmers braved the temperatures for what is doubtless an annual ritual. "A very strange stranger it must be," Jane Austen wrote in *Persuasion*, "who does not see charms in the immediate environs of Lyme, to make him wish to know it better."

How many amid the throng were conscious of Lyme's literary heritage? The Cobb, where Austen's Louisa fell on the steps, is also where local resident John Fowles saw the imaginary figure of a woman staring out to sea. She became Sarah Woodruff in *The French Lieutenant's Woman*, who in turn, to the regret of all who admire that novel, became Meryl Streep in the film adaptation directed by Karel Reisz. The lonely figure "obstinately" refused to budge, Fowles wrote in an essay on the germination of his novel; "it had to be this ancient quay—and as I happen to live near one, so near that I can see it from the bottom of my garden, it soon became a specific ancient quay"—the Cobb.

The original film poster was offered for sale, at a hefty price, in the window of the Sanctuary Bookshop on Broad Street, within sea-spray distance of the front. It is a roomy place, colorfully painted, with a "Booklovers' B&B" next door. Inside, we were met by an array of children's books, with possibly every *Beano* album and Enid Blyton title in existence. We browsed a shelf labeled "Gems and Gemmology"—a perambulatory first—and inevitably the small selection of Fowles titles. Was it time for another look into *The Magus*, as exciting to the youthful reader as *Five Go to Smuggler's Cove* was to the infant one?

We settled instead for his collection of essays, *Wormholes* (1998). It is not his best title (marginally better than *A Maggot*) but the book's varied contents are united by a common thread: enthusiasm. As an "occasional" writer of literary journalism, Fowles seldom did anything he didn't wish to do. There are pieces on authors ranging from Conan Doyle to Claire de Duras, whose *Ourika* is the hidden influence on *The French Lieutenant's Woman*. The material on Greece, which gave him *The Magus*, verges on repetition, but Fowles always writes lovingly of that country, not least when describing its "birds, flowers and insects," which mean as much to him in any new country "as the humans and their artificial world."

Leaving the Sanctuary £6.50 lighter but otherwise richer, we marched uphill to Belmont, the eighteenth-century villa in which the author lived until his death in 2005, recently restored to a pre-Fowlesian condition. The gates were open, and a bit of creative trespassing seemed worth the risk. The house has been painted a frosted pink, giving it a resemblance to a birthday cake, and much that Fowles loved has been removed, but the felling of trees in the terraced garden has had one beneficial effect: there is now a clear view of the "specific ancient quay," the Cobb, that inspired his undervalued novel.

January 22

The T. S. Eliot Prize for poetry has been awarded to Sarah Howe, for her book *Loop of Jade*, which explores her dual British and Chinese background. It is the latest in a series of successes on the British prize circuit for persons of color (the term recommended by the *American Heritage* style guide for people of "non-Caucasian heritage"). Last year's Man Booker Prize went to *A Brief History of Seven Killings* by the Jamaican author Marlon James, while the Forward Prize for Poetry was won by Claudia Rankine's *Citizen*, a series of meditations on the African American experience; the Forward Prize for best first collection was awarded to *Small Hands* by Mona Arshi, born in London to Punjabi Sikh parents. Diversity is all the rage in publishing, and the current scene speaks in varied tongues. A good thing, too, you no doubt think.

The Brooklyn-based poet Morgan Parker is not so sure. "When one of us wins, we all win. That's the mantra that marginalized folks have internalized for centuries," Ms. Parker wrote on her Poetry Foundation blog before Christmas. It is not a mantra that inspires her. "When writers of color become a filled diversity quota, it's a matter of time before we become a token." Success can be just another form of victimization. Prominence given to a designated POC author comes "at the cost of an opportunity" for another. "You will never stop wondering if your attention and success is only because of your race or gender or orientation. You will never stop wondering if you are being exoticized."

She is not the only one to feel that inclusion is exclusion by other means. All the prizes in the world won't help Wendy Xu to feel she is being appreciated solely for her talent. Ms. Xu is the author of *You Are Not Dead* and the winner of a Patricia Goedicke Prize. "When I win," she says in a statement cited by Ms. Parker, "I feel alienated from my POC peers, worrying over the knowledge that there is still not nearly enough space given to our voices. When I don't win, I'm sometimes hard on myself for not presenting a version of my identity that is most attractive (recognizable) to white gatekeepers."

Ms. Parker, whose book *Other People's Comfort Keeps Me Up At Night* is published by the women-only Switchback Press ("It's important that women and marginalized folks have a place where they can feel safe"), takes recognition even harder. "Your humanity will start to get lost," she writes of non-POC approval. "You will be ashamed of your ambition." Her blog closes with another mantra, for the benefit of both Ms. Xu and the gatekeepers: "You have enough. You have enough. You have enough. You have enough. It is getting better. They are doing what they can. They are trying. They are trying. They are trying."

February 12

A recent perambulation produced a copy of James Thorne's *Handbook to the Environs of London*, published in 1876 and reissued in 1970 by Adams & Dart of Bath. Thorne's aim was to provide historical, topographical, architectural, and social accounts "of every town and village and of all places of interest within a circle of twenty miles round London." By town and village, he meant what we now call districts: Chiswick, Finchley, Twickenham, etc. Thorne was alert to writerly presence. Thumbing through his 800 double-columned pages, we met Milton in Chalfont St Giles, Thackeray in Ealing, Coleridge in Hammersmith, Keats, Leigh Hunt, and others in Hampstead. The history of London and environs is inseparable from the literature it has produced.

Armchair browsing took us to the South Buckinghamshire village of Stoke Poges, north of Slough. "Many churchyards have claimed the inspiration of Gray's Elegy," Thorne writes, but "it is to Stoke that the glory must be assigned." *Elegy Written in a Country Churchyard* opens with some of the most famous lines in literature: "The curfew tolls the knell of parting day, / The lowing herd wind slowly o'er the lea . . ." (see also June 20, 2011). But is the world at large aware that Thomas Gray's churchyard is just forty minutes from Central London? We were not, and so off we went.

St Giles Church stands about a mile outside Stoke Poges. We approached across Gray's Field, at the hour of what, in early February, might be called "parting day." No curfew or anything else tolled the knell, and there was no lowing herd, only a scattered troupe of dogwalkers, one of whom provided directions. Gray's "glimmering landscape" brought the sounds of "twitt'ring" swallows, a "droning" beetle, "the cock's shrill clarion"—and "from yonder ivy-mantled tow'r / The moping owl does to the moon complain." We didn't hear those, though at other times we might have done. We saw and heard a flock of noisy magpies, passed five docile horses, alarmed a few rabbits, and surprised a grey heron fishing in a stream that runs through Slough and eventually reaches the Thames. None seemed troubled by the cars whizzing by.

The *Elegy* is a melancholy meditation on mortality and the vanity of human aspiration: "Can Honour's voice provoke the silent dust, / Or Flatt'ry sooth the dull cold ear of Death?" Gray's thoughts are not with "the pomp of pow'r" but with unfulfilled potential beneath the sod: "Some mute inglorious Milton here may rest." All around, memorials are "With uncouth rhymes and shapeless sculpture deck'd."

Gray himself is buried here but, in what can be seen as a fitting paradox, has no gravestone. In 1753, he built what Thorne calls a "plain tomb" for Dorothy Gray, "careful tender mother of many children, one of whom alone had the misfortune to survive her." It stands outside the east end of the church. When he was laid beside her in 1771, "no friendly hand added an inscription to his memory." A rather clumsy and imposing monument was later erected in the field beyond.

We plodded back across Gray's Field to the elegiac phrasing of a song thrush, noting that the horses had obligingly wound o'er the lea.

May 6

Does it say something about a city that it draws heavily on writers in naming its streets and buildings? The thought occurred to us in Camden Town the other day, as we passed Bernard Shaw Court, St. Pancras Way, as dismal a housing block as it is possible to imagine. Not even Major Barbara could have found a moral bromide to lift the spirits of the hapless souls drifting in and out. Do Paris and Rome contain similarly cheerless tributes? Nearby are the more sightly terraces of Rochester Place, Rochester Mews and Rochester Square. This presents a different riddle. Surely not *that* Rochester, he of the "stiff-pricked clown" and "well-hung parson" and others unsuitable of mention? (It's him all right, as adjoining Wilmot Place attests.)

You doubtless know Keats House in Keats Grove, Hampstead, but what about Keats House, Camberwell, Keats House, Pimlico, Keats House, Crayford, Keats Parade and the several Keats Ways? A recent errand led us to Shelley Gardens, Wembley, abutting Byron Road. No poet is as much honored in London as Byron: forty-one avenues, courts, closes, streets, and places are named after him.

Shakespeare has only twenty-one, but his creations help him. Hamlet merits nine namings, Ophelia one, in Cricklewood, next to Elsinore Gardens. There is an Othello Close in Kennington. Innocent, unwitting souls live in Macbeth House, Hoxton. Surely the planners intended a different Macbeth? Given that it is next to Ben Jonson Court, it appears not. It isn't the only one: on an estate in the Essex town of Colchester, you may walk from Macbeth Close along Hamlet Drive to Ferdinand Walk, giving on to Prospero and Ariel Closes, exiting via Miranda Walk. Not even there are folk forced to live in Lady Macbeth Alley or Iago Wynd. There are two Austen Roads in London—this brand will grow—and one Jane Austen House.

We wondered, as Bernard Shaw Court faded from view, who is the most modern writer to have been commemorated in London bricks and mortar. In Brixton, they have a Langston Hughes Walk (d. 1967) and a Pablo Neruda Close (d. 1973); those are outdone by Alice Walker Close and Derek Walcott Close, both nominees being still with us.

Back to our question: What does it say about a city that it hurries to name its streets and closes in this way? Brixton is saying something by choosing the African-American Hughes. But what? Is it over-sceptical to suspect that more people tread

Hughes Walk in an hour than read his poems there in a year? Some Macbeth House residents must know the character of the king under whose ominous shelter they dwell—those who do surely wish they lived in nearby Arden House instead—but whether it matters to most seems doubtful. Speaking of himself and his literary contemporaries, Gore Vidal once said: "In the future we won't be read; we'll be photocopied." Change that to terraced.

September 2

Do you read reviews of your books? We never do. We're in good company. Asked by an audience member at an event how she felt about the poor reception of her latest, *In Other Words*, Jhumpa Lahiri "fell silent, pursing her lips. . . . 'I don't read reviews,' she said." Jeanette Winterson doesn't read them, "because by then it's too late—whatever anyone says, the book won't change." A. L. Kennedy leaves it to her publisher to "tell me how they're going." Not only can John Banville not read reviews of his books, he can't stand the books themselves. "They are an embarrassment to me," he told the *Irish Independent*. The Scottish novelist Ronald Frame isn't reviewed as much as he once was, but he won't have noticed. "The reviews, I was told, were welcoming," he said of *Havisham* (2014). "I never read my reviews—truly!"

Ian McEwan is the same. His new novel, *Nutshell*, is released this week. In a *Guardian* interview, he admitted that he expects the reviews to be "wildly varied," but naturally he won't be reading them. His wife provides edited summaries, steering clear of the worst ones. When he happened to see that "some troll-like person on the *Spectator*" had declared his previous novel, *The Children Act*, to be "unforgivably bad," he simply "had to turn my head away." At the same time, he claims, unconvincingly, that it made him smile. Not only him. "When I told Julian Barnes, he fell about laughing. I mean, how bad can I get?"

Or how unobservant? We have the *Spectator* review to hand. It begins by stating that *The Children Act* "could hardly be more attuned to the temper of the times" and ends by comparing it to James Joyce's long story "The Dead." Not bad. In between, the writing is judged "lazy" and the plot development "improbable"; but the phrase "unforgivably bad" is not there.

The "troll-like" reviewer—troll-like in the Nordic sense or in the computerish way?—was Cressida Connolly, daughter of the celebrated critic Cyril. She has written books of her own, including one about happy childhoods. On the basis of a single encounter many years ago, she seemed to us as untroll-like a figure as it is possible to be (in either sense). The sole appearance of the word "unforgivable" in the *Spectator* review of *The Children Act* is in the headline, and it isn't linked with "bad." So wind back the film, Mr. McEwan. Let Julian Barnes rise up from his fallen-about hilarity. The wistful smile can remain in place. Two years of suffering over an unforgivably bad review that never happened! All you had to do was read it.

September 16

A curious publication reaches us from Patrician Press of Essex: *Robert Macfarlane's Orphans*, poems by Martin Johnson. In a covering note, the author describes it as "my first proper book," yet the words it contains are largely those of the popular "new nature" writer Robert Macfarlane. Mr. Johnson has extracted his favorite passages from several of Macfarlane's books, and reworked them, "to release the poetry . . . in his prose." Take this brief passage from *The Old Ways*, in which Macfarlane describes the poet Edward Thomas:

> When he's happy? Oh, then the days are fine. The house is filled with stories and rhymes. . . . His voice is deep and his songs are various.

Mr. Johnson drew inspiration, and concocted a poem, "His Moods":

When he's happy
Oh, then the days are fine
The house is filled with rhyme
And stories; his voice deep,
His songs various.

Only the poet can say how much thought went into the suppression of a question mark and the transposition of "stories" and "rhymes." Here is another poem, "Miles to go":

So it was down, steeply down,
across shale slopes,
stones flowing in the sunlight,
horses skidding on front hooves . . .

And here is the Macfarlane original: "So it was down, steeply down, across shale slopes, the stones of the path flowing in the sunlight, the horses skidding on their front hooves. . . ."

This manner of borrowing is not new. One of the most famous acts of literary appropriation, Hugh MacDiarmid's use of a prose passage by the Welsh writer Glyn Jones to create the poem "Perfect," was widely discussed in the *TLS* in 1965. It was agreed, even by Jones, that MacDiarmid had produced something new—indeed perfect—though he had changed scarcely a word.

Some readers may feel similarly about Mr. Johnson's endeavors. Others might wonder if new-nature writing is enriched when "I sat with my back against the warm wall, facing the sun and the mountain, narrowing my eyes" (Macfarlane) is transformed into "I rested, / my back to the warm wall, / facing the sun / narrowing my eyes" (Johnson).

The kindly Macfarlane gave his blessing to Johnson's book, referring in a letter to "the fossil poems you've prised from the strata of my paragraphs." We've even caught a touch of it ourselves. Seeing the prosaic information that *Robert Macfarlane's*

Orphans is "Copyright © Martin Johnson 2016," we felt the urge to release the poetry in that line:

> Copyright
> © Martin
> Johnson 2016.

October 28

J. H. Prynne is the magus of incomprehensibility. No one does it with more conviction. Open a Prynne text at random and—it's there, the magic touch:

> Never or, will to it, nerve throw past most
> over soon after, and grasp again offensive
> likely before ever mud downwards cut, snip
> relative to next time beset play genuine it
> break

Since *Force of Circumstance* (1962), his first book, Prynne has inscribed secret codes, seldom flirting with communication. He takes English words and arranges them in a syntax of which only he and a few devotees know the purpose:

> By the or and or other near true, yet as done
> to allow this for also, for the for than
> over far found extravagant inlet

Or we thought he knew. From an interview in the Fall issue of the *Paris Review*, we learn that even Prynne the Life Fellow of Gonville and Caius College, Cambridge, has scant idea of what Prynne the poet is getting at. His *Paris Review* interviewers cunningly ask him to comment on a passage of his own work, which one reads aloud: "For sure not in good likeness, profile in slant along the catchment / proposed, the speech corridor," etc. The recital over, Prynne is nonplussed. "Well, I wouldn't like to be confronted with a passage like that, now that we've propounded it. I'd walk out, I think."

In 2011, Prynne had "one of those feelings that I sometimes have, that maybe I'm about to write something." He checked into a hotel in Thailand, carrying one book in his luggage: V. Adrian Parsegian's *Van der Waals Forces: A Handbook for Biologists, Chemists, Engineers, and Physicists.* He began to write a poem. "I had no idea what its subject matter was going to be. I had no idea about its range of material. I had no idea about its prosodic formulism." After four or five hours of "feverish" writing, he would break off, perhaps to read *Van der Waals Forces,* before continuing:

> By the time I got to page twenty-plus, I had no idea what the rest of it was about, because I'd never once turned the pages back to see what the earlier writing had been doing. . . . Some of the things I wrote down astonished me. I'd think, Did I write that? Don't ask! Did I mean that? Don't ask!

The interview is also of interest for revealing Prynne's political standpoint, a brand of old-school Maoism:

> The narrative that Mao Zedong invented and devised to produce a native Chinese style of Marxism was and is still extremely interesting to me. . . . It's still an active part of my thinking practice, which is curious because it's no longer part of the intellectual world of the Chinese. . . . I would have been more comfortable in the bad period of Chinese Maoism than I am in the good period of post-Maoist China.

Politics have informed the poetry. Discussing his own book *Down where changed* (1979), Prynne states that it is one of several to have conducted a "part argument against clemency. The argument is that mercy is a serious disruption of the moral order . . . and that means that mercy is an extravagant extra." When next confronted by an inscrutable Prynne poem, and hearing yourself mutter, "Have mercy, old boy," understand that there is none.

2017

January 13

The industrial dispute at the Basement Labyrinth continues, and proof-reading on *The TLS Reviewer's Handbook* is at a standstill. But there is no rest for the wicked and our work continues. We avoid: "*curate* (except in relation to art galleries); *the jury is still out* (except in relation to criminal proceedings); *roller-coaster ride* (except in relation to fairgrounds)."

Meanwhile, an in-house reader has gifted us (we avoid *gift* as a verb) a small volume with a stiff blue canvas cover: *The Times Style Book*, "Revised November 1970," with a foreword by the paper's then editor, William Rees-Mogg, who probably compiled it. His advice on "plain English prose" for journalists, including literary journalists, is still valid: "It should be simple and clear. It should not sound affected, and should be neither archaic nor exaggeratedly contemporary in tone." The second point is worthy of note: avoid the matey parenthetical interjection: "I know, I know" or "I made the last one up" or "whisper it."

While most of the entries in the 121-page book are still applicable, others sound quaint, if not comic: "pygmy, pygmies; but *HMS Pigmy*." The thoughtful writer nevertheless pauses over them for a moment, if only to ponder the reason for their inclusion. Here are a few Rees-Moggisms:

Artiste	prefer singer, dancer, conjurer, etc;
best man	Mr Jones was best man. *Not* the best man was Mr Jones;

cheap	goods are cheap, prices are not;
comprise	commonly misused. Nato comprises 15 countries: 15 countries do not "comprise" Nato;
crescendo	almost always misused when out of a musical context;
fan	prefer "supporter" for football enthusiasts;
phone	permissible in headings only;
sack	avoid in the sense of "dismiss".

Amid the general advice, we were charmed by "semicolons are unjustly neglected." This would be a suitable subtitle for *The TLS Reviewer's Handbook* once the work is carried out. Rees-Mogg: "Carry out—*Do* is often better. 'The work was carried out.' 'The work was done.'"

February 3

The latest book by HRH the Prince of Wales, Prince Charles, is *Climate Change.* It is a Ladybird Book, with twenty-four pages of text and the same number of illustrations. If there is anyone who doesn't yet know that "Extreme weather events such as heatwaves, droughts, floods and storms can cause major damage and disruption, with large financial costs and sometimes loss of life," this is the book for them. To write it, Prince Charles teamed up with Tony Juniper and Emily Shuckburgh. Under the guidance of David Warrilow, OBE, of the Royal Meteorological Society, seven leading university professors "peer reviewed," as Charles tells us proudly, a text that is the length of a sizeable *TLS* or *LRB* article. Seven more high-level academics offered "additional advice," the details of which are unspecified. A "vital role" was played by "the Project Director" at Ladybird, Kristina Kyriacou, who directed a four-strong team which in turn acknowledges "the special role played by the University of Cambridge Institute for Sustainability Leadership."

Their combined scientific expertise enabled the production of sentences such as: “Severe and rapid climate fluctuations like those at the end of the last Ice Age probably contributed, along with hunting by humans, to the extinction of large mammals such as the woolly mammoth.” On the facing page is a picture of a cuddly mammoth in a snowy landscape being set upon by two uncouth lads with spears.

Other new Ladybird Expert books include *Evolution* by Steve Jones and *Quantum Mechanics* by Jim Al-Khalili, written all by themselves.

ROLL OVER, BEETHOVEN. A friend sends us a clip of the late-1950s singer Ricky Nelson performing the song “Fools Rush In,” with lyrics by Johnny Mercer: “Fools rush in where angels fear to tread / And so I come to you my love / My heart above my head . . .”—continuing to the delightful twist in the second verse: “So open up your heart and let / This fool rush in.”

As stated here before, many French pop songs of the 1950s were the work of poets and novelists, but the English-language song offers little in return. Or so we thought. Perhaps great literature can provide a response? What other pop songs in addition to “Fools Rush In” take lines of poetry (in this case by Alexander Pope) as a starting point?

Another Mercer song that comes to mind is “Days of Wine and Roses,” filched from the poem by Ernest Dowson: “They are not long, the days of wine and roses / Out of a misty dream / Our path emerges for a while, then closes.” On his first album, the guitarist and singer John Renbourn set to music a poem by John Donne—“Go and catch a falling star, / Get with child a mandrake root”—though that is not quite the same thing. Neither is John Dankworth and Cleo Laine’s “Dunsinane Blues,” which tells the story of the Scottish king in swing style: “‘Macbeth,’ said an apparition, / ‘Shall never vanquished be until,’ / Said the apparition, / ‘Great Birnam Wood to High Dunsinane Hill.’” In 1976, Paul McCartney and Wings released an album, *Tripping the Light Fantastic* (cf. Milton’s *L’Allegro*: “Come, and trip it as ye go, / On the light fantastick toe"), though no song on the disc bears the title. There must be others. Tell Tchaikovsky the news.

February 10

Inside every toughie there is a softie trying to get out. When we saw *Poems That Make Grown Women Cry*, edited by Anthony and Ben Holden, we reached for a precautionary hankie. It was after reading the same team's previous book, *Poems That Make Grown Men Cry*, that we realized that all around us men were contemplating verses and bursting into tears. Hard hearted as we are, we hadn't even noticed.

Now it's the ladies' turn. The stories they tell, in presenting their chosen item, are often affecting but they didn't make us cry; nor, in most cases, did they make the grown women cry. Mariella Frostrup chooses Yeats's "When You Are Old." She hopes to "spare my own daughter my circuitous route to romantic fulfilment" but she doesn't cry. Bella Freud reads "The Walrus and the Carpenter" and points out that the walrus cries, which is not the same thing. Joan Baez recalls a poem by Leigh Hunt that made her father cry but the singer remains dry-eyed. Does Marina Warner gush over Constance's speech from Act III of *King John*, "Grief fills the room up . . ."? Apparently not. Each time Maggie Gee reads Larkin's "Dublinesque," she thinks of Kitty Mrosovsky "who died too young," but she doesn't cry, or not in the pages of *Poems That Make Grown Women Cry.*

"I've read these lines as a reflection on women's writing," says Elena Ferrante of Emily Dickinson's "I Took a Power in My Hand." "I wish all Emilys not to be small by nature." Noble though the desire may be, it is none the less not lachrymose. Diana Athill, Pam Ayres, Helena Kennedy . . . not a wet eye in the house. The only one we could find came from Tina Brown, the formidable former editor of the *New Yorker.* She claims that "Perfection Wasted" by John Updike "breaks me up every time." You have to laugh.

March 10

Roll over, Beethoven. The idea is to find pop songs that derive from classic literature (note: not settings of poems). Christopher Wiseman of Calgary alerts us to "Jenny Kissed Me" sung by Guy Mitchell in 1952. The title is Leigh Hunt's: "Jenny kiss'd me when we met." The American composers Sid Tepper and Roy Brodsky blended four of the poet's eight lines into the final verse:

> Say I'm weary, say I'm sad,
> Say that health and wealth have miss'd me,
> Say whatever else you may,
> But say that Jenny kiss'd me.

In a later version, Eddie Albert recited the poem in the middle of the song. In "Are You Lonesome Tonight," Elvis offered a spoken interlude, beginning, "You know someone said that the world's a stage / And each must play a part . . ." (cf. *As You Like It*). The song was written by Roy Turk and Lou Handman in 1926.

James Connelly of Massachusetts notes that the refrain and title of "Into Each Life Some Rain Must Fall"—"Into each life some rain must fall / But too much is falling in mine"—were adapted by Alan Roberts and Doris Fisher from Longfellow's poem "The Rainy Day": "Into each life some rain must fall, / Some days must be dark and dreary." A delightful recording by The Ink Spots and Ella Fitzgerald reached Number 1 in 1944.

March 24

The Summer of Love, 1967, is fifty years old. It happened just in time. Before 1968 was out, Martin Luther King and Robert Kennedy had been assassinated, the My Lai massacre had taken place in Vietnam, students were tearing up Paris, Enoch Powell foresaw rivers of blood, and Soviet tanks had doused the Prague Spring. But we'll always have '67. It was during this season that Timothy Leary urged a crowd at Golden Gate Park to "Turn on, tune in, drop out." In Carnaby Street it was decreed that "All you need is love."

Among the minor events of that year was the publication of a poetry anthology with a title borrowed from the Beatles: in *Love, Love, Love,* edited by Pete Roche and published by Corgi, thirty-one poets were assembled, "with an average age of around twenty-five." Mr. Roche pointed out that many felt "a closer affinity with some of today's better pop lyricists than with the poets who were in vogue in the 1950s." They were answering "the increasing demand for living poetry, for poetry that talks to people in a direct and comprehensible way."

It sounds very 60s, but it's as old as poetry itself. Homer met that demand, as did Shakespeare and Robert Burns. Poets are still trying to talk to people in a comprehensible way, though the talk has grown talkier. The trouble started in the era of *Love, Love, Love*: "you will bring me flowers / every morning when you wake / and look at me with flowers in your eyes." That was one way of talking. Another was, "Electronic baby, / Let me plug you in / To the direct current / Of my desire." Adrian Mitchell tried to go in the opposite direction. Not many people talk like this:

> Peace is milk.
> War is acid.
> The elephant dreams of bathing in lakes of milk.
> Acid blood
> Beats though the veins . . .

Writing in 1967, Roche did not specify which pop song writers he had in mind. Nothing here rivals the lyrics of the Incredible String Band, Bob Dylan or even the better Donovan, which, however, no matter how bewitching they are when set to music, are liable to fall flat on the page.

We retain a fondness for Leary's dictum. Turn on, tune in, drop out could be useful in our era of self-help. Turn on to whatever turns you on (try to avoid drugs); tune in to idle musings; drop out of self-imposed smartphone thought control.

Love, Love, Love came to us on a recent visit to Walden Books in Camden Town, where people were tuning in to the outdoor book barrows.

Roll Over, Beethoven. In tribute to the late Chuck Berry, we spin some more discs that take their cue from classic literature. The original example was "Fools Rush In" written by Johnny Mercer and sung by Ricky Nelson, among others. A reader from Essex reminds us that Pope's line was also adapted, less elegantly, by Bob Dylan in the song "Jokerman": "Fools rush in where angels fear to tread, / Both of their futures, so full of dread."

The Everly Brothers turned to *Romeo and Juliet*, Act V, to kick off their little-known B-side, "Empty Boxes" (1967). The Bard:

> A beggarly account of empty boxes,
> Green earthen pots, bladders and musty seeds,
> Remnants of packthread and old cakes of roses,
> Were thinly scattered to make up a show . . .

Which Don and Phil turned round as "A beggarly account of empty boxes: / That is all I own in this world, / Oh Diana."

It would be nice to report that Chuck Berry himself made a musical allusion to the Ninth Symphony or the *1812 Overture* in the witty song that gives a title to this series. Alas, no; he did, however, play with a classic nursery rhyme: "Hey diddle, I am playin' my fiddle / Ain't got nothin' to lose. / Roll over Beethoven and tell Tchaikovsky the news."

April 28

The death in March of Robert Silvers, the editor of the *New York Review of Books*, brings to mind a peculiar feature of the American literary scene: the longevity of mid-century magazine editors. Silvers was one of the founders of the *NYRB* in 1963 and he died with blue pencil, so to speak, in hand: a reign of fifty-four years.

William Shawn worked at the *New Yorker* for exactly the same length of time: from 1933 as "managing editor for fact" and then, from 1952 until 1987, as editor-in-chief. Shawn took over from Harold Ross, who had been in charge of the *New Yorker* for twenty-seven years, from its founding in 1925. Another long-serving editor was George Plimpton, who in company with a few friends started the *Paris Review* in 1953. He too died with blue pencil in hand, in 2003. Norman Podhoretz edited *Commentary* for thirty-five years, beginning in 1960.

All lag behind William Phillips of *Partisan Review*. In partnership with Philip Rahv, Phillips founded *Partisan* as a left-wing journal in 1934, and died clutching that by now worn-out blue pencil in 2002, outstretching Silvers by over a decade.

In most cases, the succeeding editors have had relatively brief tenures. First to follow Shawn at the *New Yorker* was Robert Gottlieb (five years). Then came Tina Brown (six). The present editor, David Remnick, is making a pitch for longevity: he has been in the chair for nineteen years. Having had one editor-in-chief in half a century, the *Paris Review* has had several in the years since Plimpton's death. *Partisan* tottered on for a few months after Phillips died, and closed in 2003.

HOW DO YOU begin writing a book? If you ask Colum McCann, he will say: "Step out of your skin. Risk yourself. Go to another place. Investigate what lies beyond your curtain, beyond the wall, beyond the corner, beyond your town. . . . Open elegantly. Open fiercely. Open delicately. Open with surprise."

This tall order comes from the first chapter in *Letters to a Young Writer*. Its own first line? "A first line should open up your rib cage." Having complied with the above, stay put. "Don't leave your desk. Don't abandon the room. Don't go off to pay the bills. Don't wash the dishes. Don't check the sports pages. Don't open the mail. . . ." Don't end this list until it has taken up the best part of a typically short chapter. If stuck, add something like, "If you are not there, the words will not appear."

Writing's a tough business. "The exhaustion of sitting in one place. The errors. The retrieval. The mental taxation. Moving a word around a page. Moving it back again. Questioning it. Doubting it." The effort of writing sentences of more than six words. For the faint of heart, Mr. McCann has this counsel: "Find your life worth living. Be in the habit of hoping. Allow yourself a little joy."

He offers no advice on pronouns in situations that call for gender-neutral usage. Mr. McCann's faceless students, readers, writers, and agents are on the distaff side, as is his imaginary editor: "She negotiates your deal. She watches you get the praise, and gets little herself. And, if you don't get the praise, she suffers." She wonders how stuff like this gets published. When it comes to the bad guys, it's the patriarchy again. In a chapter called "Embrace the Critics," Mr. McCann advises:

> Don't stew. Don't lash out. Don't talk behind his back. Walk up to him at the bar or coffee shop. Ask him if you can buy him a drink. Watch him sip. Thank him for the review. Pause for a moment, then tell him—with a straight face—that it was the worst-written review you have read in a long time.

Which will teach him a lesson. Or elicit a laugh. Better to stew. But if you insist. Tell her to make ours a double.

September 1

This is "the story of a penny" transposed to that of a book. Browsing in the Amnesty Bookshop, Hammersmith, the other day, we lighted on a copy of *The Labyrinth* by the Scottish poet Edwin Muir (1949). Almost seventy years old, it was nevertheless a "tight, clean copy," with a somewhat tattered dust jacket, sporting a beguiling labyrinth.

We might have put it back had we not noticed a previous owner's signature on the endpaper: "Alan Ross." In later years, the editor of the *London Magazine*, Ross was a regular reviewer of poetry and cricketing lore for the *TLS* in the 1940s and beyond. The copy of *The Labyrinth* now in our hands was a review copy: we know so because a slip of paper was tucked between the pages:

Messrs Faber and Faber Limited
have pleasure in sending for review
THE LABYRINTH
scheduled for publication on
24th June, 1949.
at 8/6 net

It appears that Alan Ross received the book for the purposes of review and never threw the slip away, perhaps because he did not dip into *The Labyrinth* much after his job was done. Only after we had paid for it at the counter did it occur to us to wonder which paper he wrote about it for. Was it not likely to be his regular supplier of commissions, the *TLS*?

A search of the archives ensued, and turned up "Poetry in England" (August 25, 1950), in which the then-anonymous author surveyed recent work by Roy Campbell, Edith Sitwell . . . and Edwin Muir. The reviewer, we discovered, thanks to the archive, was Alan Ross. He quoted these lines:

There is no answer. We do here what we will
And there is no answer. This is our liberty
No one has known before . . .

They come from "The Usurpers," which we found on page 40 of our newly acquired copy of *The Labyrinth*. From the Russell Square headquarters of Faber and Faber, it had traveled in 1949 to the *TLS*; from there, it was posted to Alan Ross; years later, it had migrated to the Amnesty Bookshop. Now it is again at the

TLS. Should we send it back to Faber and Faber, addressing it to T. S. Eliot, Esq, poetry editor, to complete the cycle? We paid not a penny for it, nor "8/6 net," but £4.

September 15

A recent headline in the *Los Angeles Review of Books* (*LARB*) caught our attention: "Is Cultural Appropriation Ever Appropriate?" Cultural appropriation is an offshoot of post-colonial studies which holds that it is a form of oppression for members of an identifiably dominant social or ethnic group to make use of the history, personages and/or habits of another, for the purposes of literature, music, art, entertainment, fashion. In short, for culture.

Many recent objections to cultural appropriation have been about white people exploring black history and black life. The classic literary example is William Styron's novel *The Confessions of Nat Turner* (1967), in which the socially privileged Southern novelist invented a narrative—and a voice: the tale was told in the first person—for the insurrectionist slave Nat Turner, who led a revolt against slaveholders in Virginia in 1831. The history of Styron's novel, and the travails he endured as a consequence of having written it, are frequently mentioned in tandem with the fact that he was supported in his endeavor by James Baldwin. "He has begun the common history," Baldwin said. "Ours."

Times have changed. The common history turned out not to be as common as hoped. Cultural appropriation was recently given an angry fizz of energy by the Black Lives Matter movement, and the events that led to its formation.

The article in the *LARB*, "Is Cultural Appropriation Ever Appropriate?" by Arthur Krystal, concerns a screenplay he wrote some years ago about Tom Molineaux, "a freed American slave who turned up in London in 1809 and quickly proved himself a boxer capable of wresting the title from the British champion." Mr. Krystal saw in the story an opportunity to range over black and white American territory, as well as Regency England. Having had no success in selling his screenplay to Hollywood, he turned it into a treatment for a television series.

It is currently making its rounds of studios, "eliciting both enthusiasm as well as regretful demurrals," he writes. "Nothing unusual about this, but this time something new had been added to the mix. As one well-known producer put it, the fact that neither the director nor the writer is black is 'a huge red flag.'" People in the film and television industry, he was told, "are going to be wary." The director Lee Daniels is straightforward: "I hate white people writing for black people. It's so offensive. So we go out and look specifically for African-American voices. Yes, it's all about reverse racism."

The subject is complex, but in one respect quite simple: the headline in the *LARB* should have read: "Is Cultural Appropriation Ever *In*appropriate?" It is hard to think of a well-read, disinterested person breaking off from *Anna Karenina* or *Heart of Darkness* or *A Passage to India* or *The Sound and the Fury* or *The Grass Is Singing*, to pen a letter of outrage to author or publisher. If the art is good, it justifies its own creation. If bad, it predicts its own oblivion. Eric Clapton might be guilty of cultural appropriation for having devoted a lifetime to the blues, but isn't the world better for it? You'd have to be Lee Daniels to say no. The blues, as it happens, are an amalgam of plantation life, African rhythm and British folksong.

We asked Mr. Krystal about the evolution of his article at the *LARB*. "I knew I was up against it," he told us, "when the phrase, near the beginning, 'I thought this particular story had a strong selling point,' worried the editors because *selling point* might evoke the idea of a slave auction." He was happy to make the change to "a decent hook," but there were "a half-dozen other phrases that I had to excise or tone down before they would run the piece."

December 1

The *TLS* in crime fiction. In spite of our best efforts, the *TLS* is apt to fall into bad company. There have been worrying incidents, including one in which a lethal gunman on Capri wrapped his weapon in a copy of the paper. Then there was Edmund Crispin's mystery *The Glimpses of the Moon* (1977), featuring the detective Gervase Fen. "Fen was not thinking about the murder. Instead he was smoking a cigarette and reading *The Times Literary Supplement*—nowadays vulgarly retitled *T.L.S*, without even a full stop after the 'S.'" (We fixed that problem, by subtracting the other two.)

Writing from Doha, Qatar, Maureen Buja alerts us to *Body Blow* by Kenneth Hopkins, published in New York in 1962. As Ms. Buja relates it, "An aged scholar, William Blow, is expecting a box of 100 volumes of the works of Robert Southey." The box he receives contains the body of a woman instead. His friend, Professor Manciple, is disconcerted: "There is a more relevant line of inquiry, Blow: Why was the body sent to you? . . . It must have been the work of an enemy!"

Being a literary man, Blow thinks hard. "There's Eapes. I handled him pretty severely in the *TLS*."

Immediately, he reconsiders. "The man was honest enough, though incompetent. If he read my review, he must have seen at once that I was right, and that a figure of the complexity of Bolingbroke can't be dismissed in a miserable little catch-penny monograph . . . besides, where would a man like Eapes get a dead body from?"

He may be incompetent as a literary critic, but Eapes is in the clear, and so are we.

INTERLUDE

"Get on with it"

J.C. followed a different set of imperatives from those I felt beholden to when writing under my own name. He was compelled to write quickly, with the buzz of office noise in his ears and the likelihood of interruption—anything from "You wouldn't be able to cast an eye over this, would you?" to "Did you see the match last night?" Without much forethought, he had to shepherd his best words into the fold marked "best order" and attempt to keep the loyal reader's interest, week after week, with a variety of content, whether the mood was gay or solemn.

The advantage of writing a column of 1,400 words, consisting usually of a minimum of three items, is that you cannot hang around. The lead item is likely to be between 600 and 800 words. There is no space for throat-clearing or scene-setting. To repeat one of the most usable of all nostrums of basic good style: *get on with it*. Get in, say what you have to say using as few words as possible while aiming for the greatest clarity, and get out. Write as if composing a letter to a friend (this takes a lot of practice). Then move on to the next topic.

Continuity between items is unnecessary—is usually undesirable—and this is another advantage to the columnist. Aim for a miscellany. After complaining about the sinister atmosphere generated by philistine but noisy bullies from the cultural-appropriation or cancel-culture camps—an atmosphere that spread during the final years of my tenure—shift in the second item to a report on one of NB's prizes.

The lighter item can make a serious point, too. Something NB drew attention to more than once was the pointlessness of awarding sumptuous real-world prizes to authors already wealthy beyond the dreams of the average scribe who has been toiling valiantly in the ranks for years. In many cases, the riches of the repeatedly rewarded writer have derived from previous prizes. Certain writers are magnets for awards.

There are plenty of examples. One we made use of was the 2018 Premio Cervantes, the leading Spanish-language literary prize. In late November of that year, it was given to the Uruguayan poet Ida Vitale, who turned ninety-five in the same month. The Cervantes brought with it a cheque for €125,000. NB of November 30, 2018 commented:

> Who wouldn't look on it fondly? Even so, Señora Vitale can barely have had time to get through the $125,000 she received at the Guadalajara Book Fair on November 24, as winner of the Premio FIL de Literatura en Lenguas Romances. In 2016, Vitale won the Premio Internacional de Poesía Federico García Lorca, which brought a handy €50,000; in 2015 the Premio Reina Sofía de Poesía Iberoamericana (€42,000); in 2014, there was the Premio Alfonso Reyes and a few years before that the Premio Octavio Paz, neither of them skinflint awards. No one should begrudge a penny of it, but the greatest reward of all for her poetry would be readers.

Having addressed these matters, we could then divulge some confidential information about the latest goings-on at the Basement Labyrinth, the secretive headquarters of NB where the constitution and rules of engagement were subject to a continual process of refinement and dispute. Communication with the Elders in the Labyrinth was restricted to smoke signals, talking drum, semaphore, homing pigeon, or a morse-like system of short and long knocks on radiators. The news might concern the vote on proposed strike action by indentured interns, protesting against being forced to accept wages for their work, or a proposal to grant them a week's annual leave away from it. Their case was that they simply had too much to do—not least the task of proof-reading the new Harry and Meghan edition of *The TLS Reviewer's Handbook*, forever on the brink of being published.

NB

2018–2020

2018

February 2

Among our most coveted awards is the Jean-Paul Sartre Prize for Prize Refusal, open to any writer who has refused a literary prize. You can turn down the Saltire Prize in Scotland, as Alasdair Gray did; you can refuse the Janus Pannonius International Poetry Prize from the Hungarian PEN Club (Lawrence Ferlinghetti), with its accompanying €50,000; but you cannot turn down a Sartre. Not even Sartre did: he refused to accept the Nobel Prize for Literature in 1964, yet his name remains inscribed in the record of the Swedish Academy as its choice of winner.

In early December, we stumbled on a blog on the subject at the *Paris Review Daily* site, by the novelist Ursula K. Le Guin. "I first learned about the Sartre Prize from NB," Ms. Le Guin wrote, "the last page of *The Times Literary Supplement*, signed by J.C. The fame of the award, named for the writer who refused the Nobel in 1964, is or anyhow should be growing fast." Ms. Le Guin flattered us by quoting from a past NB: "So great is the status of the Jean-Paul Sartre Prize for Prize Refusal that writers all over Europe and America are turning down awards in the hope of being nominated for a Sartre." As we noted at the time, and Ms. Le Guin repeated it, "The Sartre Prize itself has never been refused."

She revealed that she too had refused a prize, during the "coldest, insanest days" of the Cold War. "My novelette *The*

Diary of the Rose was awarded the Nebula Award by the Science Fiction Writers of America. At about the same time, the same organization deprived the Polish novelist Stanislaw Lem of his honorary membership." Hence, no Nebula for Ursula Le Guin.

We contacted Ursula Le Guin afterwards, thanking her for her remarks—the essay is more wide-ranging than we are able to indicate here—and requesting permission to bestow an honorary retrospective Sartre, which she graciously accepted. We also asked if she might be minded to write again for the *TLS*, as she used to do. She replied charmingly: "I'd say yes if I thought I could promise work, but I really can't any more, my energy is too unreliable. And I hate to let people down."

We didn't know then what she was referring to. Ursula Le Guin died on January 22, aged eighty-eight. She left us with an idea, however: "I do hope you will recommend me to the Basement Labyrinth so that I can refuse to be even nominated, thus earning the Pre-Refusal of Awards Award, which has yet to be named."

It has a name now: The Ursula K. Le Guin Prize, for writers who refuse shortlisting, longlisting and any other form of nomination for literary prizes.

A footnote. As if to prove that there is no limit to the ironic outcome of fame, it was reported in 2021 that the first Ursula K. Le Guin Prize for Fiction would henceforward be awarded on October 23, the author's birthday.

February 9

It's hard to be a critic these days. Literary judgment is apt to be mistaken for something else: misogyny, racism, elitism, or just snobbery. In the course of an article in the *New York Times* late last year, in praise of the "Instagram poet" Rupi Kaur, Carl Wilson stated: "Fights about artistic taste are nearly always about submerged social hostilities—putting down the audiences as much as the artists." Fights about artistic taste used to be about art. It represents a major cultural shift if that has ceased to be the case.

When Rebecca Watts wrote in severe terms in the January–February issue of the poetry journal *PN Review* about two collections of verse—Kaur's *Milk and Honey* and Hollie McNish's *Plum*—she was taken to task by a variety of folk for being narrow-minded, fearful of advances in poetry, and plain "mean-spirited." The last remark was made by Don Paterson, himself a poet and the poetry editor at Picador, publisher of *Plum*:

i wish i was as strong as a dung beetle
i wish i was as nice as a dung beetle
clearing those huge piles of crap

Invited on to *The World at One* on BBC Radio 4, Lemn Sissay relied on a common philistine trope to criticize Watts and defend McNish. "There is a new horizon in poetry. Hollie McNish is it. Some people are cowering in the dark from this horizon." The notion that the critic was exercising literary judgement and defending evaluation did not arise.

"Why is the poetry world pretending that poetry is not an art form?", Ms. Watts asked in *PN Review*. "I refer to the rise of a cohort of young female poets who are currently being lauded by the poetic establishment for their 'honesty' and 'accessibility'—buzzwords for the open denigration of intellectual engagement and rejection of craft that characterizes their work." Here is a sample of Rupi Kaur:

when i am sad
i don't cry, i pour
when i am happy
i don't smile, i beam
when i am angry
i don't yell, i burn
the good thing about
feeling in extremes

is when i love
i give them wings . . .

Ms Watts wished to measure whatever talent Ms. Kaur might possess against what used to be called "the tradition"—a tradition Don Paterson has made ingenious and artistically profitable use of. Interviewed about the scrap, he said: "There are some of us who think that poetry is a way of cleaning the lies out of language, and lending our lives some meaning," an implied slight against Ms. Watts. She might have replied that criticism is likewise a way of cleaning the lies out of rhetorical statements about poetry, and that it was part of her job to try. It seems unfair to criticize the critic for having a try at criticism.

February 23

May '68 will soon be upon us. Expect to hear a lot about the fiftieth anniversary of the "revolution that never was" in Paris. Before that, there was the assassination of Martin Luther King (April 4). Robert Kennedy, in his prime, was shot in Los Angeles on June 5. On August 21, 1968, Soviet tanks entered Prague, halting a cautious process of reform. Days later, eight demonstrators were arrested in Moscow's Red Square. The soundtrack, if you like that kind of thing, was "Sunshine of Your Love" (Cream), "People Got to Be Free" (the Rascals), and "Revolution" by the Beatles. May '68 was the month that John officially left his wife and took up with Yoko.

The Walls Have the Floor is a record of the graffiti collected by Julien Besançon in Paris in 1968, while covering *les événements* as a journalist. Some of the students' and workers' statements sound as if they were concocted for a novel or a film: "Embrace your lover without dropping your rifle"; "There is no Revolutionary thinking. There are only Revolutionary acts"; "To challenge the society in which we live we must first be capable of challenging ourselves."

The reader encounters an essentially French philosophical tint. In Prague they might also have been thinking, "The Revolution must cease to be in order to exist," and perhaps even spraying it on the walls, but they had a different revolution in mind. What on earth would Czechs, oppressed by the Communist Party and its secret police, have made of "We're reassured. 2 plus 2 no longer makes 4"?

The French regime in the making did not promise liberalism. "We want to smash," was the writing on the wall at the Sorbonne. "The outcome of every thought is the cobblestone." The enemies were the police, the bourgeoisie, and the professoriate. In fact, enemies were everywhere. "Art is dead, let us liberate everyday life." "Kill the bureaucrats." "The new society must be founded on the absence of all egoism." There was to be "No liberty for the enemies of liberty"—a typical Newspeak thought that was heartily embraced by those commanding the Soviet tanks in Prague.

Lenin was a source of wisdom, though it might have pained the much-derided profs to read his mantra, "Education, education, education," scrawled on the classroom walls. Especially where it was written above the slogan, "All power to the free Soviets."

It was fun (for some) while it lasted. De Gaulle fled to Baden-Baden and eventually resigned in April 1969, though he had won a general election in the meantime. *The Walls Have the Floor*, "an immediate transcription of the discourse that student revolutionaries were inventing in the heat of their struggle," as Tom McDonough says in his rousing foreword, was originally published in France in 1968 as *Les Murs ont la parole.*

May 25

A friend of ours from up North got in touch after reading about *The Ink Trade*, a new collection of Anthony Burgess's journalism. In 1980, Burgess contributed to a symposium in the *New Edinburgh Review*, a quarterly literary magazine with which our correspondent was involved. The topic was book reviewing. Authors were asked to reply to two questions:

1. What do you consider to be the main purpose of book reviewing?
2. What effect is a review likely to have on the author; on the public; on sales?

Our friend came across Burgess's typewritten copy in a drawer, while searching for something else. "It hasn't been published since," we are told. Given that the business of the *TLS* is book reviewing, and that Burgess in his prime was a frequent contributor, we thought his responses might interest readers. What is the purpose of book reviewing anyway? Here is what Burgess wrote from Monaco, on January 16, 1980:

1. Book reviewing in Great Britain is cognate with book advertising in Great Britain: it is a means of telling readers of newspapers what new books are available. It differs from advertising in that it evaluates the books according to theories of value which the reviewer holds empirically, while the advertisement merely tells the reader that the books are unequivocally good. Unfortunately, reviewing is rarely true criticism. Reviews are too brief to say much. In the days of the old *Edinburgh Review* there was room to expound a whole aesthetic and to consider an author in terms of it. The *TLS* sometimes deals at length, and often admirably, with new books, but very rarely with books that people actually buy. It is a scholar's periodical.
2. Reviews are mostly ignored by the general public. The books that sell best—Harold Robbins, Barbara Cartland etc—are hardly ever reviewed. At most, they are noticed scathingly. No author has ever, since the days when Arnold Bennett could make or break a reputation in the *Evening Standard*, either benefited or suffered from reviews. My most popular book

> was, however, publicised on television, which may be regarded as a medium having an impact on readership, but it was so thoroughly covered that there was no need for anyone to read the book. It is pleasant to know that people whose taste one approves of read one's books and write about them; one gains an indication of whether one has been understood. It is only the lengthy critical article, as in American magazines, or the book on one's work, America again, which is really helpful to the author. A good critic is of immense value: he sees the undertext or the symbols which the author's unconscious has contrived but his working conscious missed. A bad review, even when written by a known idiot or bloody minded swinger like Geoffrey Grigson, can be very upsetting. Most authors these days refuse to read reviews.

He signed off: "Lang may your lum reek."

The offensive opinion of the bloody minded swinger didn't fade: it is referred to in an article included in *The Ink Trade*. There, Burgess writes: "I still smart from a review excreted by the late Geoffrey Grigson. In noticing a volume of essays I had published, he said: 'Who could possibly like so coarse and unattractive a character?' This, I think, was unjust and impertinent."

Had we been invited to contribute to the *New Edinburgh Review* symposium, we would have said that reviewers should ask more awkward questions of books than they tend nowadays to do, but should strive not to be unjust, and avoid being impertinent. Other contributors in the Spring of 1980 included Douglas Dunn, George Mackay Brown, Robert Garioch, Norman MacCaig, Peter Porter, and Alan Ross.

June 15

Mary Wilson, née Baldwin, wife of Harold Wilson, Britain's prime minister from 1964 to 1970 and from 1974 to 1976, died on June 6, aged 102. She published two books of her work, a *Selected Poems* in 1970, which is said to have sold 75,000 copies, and *New Poems* in 1979. Her social views made their way into a poem cited (with an unkind sneer) in the *TLS* in 1970, which has at least as much relevance today as during her husband's term:

His feet are bandaged, his clothes are rags,
All his possessions in paper bags.
"Lay-about, drop-out!" you glibly say
And hastily look the other way.

Mary Wilson had the distinction of being mentioned in the poems of other prominent versifiers. John Betjeman, a close friend, wrote in rhyme about their outing to Diss in Norfolk, her birthplace:

Dear Mary,
Yes, it will be bliss
To go with you by train to Diss,
Your walking shoes upon your feet;
We'll meet, my sweet, at Liverpool Street.

She also features in Andrew Motion's elegy for Philip Larkin, "This Is Your Subject Speaking," published in the *TLS* in February 1986. Larkin is talking:

You know that new anthology?
The one that Mary Wilson edited—
the favourite poems of the famous?
Have you seen it?
Callaghan and Mrs T and I
all chose Gray's Elegy. . . .
Why wasn't I prime minister?

August 10

Is there still such a thing as literary taste? Of course there is, you reply. Dickens is better than Dick Francis; Trollope (Anthony) is superior to Trollope (Joanna); Graham Greene beats Jane Green. Only a reader without taste would dispute it.

Or you might think it's all relative. People today learn more about life and derive greater pleasure from *EastEnders* than from Shakespeare. Val McDermid has wider appeal than Hugh MacDiarmid. No one can prove that it's more worthwhile to read Dylan Thomas than to listen to Bob Dylan, and anyway only one of them has won the Nobel Prize in Literature.

Both sides would at least agree that current notions diverge from what Arnold Bennett had in mind when he wrote a book in 1909 called *Literary Taste*. Bennett meant taste not in the I like it, don't like it, turns-me-on, not-my-thing sense, but as a shared goal of education, a recognized attribute among people who value the best that has been thought and said. Bennett sought to introduce readers to Charles Lamb, Carlyle, and Macaulay. He advised the apprentice reader to avoid living authors (the likes of Conrad and Hardy), the reason being "simply that you are not in a position to choose among modern works." You first have to develop taste. Few guides to good reading would say now, as Bennett did, "If you differ with a classic, it is you who are wrong, and not the book." Stating of a book that it's good just because you happen to like it is whimsy, not taste.

Bennett was assuming an aspiration to acquire taste by way of mastery of the canon. Among critics, Hazlitt was his favorite. "If you chance to read Hazlitt on Chaucer and Spenser, you will probably go out and buy these authors, such is his communicating fire!"

All this is touchingly dated. Hazlitt? Spenser? Lamb? Bennett himself was aware that taste changes. In one passage, he writes that the learned people of his day (circa 1909) are forever claiming there are no decent authors any more. "It is a surety that in 1959 gloomy and egregious persons will be saying, 'At the beginning of the century, there were great poets like Swinburne, Meredith. . . . But whom have we to take their place?'" No doubt they did. And today they are saying much the same.

In the formation of a catholic taste, there is nothing more useful than reading itself. Every literary guide since 1909 has said the same. But Bennett had another recommendation, which we find likeable: "Buy! Buy whatever has received the *imprimatur* of critical authority. Buy without immediate reference to what you read. Surround yourself with volumes as handsome as you can afford." They don't only furnish a room. "Literature, instead of being an accessory, is the fundamental *sine qua non* of complete living."

It needn't cost a lot: this 1938 Pelican Special reissue of *Literary Taste*, eighty years old and still sturdy, cost 99p at Oxfam Books, Turnham Green.

CRESSIDA DICK, the Commissioner of the Metropolitan Police, recently criticized "hypocritical" middle-class users of cocaine, who snorted with eyes turned away from the social and personal problems caused by drug-taking lower down the social ladder.

We're happy to agree, but feel obliged to note that Ms. Dick's most celebrated crime-fighting precursor was an enthusiastic cocaine user. As he attended Sidney Sussex College, Cambridge, and had an extensive knowledge of the sciences, he can probably be called middle class. There is now a museum dedicated to him.

No one ever called Sherlock Holmes a hypocrite. According to a new Handbook, *Biographic Sherlock* by Viv Croot, he used cocaine "to escape the stagnating banality of daily existence." Only Watson disapproved.

It started in 1881, when Holmes was twenty-seven. In *A Study in Scarlet*, Watson voices his suspicions. By 1888 (*The Sign of the Four*), Holmes was shooting up three times a day, but by 1897 ("The Adventure of the Missing Three-Quarter") he was clean. Ms. Croot reminds us that cocaine and opiate-derived drugs were not illegal. In a technical note, she writes that Holmes "always used a 7 per cent solution of cocaine hydrochloride." If you're one of the hypocrites, you'll know what that means.

Biographic Sherlock bulges with information. What was Holmes's favorite weapon? Not his Webley Bulldog revolver, which he used mainly for indoor target practice, nor the standard cudgel, which he drew only once. He was good with his fists, and was a master of Bartitsu, "a blend of ju-jitsu, boxing and stick fighting," all the rage in London at the turn of the century. His readiest weapon sounds rather chic: a "loaded hunting crop."

How much did Holmes earn? For a case in 1883, he received £1,000; in 1888 and 1890, the same amount is mentioned, but in 1895, working for the British government to retrieve secret military plans, he accepted an emerald tie-pin, as "a gift from a grateful monarch." Thanks, ma'am, but the price of coke is going up.

Not even Ms. Croot can solve a case we have long worked on: was Watson Scottish? He studied medicine at Edinburgh; his surname and middle name—Hamish—suggest he might have been born there. Elementary? Ms. Croot does not say.

August 17

A Visit to V. S. Naipaul (1932–2018)

In 2007, a friend of ours interviewed V. S. Naipaul, who has died aged eighty-five, at his home in Wiltshire for a profile in a national newspaper. We asked for some recollections. This is what he told us:

> The first problem was finding the place. I'd been given the address "Dairy Cottage, Salterton"—that's all. It sounded delightful, but Salterton is one of those strung-out villages with no particular center, and it took enquiries at some neighboring grand places to locate the modest, modern house. The sole picture on the wall of the room in which we sat was a portrait of V. S. Naipaul. "She insisted on that," he said, referring to his wife Nadira.
>
> I knew that Naipaul held his father in high esteem. Seepersad Naipaul was a journalist and writer of stories. So I

began our interview with what I thought was a clever question, hoping for some discussion of family background. "How would you describe your father to someone you happened to meet on a train?"

Naipaul looked at me with a mixture of pity and perplexity. "But I *wouldn't* talk about my father to someone I'd met on a train." That appeared to be that, but then he allowed himself to be drawn a little and told me how he had depended on his father's writing "to get a knowledge of my background," otherwise obscure to him. "And for the example he gave me of a literary labor."

Naipaul had come to Wiltshire from London but was always keen to stress his estrangement. Several times in our conversation he used the phrase "floating man." He was not a figure like Anthony Powell or Evelyn Waugh, "who retired from city life, in order to become the Writer in the Country." He returned to Powell and Waugh later in our conversation, when he passed out verdicts on other writers. His disobliging views on Jane Austen and E. M. Forster were by then well known. *Brideshead Revisited* was "a very, very bad book," he said. Waugh wrote of the aristocracy "with a kind of feminine longing." Powell was a friend, which made his reaction to *A Dance to the Music of Time* all the more embarrassing. "I was appalled."

There were other disappointments. Graham Greene's protagonists were just "being moved from one seedy background to another. There was nothing for me in it." But the greatest scorn was reserved for Chinua Achebe, to whom the Man Booker International Prize had been awarded weeks before our meeting, an accolade accepted elsewhere with unquestioning admiration.

From the transcript of my recorded interview: "Have you read *Things Fall Apart*? I think it's an *appalling* book. It's one of these things that people talk about but don't consider. It's a primitive piece of writing about primitive people . . .

and that's something that's very limited. You couldn't do another piece of writing about those people."

Achebe's attack on Conrad's approach to Africa was "very foolish. Too many people talk about Conrad in a foolish way. They object to the title *The Nigger of the 'Narcissus.'* They've not read the book. It's the opposite of anything racial. Conrad gives the man standing." His objection to early Conrad was that he found it "too mannered." The only writer about whom he spoke with enthusiasm was Maupassant, whose stories he was reading. "I was dazzled." But not even Maupassant left an impression on his own work. Naipaul floated alone.

In her memoir *Stet,* Diana Athill wrote of her exasperation while working as Naipaul's editor at André Deutsch, but for the stretch of an August afternoon, with Nadira next door—Naipaul's face took on a happy sheen each time she entered the room—he was a cooperative and interested interlocutor. The encounter lasted some three hours, longer than I had expected.

Did I believe him when he claimed to be ignorant of his one-time friend Derek Walcott's praise of his books, which I recounted? ("I had no idea of this, you see.") No, I probably didn't. Did I take him seriously when he said of *The Enigma of Arrival*: "To my amazement I heard that they liked it at the Palace. I was asked to go to lunch, and this was a book talked about among the courtiers"? Yes, I probably did.

THE *TLS* IN LITERATURE: expansion into overseas territories. Lydia Davis writes to tell us of "Examen de la obra de Herbert Quain" (A Consideration of the Work of Herbert Quain) by Jorge Luis Borges. Ms. Davis passed us the passage in the original, which reads in part:

> Quain ha muerto en Roscommon; he comprobado sin asombro que el *Suplemento Literario del Times* apenas le

> depara media columna de piedad necrológica, en la que no hay epíteto laudatorio que no esté corregido (o seriamente amonestado) por un adverbio. El *Spectator*, en su número pertinente, es sin duda menos lacónico. . . .

Finding that our O-level Spanish isn't what it was, we asked Ms. Davis, a distinguished translator from French, if she would care to attempt a version of the Borges. She agreed to do so, and we offer her rendering (modestly referred to by her as "rough") of the opening paragraph:

> Herbert Quain has died in Roscommon; I have confirmed without surprise that *The Times Literary Supplement* barely gives him half a column of necrological pity, in which there is no laudatory epithet that is not corrected (or seriously admonished) with an adverb.
>
> The *Spectator*, in its relevant number, is no doubt less reticent and perhaps warmer, but likens Quain's first book—*The God of the Labyrinth*—to one of Mrs Agatha Christie's, and others to those of Gertrude Stein: allusions that no one will consider self-evident and that would not have pleased the deceased. . . .

September 21

The *Village Voice*, pioneer of the alternative press, has a voice no more. Among its founders, in 1955, was Norman Mailer, who became a vigorously argumentative columnist. *Voice* mainstays included Nat Hentoff (jazz), Jules Feiffer (cartoons), Robert Christagau (rock criticism) and Richard Goldstein (ditto, plus gay life). In the 1980s and 90s there was a freestanding *Voice Literary Supplement*. Three Pulitzer Prizes came the way of the *Voice* between 1981 and 2000. For many years, the paper occupied impressive premises in Cooper Square. On entering, one felt the heat of a hundred typewriters.

No decent newspaper deserves to suffer a demise as prolonged as that of the *Village Voice.* Things started to look bad when it went free in 1996. Several regulars, including Hentoff and Christagau, were laid off after a change of owners in 2005. It changed hands again in 2013, and again in 2015. Editors didn't stay long. Anyone who has worked in journalism since the invention of printing recognizes these auguries. But the worst portent of all came last year, when the *Voice* ceased print publication and went online only. On August 31, the newest new owner, Peter Barbey, announced that the *Village Voice* would stop production altogether.

Different theories have been put forward about "what happened." One is that New York itself has changed—not least in Greenwich Village, which gave the paper its name and identity—and that the voice in which the journal once spoke no longer made sense. "Bohemia, nonconformity, one thriving avant-garde arts scene replacing another thanks to a talent pool regularly refreshed by new arrivals with more ambition than rent money, even a belief in New York itself as the nation's cultural capital." That menu, according to old hand Tom Carson, is no longer available.

Another reason for the silencing of the *Voice,* Mr. Carson wrote in an article in the *Baffler,* "is that 'we won.' The cultural and political assumptions and insights once confined to the *Voice*-defined margins have long since been absorbed into the mainstream." In that sense, he concluded, "the *Village Voice* folded simply because its work here was done."

Wouldn't it be pretty to think so? It led us to ponder what we've won just in recent years: Islamic terrorism, armed guards at US schools, security patrols at London synagogues, impossible rents in New York and London, rising tuition fees, debasement of political discourse, online shaming and scapegoating, Twitter mobs, campus no-platforming, cultural appropriation, the negation of critical judgment by identity politics, censorship of incorrect ideas. If you can think of any more ways in which we won, let us know.

Nov 16

What happened to all the Catholic writers? Once, their name was Legion. Graham Greene is probably the most reputable, part of the attraction being that he delighted in the disreputable. Evelyn Waugh converted to Catholicism in 1930, at the age of twenty-seven, explaining later that he had realized that life was "unintelligible and unendurable without God." Muriel Spark, a protégé of both Greene and Waugh, left behind her Jewish family background and Edinburgh's Calvinist air, to embrace the Roman faith in the mid-1950s. These three were converts; Anthony Burgess was a cradle Catholic. Hilaire Belloc converted from having lapsed, if that makes theological sense.

French literature of the twentieth century is rife with what are sometimes referred to as "left-footers," from Paul Claudel to Paul Valéry, François Mauriac to the late Jean d'Ormesson. But what of the twenty-first? In our age of brutalist profanity, who will guide us through death's dark vale? David Lodge and Piers Paul Read are perhaps the closest we have to inheritors of the Catholic strain in literature.

These meditations were prompted by a perambulatory acquisition, *Altar & Pew*, edited by John Betjeman, a little anthology in the Pocket Poets series published by Vista Books in the 1950s. The topic is "Church of England verses," but you won't find any more of those nowadays than you will Catholic novels.

Betjeman includes Herbert, Wordsworth, Blake, Hartley Coleridge, a bit of irreverent dialect Tennyson ("niver not speäk plaain out, if tha wants to git forrards a bit, / But creeäp along the hedge-bottoms, an' thou'll be a Bishop yit"), and a verse by Thomas Hardy about being bored in church. At least he got a poem out of it.

It is hard to imagine a successful contemporary writer saying, as Waugh did, that he or she found life unintelligible without God. Much more trendy to say the opposite: that life is unintelligible with Him. Betjeman's anthology ends with Philip

Larkin, the youngest writer in the book (thirty-seven at the time of publication). The poem is "Church Going":

> Once I am sure there's nothing going on
> I step inside, letting the door thud shut.

Altar & Pew cost us £1 from a Charing Cross Road barrow. The next time we're in church, with something going on, we'll add a further £1 to the collection.

2019

January 4

We read, the other day: "Atticus Finch has inspired legions of lawyers, been memorialized with a public sculpture, and had professional-achievement awards and a nonprofit organization named after him. . . ."

Atticus's honor has been somewhat tarnished since the appearance of *Go Set a Watchman* (2015), Harper Lee's follow-up to *To Kill a Mockingbird.* It made him out to have had dubious associations in the segregated South. So far, however, the monument located at the Old Courthouse in Monroeville—Lee's home town and the model for the fictional Maycomb—stands firm. Erected in 1997 by the Alabama Bar Association, it presents Atticus Finch as "a great and noble lawyer . . . who knows how to see and to tell the truth, knowing the price the community will pay for that truth."

Which set us wondering: what other fictional characters of the past 200 years have had public monuments installed in their honor? There is a statue of Peter Pan in Kensington Gardens, though it barely corresponds to our imaginary conception—which is the trouble with real representations of unreal figures. Every statue of Sherlock Holmes shows him in a deerstalker, which Conan Doyle never placed on his head. There is one outside Baker Street Tube station and another at the top of Leith Walk, Edinburgh. In both, he is about to draw on a meerschaum pipe. Even the victims of the crimes he investigated would shun him for doing so today. A statue of a rather camp Tom Sawyer and an earnest Huck Finn was unveiled in Hannibal, Missouri, in 1926. But no sign of Huck's sidekick, Jim. Why not?

A life-size statue of a young boy holding an outstretched bowl with a spoon in it—saying, "Please, sir, I want some more"—was donated to the City of Houston by the sculptor Trace Guthrie. There isn't one in Clerkenwell, where the boy asked for it. There must be more public monuments to people who exist not only in the pages of books but—their true residence—in our imaginations.

January 25

A rhetorical question stalked Saul Bellow during his final years: "Who is the Tolstoy of the Zulus, the Proust of the Papuans?" Picture a privileged white male smirking. "I'd be happy to read them."

But Bellow never wrote those words. The journalistic "scandal" of his contempt for multiculturalism and minority races, he later insisted, grew out of casual remarks made to a reporter. His intention had been to affirm a distinction between literate and non-literate societies. In any case, he asked later in a *New York Times* op-ed (March 10, 1994),

> Why did my remarks . . . throw so many people into fits of righteousness and ecstasies of rage? France gave us one Proust and only one. There is no Bulgarian Proust. Have I offended the Bulgarians too? We, for that matter, have no Proust either: should the White House issue a fatwa and set a price on my head for blaspheming against American high culture?

Few readers would make a claim for a Tolstoy of Zulu (or Bulgarian) literature. But one African writer deserves a place in this year's list of literary anniversaries. Sibusiso Nyembezi, who wrote several novels in the Zulu language, also known as isiZulu, would have been 100 this year (he died in 2000). Nyembezi translated Alan Paton's *Cry the Beloved Country* into Zulu in 1958, as *Lafa elihle kakhulu*. His own novel *Inkinsela Yase-Mgungundlovu* 1961) was translated into English as *The Rich Man of Pietermaritzburg* and published by Aflame Books in 2008.

Our knowledge of Zulu is not what it was, but with the help of the translator Sandile Ngidi we can offer a taste. In this brief passage, one man meets another to discuss business:

> nakho lokho okwenziwa nguNdebenkulu kwamcasula uMkhwanazi ngoba yena wayefuna ukuba baqede lolu daba ngaphambi kokuba bafundane namaphepha. . . .

Which in *The Rich Man of Pietermaritzburg* becomes: "Mkhwanazi found this annoying—he would've preferred them to finalize the matter at hand before reading the newspaper."

Not Tolstoy—we haven't read the whole thing—but demonstrably not the product of an exclusively oral culture.

February 1

Nothing blows the winter blues away like a brisk perambulation. And few things are more rewarding on such a walk—in this case along still-charming Cecil Court, in the center of London's West End—than a good bibliography. Warren Roberts's *Bibliography of D. H. Lawrence* was published by Rupert Hart-Davis in 1963.

You may think you know something of the publishing history of *Lady Chatterley's Lover*. Only by browsing in Roberts do you realize how much you didn't know. The novel is "unquestionably one of the most interesting bibliographical specimens of the century. It has been pirated, expurgated and bowdlerized, condemned and confiscated, translated into many languages and published in many formats."

The first edition, privately printed by Tipografia Giuntina of Florence, consisted of 1,000 copies, which went on sale in July 1928 at £2 each. A "cheap paper issue" by the same company followed in November. There was a Paris edition in 1929, an "authorized expurgated" UK edition from Martin Secker in 1932 and another from Knopf in the US that year.

Roberts tells us that *Lady Chatterley* exists in three separate manuscript versions, and that each has been published: the "first manuscript edition" in 1944, the "second manuscript" ten years later, and finally the "unexpurgated American edition," published by Barney Rosset at Grove Press in 1957. Penguin followed, after the Old Bailey trial in 1960, printing 200,000 copies.

That was that—except for the parodies. *Lady Chatterley's Husband* was published in 1931. Next came *Sadie Catterley's Cover* (1933). By the time of *Lady Chatterley's Second Husband*—with a preface by André Malraux—it takes on a touch of *Bride of Frankenstein*. There have been two books called *Lady Loverley's Chatter*, including one in the US in 1960, claiming to be "abridged, censored, expurgated, incomplete," suggesting weariness about the lady. The cover showed an ample woman being embraced by a skinny man. We haven't even mentioned the piracies, of which there were at least eight by 1932, all listed by Roberts.

No one actually believed that *Lady Loverley's Chatter* was written by the author of *Lady Chatterley's Lover*. But under "Spurious Works," Roberts lists *Dirty Words*, a pamphlet that appeared in 1931. "There is no evidence to show that the essay was written by D. H. Lawrence," he writes.

Much else was, however. The reader of the bibliography is amazed all over again at Lawrence's prodigious output. The year 1923 saw *Kangaroo* (novel) and *The Ladybird* (three novellas); *Birds, Beasts and Flowers* (poetry), *Studies in Classic American Literature* (criticism), a translation from the Italian, *Mastro-Don Gesualdo*, by Giovanni Verga, as well as sundry periodical works. The previous October, he had published *England, My England* and *Fantasia of the Unconscious*, and in the spring *Aaron's Rod*.

Whatever happened to productivity of the Lawrentian kind? In decent condition, dust jacket and all, our SAD-defeating *Bibliography* cost £4 from Peter Ellis of Cecil Court.

March 1

When the revised edition of *The TLS Reviewer's Handbook* finally emerges, there will be this brief entry: "*Brit*: avoid." *Dreyer's English: An utterly correct guide to clarity and style*, by Benjamin Dreyer, "copy chief of Random House," uses it throughout. *Dreyer's American English* would have been more accurate. You might ask: if not "Brit," what? Briton? British person? Not "English person," please. Mr. Dreyer resorts to "Englishpeople" at one stage. Shudder. Bring back the Brits.

Mr. Dreyer is a useful and mostly amusing guide, even if he is fond of setting up Brit usage as a foil. "Please leave 'whilst' and 'amidst' and especially 'amongst' to our cousins"—that's us, the Brits—"'while' and 'amid' and 'among' will do just fine." You won't find the first lot in the *TLS*, old chap (Mr. Dreyer likes that sort of thing, too). One of those cousins seems once to have offended him: "The Brits think that the word 'gotten' is moronic, and they're not shy about telling you so." The Brits we know are not shy about telling you it's just American, like many other things, including "Brits." Even the shyest cousin will happily talk of "ill-gotten gains." Or of a common British usage that has been forgotten by Mr. Dreyer.

Dreyer's English has numerous examples of how we are divided by language. Americans eat zucchini, eggplant, and arugula; in Britain, they eat courgettes, aubergines and rocket. "We ride in elevators, they ride in lifts. They pump petrol; we pump gasoline." Rather, we "go up" in the lift, or down; and no Brit cousin of Mr. Dreyer's ever said, "I'll just pump some petrol." The over-sensitive Mr. Dreyer feels that "Brits laugh at us for doing math, because they do maths."

Dreyer's English contains a section on "easily misspelled words." Here are a few: batallion; bouy; centenniel; dacshund; daquiri; diptheria; doppleganger; ecstacy; elegaic; emnity; fuschia; garotte; gutteral; infinitisemal; inocculate; millenium; miniscule; occurence; paraphenalia; pharoah.

Did we fool you? Probably not. Battalion: two *t*'s, one *l*; buoy, not bouy; dachshund, two *h*'s; we leave the rest to you.

Another section is "The Trimmables," of which a few examples speak for themselves: added bonus; advance warning; all-time record; cameo role; closed fist . . . we've all used them. While we're at it, close proximity; end result; exact same; fall down (Dreyer: "What are you going to do, fall up?"); fellow countryman; and last of all, last of all.

Mr. Dreyer has lots of good advice for us. Our advice to him is not to say "Queen Elizabeth" when referring to the Queen—no Brit would do so: "the Queen" will do—and to avoid "alternate" when the meaning is "alternative." "Pseudonyms are not alternate identities"? Come on, Mr. Dreyer. As for "Bound galleys are sent out to people who, hopefully, will provide the publisher with a blurb . . .", it is to be hoped that future editions of *Dreyer's English* will set that right.

We like it when he says (to his American readers), "*The Times* is a UK newspaper"—"British newspaper" would be better—"whose name is not, never has been, and never will be, *The London Times*." But are you serious, Mr. Dreyer, when you claim that the origin of "brownie points" is a mystery?

March 15

During those alarmingly clement February days, a minor perambulation found us loitering in Ravenscourt Square, situated between the eastern fringe of Chiswick and the western one of Shepherd's Bush. The "square" is, in fact, a street, with two short cul-de-sacs jutting from it, on which stand some impressive villas. On the wall of one, we saw an old London County Council blue plaque:

"OUIDA"
1839–1908
NOVELIST
lived here

The real name of Ouida was Maria-Louise Ramé. She was born in Bury St Edmunds, the daughter of a French wine merchant. The sight of the plaque set us wondering: what other writers have gone under a single name?

There is Colette (Sidonie-Gabrielle Colette) and there is Saki (Hector Hugh Munro). We have always had a soft spot for the novel *Olivia* by Olivia, the author's real name being Dorothy Bussy, née Strachey, sister of Lytton. Stendhal was the pen name of Marie-Henri Beyle. Jean-Baptiste Poquelin is little spoken of; his alias, Molière, more so. German literature offers Novalis, full name Georg Philipp Friedrich Freiherr von Hardenberg (1772–1801). Ossian was the pen name of the eighteenth-century Scottish literary fraudster James MacPherson.

If you have read any of Ouida's forty or so works of fiction—*Moths* or *Pipistrello* or *Dogs*—and think we ought to follow, please say so.

March 22

Eric Hobsbawm is famous for his works of history—*The Age of Capital*, *The Invention of Tradition*, etc.—and notorious for believing that the attainment of a communist utopia would justify the bloodiest human sacrifice. David Kynaston referred to both in his review of Richard J. Evans's biography (*TLS*, March 8). He also alluded to a third part of the historian's intellectual make-up: his love of jazz. It is evoked as a diversion from labors in the archives and the breaking of millions of human eggs to make the perfect social omelette. But the book Hobsbawm wrote on the subject is seldom discussed.

The Jazz Scene was published in 1959, under the name Francis Newton (a pseudonym worthy of excavation; but that can wait for another time). It is a straightforward account—the opening chapter is called "How to Recognize Jazz"—with good recommendations for both listening and reading. Kynaston quoted some disobliging views about Miles Davis, but in *The Jazz Scene*, Newton includes Davis among those whom "the jazz listener ought to be able to identify after a few notes," an essential quality in top-level players. He even suggests *Miles Ahead* (1957) as a "superb example of modern big-band arrangement; a sort of concerto for the leading 'cool' player."

It is not for us to say if Newton's literary style is drier than Hobsbawm's. But few jazz enthusiasts nowadays are inclined to think in terms like these: "we can now see that 'modern' jazz developed logically out of the middle period, partly as a prolongation of it, partly as a reaction to it." Newton could be technical. When he observes that "Bop rhythm no longer indicated the beat, except perhaps by a legato agitation of the cymbal," the head might nod but the foot won't tap. There are better insights: bebop was "musicians' music," and as such not always attentive to the audience's primary demand—to be entertained.

Familiarity with the career of Newton's alter ego naturally leads the reader towards the final chapter, "Jazz as a Protest." Some views seem commonplace now—"jazz was originally the music of an oppressed people" and so forth—but others strike the modern reader as unusual:

> The belief that the American negro in some sense represented desirable elements which white civilization lacked has been widespread . . . since the black-faced minstrel shows first became a standard type of popular entertainment in the second third of the nineteenth century.

Here we see the great left-wing historian approving of blackface—practically a capital crime these days—as a form of homage. "The search for the pure, the innocent, the 'natural' counterpart to modern Western bourgeois society is as old as that society itself."

Insights like these stamp *The Jazz Scene* as the work of an independent thinker. The reputation of the communist historian Hobsbawm has weathered persistent criticism of his defence of murderous Soviet methodology; but if the thought police get wise to the jazz critic Newton's liking for minstrelsy, it will never recover.

WRITERS WHO GO by one name only, contd. We cited Ouida, Colette, Olivia (author of *Olivia*), Stendhal, and others. Are there more, we wanted to know? Yes, there are. François-Marie Arouet, for a start, known as Voltaire. The author of *Le Grand Meaulnes* is seldom spoken of other than as Alain-Fournier. He did have a first name: Henri.

Peter Cogman writes from Southampton to say that our mention of Colette "leads to her first husband, Henry Gauthier-Villars, known as Willy." Early Colette novels, such as *Claudine*, were published originally under one name only—that of Willy. The charitable explanation is that "Willy" was a successful brand. Authorship was later attributed to "Colette et Willy." Eventually, justice was seen to be done, and Colette alone is now the author of most works by Colette. Willy (1859–1931) was nothing if not industrious. Among the other pseudonyms he used were L'Ouvreuse (the usherette), Henry Maugis, Boris Zichine, and Jim Smiley.

More than one reader has reminded us of the novelist and poet Bryher, originally Winifred Ellerman (1894–1983). Then there is Sapper, author of the Bulldog Drummond novels, in reality H. C. McNeile (1888–1937). Heading back to France, we are reminded of the philosopher Alain, aka Émile-Auguste Chartier (1868–1951). And that is the last—single—word on the subject.

April 5

We suggested in our discussion of *The Jazz Scene* by Francis Newton that the pseudonym chosen by the historian Eric Hobsbawm for his music writing was "worthy of excavation." So, one reader challenged: excavate.

The Francis clearly derives from Hobsbawm's devotion to the French revolution and Robespierrean principles of *liberté, égalité, fraternité*. The most celebrated Newton in English history is Isaac, a revolutionary, like Hobsbawm himself, though in a different sphere, and in action, not sanguinary theory. Had the perfect society desired by Newton/Hobsbawm been realized, the "new town" would have been, in microcosm, the new world. Call it brave, if you like.

May 3

A common cry in the *TLS* office, among those whose job it is to observe correct form, is, "Where is Richard Brain when we need him?" Richard, who worked at the *TLS* from the early 1980s until his retirement in the new century, was the man to go to when you needed to know if a marquess ranked above an earl, and how a baron stood in relation to both. "In descending order of rank," Richard might reply, looking up from a proof covered in his snakes-and-ladders emendations, "they are: duke, marquess, earl, viscount, and baron." Does it mean, then, that the title of baron denotes the lowest grade in the peerage?

After an eloquent pause (how could anyone not know?), and still gazing over the tops of his half-moons, Richard would reply: "Quite so."

A baronet, on the other hand, is something different—not a peer, and in rank below a baron. Everybody knows that.

Richard came to mind the other day when we stumbled on a book, *Written and Spoken Guide to Titles and Forms of Address* by L. G. Pine. It is not a modern guide, as may be observed from one of its infrequent nods to the common man. "Today it seems to me more of a distinction to be called Mr. than Esquire since the latter must be shared with everyone whom the sellers of book clubs or football pools may wish to approach." Mr. Pine—and despite trailing his "B.A. Lond., F.J.I., F.S.A.Scot." after his name he was still a humble mister when he wrote his *Guide to Titles* in 1959—makes "Esquire" after a name on an envelope sound vulgar; now it might appear affectedly posh.

We approach Mr. Pine's work in a spirit of awe similar to that in which we open a specialized guide to Eurasian warblers or the lesser moths: someone has taken the trouble to know all this, to classify it, and—in a book such as *Guide to Titles*—to simplify it for the likes o' us.

Let's get to the important bit: how to address the Queen? Our old friend Richard is no longer here to advise, but Mr. Pine is happy to do so. If writing, begin, "To the Queen's Most Excellent Majesty"; and conclude, "I have the honor to remain, Madam, Your Majesty's most humble and obedient servant." If invited to the Palace to have your own title bestowed, begin, when presented to the Queen, "Your Majesty." In all that follows, "Ma'am" will do.

When addressing a newly created knight, e.g. Sir John Smith, use "Dear Sir John"; his wife is "Lady Smith." When it comes to a duke, Pine recommends beginning, "My Lord Duke" (in speech, "Your Grace"). But think about it. Would you? No. Consider the dukes of your acquaintance. Do they expect the full "My Lord" routine? We suspect not.

Even Pine feels the same way. "Usually, when I have to write to a peer, I write 'Sir', and conclude 'I am, Sir, yours faithfully'. This gives an air of formality while avoiding the abject style, 'Your creeping, humble and obsequious slave, etc'." Good old Pine. Note that we've dropped his title.

June 7

It's an attractive thought—a collection of sayings, remarks, and aphorisms by the painter Jean-Michel Basquiat. And *Basquiat-*

isms, edited by Larry Warsh and published by Princeton University Press, is an attractive book. He makes the contents sound good, too: "this book provides a glimpse into Basquiat's incredible mind. . . . May his words and thoughts enliven your thinking today as much as they have inspired me for many decades."

Who wouldn't wish to be inspired? "The more I paint, the more I like everything" is the first entry in *Basquiat-isms*. The second entry: "Believe it or not, I can actually draw." Third: "I start with a picture and then finish it."

We like a slow start as much as anyone. With "Everything is well stretched even though it looks like it may not be," we thought we saw the incredible mind moving towards something more koan-like—the kind of thing your Zen master comes out with. But the next Basquiat-ism is about cropping paintings. It turns out "stretched" refers to canvases.

Mr. Warsh is inspired by the revelation, "A lot of the figures in my paintings are self-portraits and some of them are just my friends." We, frankly, are not. Basquiat doesn't listen "to what art critics say." Show us an artist who does. He likes "kids' work more than work by real artists." He likes Picasso's *Guernica*. He liked Rauschenberg "when I used to live in the Lower East Side." He "never learned anything about art in school."

Tooled in gold leaf on the back cover we found a Basquiat-ism we could believe: "I don't like to discuss art at all." Fine by us, Mr. Warsh. So why *Basquiat-isms*?

June 14

Recent enjoyment of novels by the Scottish writer George Blake leads to the announcement of a new series: Writers Who Are More or Less Forgotten. It is fitting that the title should be cumbersome. We mean something more than neglected. Who would take it as an honor to be the subject of the launch?

The best-known novel by George Blake (1893–1961), the only one that continues to live in a literary sense—by being read—is *The Shipbuilders* (Faber, 1935). Blake was forty-two years old and it was his fourteenth novel. By our count—accurate information is not all that easy to find—there were a dozen more to come.

The Shipbuilders perches on the twin platforms of the Blake oeuvre: ships and families. The theme is the demise of the great West of Scotland yards during the Depression, and what it means for the communities dependent on them. Blake splits the narrative between the wealthy yard owners, the Pagan family—decent folk, but removed from everyday strife—and the hand-to-mouth existence of the riveter Danny Shields. The novel is worth it alone for the scenes in sour pubs and on Glasgow football terraces. It is a tale of high and low life, but also of the middle. Danny's wife thinks she'll do better without him, now that the yard has closed.

Blake's later novels were published by Collins, which had a strong Scottish connection in the 1940s and 50s. *The Constant Star* and *The Westering Sun* also chart the declining fortunes of shipbuilding families. Other novels are set in the fictional Garvel, which resembles the port of Greenock. This renaming device, seldom used now, has an old-fashioned feel. *The Last Fling* concerns yet another clan, presided over by John Mill, whom we meet on his deathbed (or so greedy family members hope). A tactful editor might have advised the author against beginning his story like this: "Above the edge of a sheet drawn up to a mouth sunken by the removal of dentures there curved a great nose, almost vulturine in its magnificence. . . ."

A milder tone prevails in *The Paying Guest,* again set in Garvel and featuring a more attractive family overseen by good Ness Nimmo. A sea-going craft is seldom out of view in a novel by Blake: in *The Paying Guest* it is the *Dulcibelle,* bought by Ness from the proceeds of a win on the football pools. Yesterday, the Nimmos were poor; today they are rich. You can probably guess the consequences.

Blake had that great thing for a writer: a job. In Glasgow, he worked for the *Evening Times* and in London for *The Strand* magazine and *John o' London's Weekly.* He had an army career, and was wounded at Gallipoli. In brief, he had something to write about. Now, he doesn't even merit that token of contemporary recognition, a Wikipedia page.* It is little consolation to be the first in our Writers Who Are More or Less Forgotten series. If you read *The Shipbuilders,* you might agree he shouldn't be.

(*Within days of this item being published, he acquired one.)

August 2

Is it OK? Not everything is these days. Joe Cain, Professor of History and Philosophy of Biology at University College London, has decided it is not OK for a lecture theatre at his university to be named after Francis Galton (1822–1911). Galton's name is "linked with racist, misogynist and hierarchical ideologies," and virtuous Professor Cain refuses to teach there.

Is it OK to read Vladimir Nabokov? The retiring editor in chief at Jonathan Cape, Dan Franklin, has said that he would not publish *Lolita* now. Is it OK to admire T. S. Eliot? ("My house is a decayed house, / And the Jew squats on the window sill," among other unprintables.) Ezra Pound? How could you, after reading his view that "Adolf" was "clear on the bacillus of kikism"? Is it OK to read Philip Larkin, racist and pornographer? William Faulkner? Oh boy. The phrase "trigger warning" might have been coined to protect the young against the traumas that lie in store for a reader of *Absalom, Absalom!* Is it OK to read William Burroughs, merciless pursuer of boys in Tangiers? What about Chester Himes, the fourth corner of the Ralph Ellison–Richard Wright–James Baldwin quadrangle? An article in the *LRB* last year offered more detail than you needed to know about how he beat black and white women black and blue.

It is not OK to like Norman Mailer. Don't even ask about Henry Miller. The question of whether it's OK to read John Updike was addressed in these pages recently by Claire Lowdon (it is) who, in the course of the article, also cast forgiving glances in the direction of Bellow, Roth, and other big male beasts.

The beast is not exclusive to America. It is really not OK to read Guy de Maupassant. If you think it is OK to adore Flaubert, you haven't opened his letters from Egypt. Is it OK to read Albert Camus, that modern saint? You know the one, whose adultery drove his wife to attempt suicide. How can it be OK to read Louis Althusser, wife strangler? It is so not OK to read Kipling's "If" that it was removed from a wall at Manchester University to protect students. It has been replaced by some deeply OK and deeply awful lines by Maya Angelou.

Perhaps it's safer not to read at all, which is what lots of people are doing anyway. Some say we should be debating these matters. If we organize a talk on the subject, will you take part? The venue is the Galton Lecture Theatre, University College London.

August 9

Writers Who Are More or Less Forgotten, part II. Does it seem strange to say of a writer who won the Nobel Prize that he is more or less forgotten? Let's begin with this test. Who is the author of the plays *Strife*, *Joy*, *Windows*, *The Pigeon*, *The Eldest Son*?

You don't know? Who wrote the novels *Saint's Progress*, *From the Four Winds*, *The Island Pharisees*, *A Man of Devon*? Whose *Addresses in America* were published in 1912?

John Galsworthy was awarded the Nobel Prize in 1932, a few months before his death at the age of sixty-five. During his lifetime, he was a successful playwright—those mentioned represent about a quarter of the plays he wrote—and his overall output is enormous. Writing in the *TLS* recently about Anthony Powell, A. N. Wilson suggested that no one reads Powell's work nowadays. This is manifestly untrue in Powell's case, but does the unkind verdict apply to Galsworthy? Everyone has heard of *The Forsyte Saga*. Mention of it in literary company, however, is apt to provoke a reference to the television adaptations of 1967 and 2002, not the novels themselves. Don't try it with us. "No one reads *The Forsyte Saga* nowadays." We just have, and it's terrific.

Another question: how many volumes does *The Forsyte Saga* comprise? The answer might surprise you: three. (Two serial sequels were published, but under different titles.) The action spans roughly thirty years, from about 1890 to 1920. The pleasure resides in seeing how "morals had changed, manners had changed," and in Galsworthy's lightly sardonic, consistently observant writing and substantial characterization. The first volume, *The Man of Property*, is resolutely Victorian. The third, *To Let*, displays a world transformed into modernity by mechanization—Tube, motor car, pianola—and by war.

Among much else, the *Saga* is a directory of changing speech habits. It was fashionable to use "chic" in the 1880s, less so in the 90s. It was chic in the later decade to refer to one's parents by their first names. Has anyone been heard to say recently, "That was a nasty jar," as one Forsyte does of another's divorce? The building of affordable housing was making London "hideous" even by the 1880s.

Of the non-Forsyte works, we are well into *Saint's Progress* (1920), a novel about the impact of the First World War on domestic life. Galsworthy's descriptions of the streets of London and their motley inhabitants are as vivid as those of any writer we can think of. He fully deserved his Nobel Prize; he does not deserve to be more or less forgotten as an agent of readerly pleasure.

August 16

Is it OK? Two weeks ago, we offered a concise history of Western Literature, with a hint to the effect that if you insist on judging writers by their personal behavior, you'll be better off not reading at all.

The question—"Is it OK to read so-and-so?"—is not a new one. A reader has sent us an article by Edward Mendelson, published online by the *New York Review of Books* earlier this year. It is headlined: "Auden on No-Platforming Pound." The event took place in 1945, when Bennett Cerf of Random House was preparing a new edition of *An Anthology of Famous English and American Poetry,* first published in 1927. The Second World War had ended, and Ezra Pound's treasonous behavior was a firm memory. Pound's radio broadcasts from Italy addressed to American troops, in praise of Mussolini and Hitler, trailing abundant anti-Semitism, resulted in incarceration in St Elizabeths Hospital. In 1945, Cerf intended to include a note to the new edition, stating that the publishers "flatly refused at this time to include a single line of Mr. Ezra Pound." They declared themselves "not only willing but delighted" to take this position.

Random House was W. H. Auden's publisher in the US. When he read about the decision early in 1946, he wrote Cerf a letter:

> The issue is far more serious than it appears at first sight; the relation of an author to his work is only one out of many, and once you accept the idea that one thing to which a man stands related shares in his guilt, you will presently extend it to others; begin by banning his poems not because you object to them but because you object to him, and you will end, as the Nazis did, by slaughtering his wife and children.

Auden felt he had no alternative "but to sever my connection with your firm which has done me the, poorly requited, honor of printing my work and from whom I have received unfailing courtesy and kindness." The "poorly requited" refers to paltry profits made by Random House, not the poet himself.

In the ensuing correspondence, Auden said that "the question of how good or bad Pound's poems are is irrelevant." An aside—"I do not care for them myself particularly"—only reinforces his disinterestedness. As for Cerf, he had difficulty in understanding, as Mendelson puts it, "what it might mean to act on principle." "Do you mean that you really insist upon changing publishers if we stick to our guns in the Pound matter?" he asked.

Auden did, and succeeded in changing the editor's mind. On March 4, 1946, Cerf wrote: "We have definitely decided that we were wrong about the Pound business." The poems would be included "in all subsequent editions of the anthology." Politeness and persuasion had got the upper hand over no-platforming. There is, after all, more than one way to win a war.

September 6

With even a minimal interest in modern poetry, you should be able to formulate answers to the following:

> What, in your view, have been the most (a) encouraging, (b) discouraging features of the poetry scene during the past decade?

The commonest responses to both parts of the question will inevitably gesture towards diversity. There are more women poets, more BAME, more LGBT, all encouraging. North of the border, someone will be discouraged by the continuing neglect of MacCaig, Morgan, Crichton Smith, Mackay Brown. Will anybody respond to (a) with news of an interesting new school, or the emergence of "a really big talent" that makes "the business of reading poetry exciting once more"? Who sets the scene for appreciation of poetry today anyway? What *is* the scene? Hollie McNish or A. E. Stallings?

The words about an exciting "big talent" are those of Philip Larkin, made in the course of his response to questions (a) and (b) when asked in 1972. A symposium on "The State of Poetry" was published in Ian Hamilton's little magazine *the Review* that year. Larkin said that the most encouraging features of the past decade (the 1960s, in effect) were the good poems. The most discouraging? The bad ones. You'd think the same answer would do today, but no one likes to say how bad the bad ones are, for fear of being accused of something awful.

The Review put the questions to thirty-five active writers, all but two of them men, all of them "white" (a debatable category, but let's move on), none outspokenly gay. Thom Gunn either was not asked or did not reply. Edwin Morgan, though he had written many poems of love and loss, had yet to come out of the closet.

Several of those questioned expressed surprise at Hamilton's choice of words. "Poetry 'scene,' is it?" (Julian Symons) "No doubt the salient development is the one (consciously?) signaled by your use of the phrase 'the poetry scene.'" (John Fuller) "The 'poetry scene' is recognizably a phrase of our own time, and stands for something very discouraging indeed." (Martin Dodsworth)

There would be no such fastidiousness now. What was the problem? The "scene" was the Mersey Scene: Brian Patten, Adrian Henri, Roger McGough. David Harsent's feeling was typical: "A nasty piece of cross-breeding between the Beats and rock music spawned a gruesome monster in Liverpool." Clive James joined in. "I can't get discouraged or even bored by the success of the Liverpudlians in particular or the artless unwashed in general." One of the Liverpudlians, gamely invited to contribute, was Adrian Henri. He could not have seen James's response in advance, but had no need to. "If I were Clive James, no doubt the answer to the question would be (a) me, (b) you!"

His reaction to the unwashed notwithstanding, James did not wish to take "the Roy Fullerish mandarin disapproval—ramrod-backed on the last bastion, defending standards to the final yawn." As chance would have it, Roy Fuller contributed too. Imagine coming on like this today: "Like the increase of educational opportunity, in the field of poetry the increased ease of publication and of public appearance has been of dubious benefit."

To read the symposium almost fifty years on is to ask oneself, over and again: Would they say the same things now? Alan

Brownjohn disliked the Liverpudlians, but detested "the poetry of modern 'folk'. . . . It is worse than the worst of Liverpool. Dylan thinks he's *good*."

What a thought. Back numbers of *the Review*, if you come across them, are always worth picking up. If only for the opportunity to marvel at how much the poetry scene has changed.

THE ROCK & ROLL A LEVEL by David Hepworth advertises itself as "a very hard pop quiz." How very hard can a pop A Level get? Try this, from a chapter titled "London":

> Which famous album covers were photographed in the following London postal codes? a) W1B 4BH; b) SW8 5BP; c) E4 8SJ; d) NW8 0AH; e) EC1V 8EN.

Abbey Road is bound to be there somewhere, so NW8 is a safe bet (correct!). With a bit of prodding, you might get a), *The Rise and Fall of Ziggy Stardust*, possibly even b): Pink Floyd's *Animals*. The other two are c) Blur's *Parklife*, shot at Walthamstow Stadium and e) *Original Pirate Material* by The Streets (City Road, Islington). Very hard indeed.

The Rock & Roll A Level is divided into examination topics: Economics, History, Law, German. Try this one: "The Beatles re-recorded two of their big hits in German-language versions. Which two?" We'll tell you later.

Meanwhile, we set our brains to the Literature paper. If you don't know this, you don't belong in the class: "Which band took their [*sic*] name from a novel published in French in 1956 under the title *La Chute*?" Even we know that: The Fall. Slightly harder is: "Which band took their name from the title of a book, published in 1925, which D. H. Lawrence described as 'the best modern book about New York'?" *Manhattan Transfer*, of course. Name the author for an extra half-point.

Under what name did David Jones become famous? Name the only country outside of the United States in which Elvis Presley performed. Which of the following never served time in prison: Johnny Cash, Chuck Berry, James Brown? Where was Cliff Richard born, and under what name?

Answers: Jones became Bowie. Elvis sang in Canada. Johnny Cash made prison albums, but didn't serve time. Harry Webb (Cliff) was born in Lucknow, India. As for the Beatles in German: "She Loves You" ("Sie liebt dich") and "I Wanna Hold Your Hand" ("Komm gib mir deine Hand"). John Dos Passos wrote *Manhattan Transfer.*

September 20

Something strange is happening to the status of James Baldwin in American culture. No member of the East Coast literary generation of the 1950s and 60s has received as much attention in recent years as Baldwin. This is partly on account of his repositioning as an identity icon: the Black Lives Matter movement's "touchstone and pinup, its go-to ideal of the writer in arms," as William J. Maxwell put it in the recent *James Baldwin: The FBI file.* Is it sure to encourage increased interest in his books as well? The signs are not always encouraging.

Take the two cases this year in which professors at American universities were suspended from teaching for using unacceptable words. Or, rather, one word—you can guess what it is. In neither instance did the teacher employ objectionable language independently. Both were doing what teachers are supposed to do. They quoted the author in class—and landed in the soup as a result.

Phillip Adamo of Augsburg University, Minnesota, was suspended after trying to lead students into a discussion of Baldwin's best-known work of non-fiction, *The Fire Next Time.* "You can really only be destroyed by believing that you really are what the white world calls a nigger." First the *New Yorker,* then Alfred A. Knopf printed the essay containing the passage, followed over the years by dozens of other publishers; a hundred critics and biographers have cited it, as Phillip Adamo recently did. He has since retired.

In June, Laurie Sheck of the New School, New York, was placed under investigation for enunciating the word in a discussion of the successful but euphemistically titled film *I Am Not Your Negro* (again, it's easy to take a guess at what Baldwin actually said). Ms. Sheck was eventually cleared, but must teachers at universities in the US and Britain hesitate in future before engaging in discussion of Baldwin's work? It appears so.

Strange in a different way was a recent pantomime in the pages of *T: The New York Times Style Magazine* dated September 8. To illustrate a lengthy essay by Hilton Als on the subject of Baldwin's second novel *Giovanni's Room* (1956), the paper organized a glossy fashion shoot. At its center are two models, one black, the other white. As an almost comical accompaniment to Baldwin's "layered exploration of queer desire," readers were treated to one picture after another of the sultry pair, gazing into each other's eyes, kissing, showering, all with fashion-house details—and prices! "Left: Salvatore Ferragamo coat, $4,200. Loro Piana sweater, $1,695. Celine by Hedi Slimane jacket, $4,460."

But hang on—David and Giovanni, the impecunious lovers in *Giovanni's Room*, are white. There are no black characters in the novel. So why the misrepresentation? In a postscript by Alice Newell-Hanson, "senior digital features editor of *T Magazine*," the story's photographer, John Edmonds, was quoted: "Baldwin came to prominence in a very different time in America, where a black artist had to write a white narrative about white characters to be avant-garde."

No evidence was produced in support of this misleading claim. Both Mr. Edmonds and Ms. Newell-Hanson evidently live in ignorance of the novels of Richard Wright, Chester Himes, Langston Hughes, Ann Petry, and others. One of the most "avant-garde" novels of the era, *Invisible Man* by Ralph Ellison, appeared in 1952. One year later, Baldwin published his first book, *Go Tell It on the Mountain*. It is scarcely avant-garde, though it is original in approach. It has an entirely African American cast. We recommend it to Mr. Edmonds and Ms.

Newell-Hanson, especially if they are ever charged with organizing another feature about a black writer, in a paper of record.

Mr. Edmonds appears not even to have read the article to which his lavish photo-shoot is a complement, for his odd suggestion is contradicted by its author. "Baldwin wanted to prove in this book," Hilton Als writes, with greater accuracy, "that he was not 'merely' a Negro writer, that he would not let his talent be defined by racial subjects."

There was plenty of real oppression around in the 1950s and after; no need to invent more, in the interests of "style" in the *New York Times*.

September 27

Ever since we published a list of writers it is not OK to read—Eliot, Pound, Nabokov, Faulkner, Larkin, Flaubert, even the sainted Albert Camus—we have been overwhelmed by readers' requests for a curriculum for safe self-improvement. What *is* it OK to read? It is not OK to read Arthur Rimbaud, hero of those thoroughly OK guys, the Beat writers. After giving up poetry, Rimbaud lived in Aden, where he traded in guns and possibly people. "There is evidence, though it is hotly disputed, that he was, briefly, a slave-trader," one writer says. Don't bother with dispute. Just bale out of the drunken boat. Verlaine? You can't go around shooting people, even if they are suspected slave traders, and then expect us to say you're OK as a poet. Talking of the Beats, how can you read William Burroughs, who shot and killed his wife in a game of William Tell?

Penguin have just reissued the works of J. D. Salinger in four attractive paperbacks, at £8.99 each. But given what we know of his wooing of the teenage Joyce Maynard, can we guarantee that it is OK to read them? It is OK to read the novels of Joyce Maynard.

You can always resort to the cinema, but be careful to dim the lights in safe spaces only. It is not OK to watch the films of François Truffaut, who made a habit of sleeping with his leading ladies. Jean-Luc Godard's mistreatment of actresses outraged even Truffaut. Not OK. Tippi Hedren, who starred in Hitchcock's film *The Birds*, claims he tried to molest her. Best avoid. Woody Allen? Enough to say that the virtuous Colin Firth has stated publicly that he will not work with him again. There is no better time to say that we won't either.

December 20

At the beginning of December, one of the judges of the Saltire Society prize for best novel of the year by a Scottish author walked out of the final meeting in Edinburgh. Lesley McDowell's colleagues voted to give the prize to *Nina X* by Ewan Morrison, overruling Ms. McDowell's favorite, the 1,000-page, single-sentence *Ducks, Newburyport* by Lucy Ellmann.

There is nothing new about disaffected judges resigning, but Ms. McDowell's candor about her motive was exquisitely in keeping with the times. Apart from *Nina X*, all the novels on the short list were by female authors. Ms. McDowell told the newspaper *Scotland on Sunday*. "There were three women on the shortlist who had all written women [*sic*]. One of the three was Lucy, whose book had been shortlisted for two national prizes and described as a masterpiece. My question was, 'What else does a woman have to do to get you to vote for her?'"

After a little thought, we came up with the answer. She must write a book that will be favored by a majority of the judges. As with parliamentary democracy and Brexit referendums, it won't seem fair to everybody, but it's the least unfair system we've got.

The triumph of identity approval over critical approval is widespread. When the 2019 Booker Prize for Fiction was split between *Girl, Woman, Other* by Bernardine Evaristo and *The Testaments* by Margaret Atwood, it was implied in certain places that race played a part in Ms. Evaristo being deprived of a whole prize, rather than half of one. Among those objecting was Lucy Ellmann: "Why in hell would you give the first black woman to win the Booker half the dough?" she asked rhetorically in a *Guardian* interview (December 7). "It's deeply mistaken and insulting."

No one bothered to ask if Margaret Atwood was happy with her divided prize. Nor did anyone trouble to remind those who favor the "first black woman" argument for giving someone a prize—a peculiar argument, when you think about it—that the Booker is awarded to a book, not an author. Some might even consider it "mistaken" to make loose statements that leave themselves open to the interpretation that because an author is black she needs all the dough.

What used to be about literature is increasingly talked of as if it's about social policy or just politics. When the Nobel Prizes for 2018 and 2019 were announced in October, there was an outcry against the 2019 laureate, Peter Handke, because of his past defence of the Serbian war criminal Slobodan Milošević. Salman Rushdie was only one of those who rushed to make his objection public—not an objection to Handke's literary ability but to his political allegiances. It would take a lot of time to read Handke's work, even in translation, and a lot of thought to reach a considered verdict on its merits. Not doing so leaves more time to tweet.

Among the pertinent questions to be asked might be: is Handke's literary output rendered irrelevant by his views, even if they are held to be obnoxious by certain readers? Is it relevant that he himself has not so far been accused of causing bodily injury to anyone? These matters appeared to interest few people. Ben Hutchinson was an exception: "Almost no one has bothered to comment on Handke's actual work," he wrote in the *TLS* of October 18. "For all the politics, it is the poetics by which posterity will judge him."

The same may be said of Lesley McDowell, Ewan Morrison, and *Nina X*. That much is clear. Less clear is why people who can't see it are selected to sit on literary prize judging panels.

2020

February 14

Does Françoise Sagan count as a more or less forgotten author? For purposes of discussion, we will say that she does. She is the latest in our series.

Everyone knows of *Bonjour Tristesse*, which, like *Les Enfants terribles* and *Le Grand Meaulnes*, keeps its title in the English version, first published in 1955. Sagan was eighteen when the novel appeared to acclaim in France the previous year. By the end of the decade, she had written another three, including *Un Certain Sourire* (*A Certain Smile*) and *Aimez-vous Brahms?* It is part of their charm that they belong perfectly to their time: of changing morals, existentialism, cool music, black polo necks, beautiful people on the Côte d'Azur, the beginnings of New Wave cinema. Sagan's tidy, intelligent, girl-meets-boy stories have their cinematic equivalent in the films of Eric Rohmer and the early François Truffaut, but the only screen adaptation of *Bonjour Tristesse* is a Hollywood affair. Directed by Otto Preminger (1958), it starred Jean Seberg and David Niven in the roles of Cécile and her louche papa. By the time she was thirty, Sagan had published five more novels and had had four plays staged.

A Notting Hill perambulation yielded the pretty orange Penguin edition of *Bonjour Tristesse*, in a translation by Irene Ash. Here are its two opening sentences:

> A strange melancholy pervades me to which I hesitate to give the grave and beautiful name of sadness. In the past

> the idea of sadness always appealed to me, now I am almost ashamed of its complete egoism.

Keen to know how many of Sagan's books are available now, we proceeded to Waterstones in Piccadilly. Only *Bonjour Tristesse* was on the shelf—but in a new translation by Heather Lloyd (Penguin Classics, 2013). Compare Lloyd's first two sentences with those of Ash:

> This strange new feeling of mine, obsessing me by its sweet languor, is such that I am reluctant to dignify it with the fine, solemn name of "sadness." It is a feeling so self-indulgent and complete in itself that I am almost ashamed of it, whereas before I had always looked upon sadness as being a worthy emotion.

At this point, the common reader is entitled to ask: Whose book am I reading? A reviewer of the earlier translation recommended it with the assurance that Sagan "writes exceptionally well," even though Sagan did not write the sentences cited: Irene Ash did. Another problem is that the 1955 edition is abridged. In an informative note to her version, Lloyd tells us that Ash acted as an unofficial editor of Sagan's novel. "A number of sentences have been removed as too frank or too suggestive for the innocent English public."

Lloyd's *Bonjour Tristesse* is twinned with *A Certain Smile* and priced at £7.99. It runs to 217pp. In a curious bit of publishing, Penguin continues to offer Ash's *Bonjour Tristesse*, with no added features: 97pp, for the same price.

February 21

In his role as *Spectator* diarist the other week, Tom Stoppard wrote: "If I were not so busy not working, I would make time to start a campaign to bring back 'he or she.' The movement to make amends for the excludingness of the male pronoun is becoming ridiculous." Sir Tom wrote in the same diary that his lockdown reading includes the *TLS*, therefore he must know that the campaign is already underway, and that its headquarters are here. We are happy to elect him honorary president.

The non-specific third-person pronoun is the most troubled of all modern parts of speech. Do you *he*? Do you *she*? Do you *his or her*? Or even *they*? Our most recent step into the arena prompted the suggestion, "Try a little inventiveness." To put it another way, go by sound. If the Stoppardian *he or she* sounds OK in the context, is it only stubbornness that makes you stick with the neutral *he*? Is it virtue signaling (what a useful term that has turned out to be) that leads you to primp your page with a *she* standing for all humankind? The virtue is all the more starkly on show when the writer is male.

You probably consider it one of those tiresome problems of modern times. Even so, you might agree with the Scottish writer James Anderson. He thinks the generic *he* is inappropriate because it is "confined to the male"; the pronoun, says Mr. Anderson, "ought equally to include the female." The up-to-date Mr. Anderson was writing in a magazine called *The Bee* in 1792. Nor was he the first to raise the issue: he was expressing solidarity with an earlier writer, who in 1789 suggested using *ou*.

That didn't catch on, as we learn from *What's Your Pronoun?* by Dennis Baron, subtitled "Beyond He & She." Mr. Baron offers a discussion of the subject with historical examples. As a way of illustrating the tricky nature of the problem, he offers various proposals based on the sentence "Everyone forgets —— passwords."

Several options are given, beginning with "Everyone forgets his passwords," proceeding via *their, his or her, her, one's,* etc. "None of them seem just right," says Mr. Baron. But (have we said this before?) try a little inventiveness. Singularize the noun, loosen up the sentence, and you'll find that "Everyone forgets their password from time to time" sounds fine.

Odd usages through the ages are helpfully organized by Mr. Baron into a chronology: one writer wanted "it" (1843), another, in New York in 1850, offered "ne, nis, nim," yet another, in 1863, proposed *er*, "a pronoun of common gender in continual use in the West of England." As early as 1871, the *OED* reported what might appear to readers today as a trendy solution: *s/he*. It came back into fashion in the 1970s.

Among other proposals for the gender-neutral pronoun—all dating from the nineteenth century—were *ve, han, un, um, hesh, hersh, hae, se, ip* and *twen*. It was another Scot, writing one hundred years after James Anderson, who recommended the use of the singular *they*. As we suggested above, it works, when it works, in a context where it sounds right. If you're really stuck, *he* resolves the problem quite elegantly.

March 6

The *TLS* in Literature, a somewhat more than occasional series. Laura Freeman brings *Poet's Pub* by Eric Linklater (1929) to our attention. How could we have missed it? It opens with a nightmare brought on by a review in the *TLS*, about a female centaur stalking a terrified poet. Saturday Keith, author of *February Fill-dyke*, wakes with relief, reminding himself that his (anonymous) *TLS* tormentor could not have been female. "Women never write in the *Literary Supplement*; or at any rate no oftener than they preach from other pulpits." But this realization fails to soften the review he read the night before. "No serious poet today can write without a theory," said the *TLS* reviewer, before quoting: "Then through the wood came the wind with a shout, / And like blue wings her long scarf flew out." Might the centaur have had a point?

His friend Quentin Cotton enters (author of the novel *A Nettle Against May*) and Keith uncrumples the accursed *TLS* to complain: "They've picked out the worst lines in the book." They always do, says the kindly Quentin. "A reviewer must amuse his public, and good poetry's dull stuff."

There is a lesson here for anyone who has ever reviewed a book, in the *TLS* or elsewhere: your words can cause pain, not to say nightmares. Saturday Keith eventually opens a pub. Is this a more worthy pursuit than the writing of poetry? If it's like this—"My love is young and very fair. / The sunlight will not leave her hair"—the answer might be yes.

July 10

Until June 27, Don Share was comfortably in place as editor of the magazine *Poetry,* founded by Harriet Monroe in Chicago in 1912 and brought to international prominence by Ezra Pound. "The Love Song of J. Alfred Prufrock" was first published in *Poetry,* as well as work by Pound himself, Robert Frost, Marianne Moore, Frank O'Hara, and almost every other bright name in modern verse.

Mr. Share is generally admired in the poetry world. The magazine he edited featured frequently in NB, though the temperature of the relationship went up and down. He took to Twitter to scold us for saying nothing more than what we have been saying for years, something increasingly evident with each month that passes: that there is no longer any critically authorized tradition of merit in poetry. Favor on the contemporary scene is fueled to a large extent by identity approval, not critical judgment.

Mr. Share was complicit in this new arrangement. The magazine under his editorship continued to publish good work by experienced poets, but he put in a lot of poor stuff, too, and he gave us a tweeted cuff around the ear for saying so. Get with it! was the message. The world has changed.

The message has now got with Mr. Share. The July/August issue of *Poetry* carried a poem by Michael Dickman called "Scholls Ferry Rd." A Twitter user called Hana Shapiro, who describes herself as Japanese-American, posted a tweet on June 25 to say that reading Mr. Dickman's poem put her into a state of "absolute shock." Ms. Shapiro "had to put the magazine down." The shock was caused by the word "negress," spoken in the poem (by and large affectionately) by an elderly woman of diminishing faculties. It is followed by the word "Hawaiian," which seems also to have shocked Ms. Shapiro, and the line "A river of Japanese businessmen cross in front of the car."

Ms Shapiro's tweet (at the time of writing she had 141 followers) caused a different form of trauma among Mr. Share's employers, the immensely wealthy Poetry Foundation. On June 27, they issued a statement:

> This poem centers whiteness and employs racist language, which is hurtful and wrong. We published this poem because we read it as an indictment of racism within white families; this was a mistake. We clearly have more work to do in considering how poems center certain voices and affect our readers. We regret not taking serious action sooner to interrogate the editorial process, and we apologize.

In the ominous warning that followed—"changes in the magazine's structure and process are imminent"—Mr. Share read an invitation to present himself at the nearest re-education camp. The sans culottes of the moronic inferno posted "WE DID IT!" and moved on.

Michael Dickman was recently named by the US National Poetry Library among "America's most exciting contemporary poets." That kind of accolade won't help if you commit an offence against certain notions of linguistic usage, even in a work of nuanced literary expression. We hear a lot about safe spaces; it appears that the imagination is no longer one of them.

At its highest point, criticism of poetry is guided by T. S. Eliot's suggestion of what a serious literary community ought to be engaged in: "The common pursuit of true judgment and the correction of taste." Otherwise, why bother? This is what Harriet Monroe founded *Poetry* for. Readers who believe that the "common pursuit" is advanced by sacking an editor for publishing a poem that shocks a passing reader are invited to write and put their case. Likewise, if you dispute our assertion that "identity approval trumps critical approval"—originally made, it so happens, in reference to an edition of Mr. Share's *Poetry*—we would welcome that, too. It would be like old times, when debate was the in-thing.

July 17

The perambulatory spirit is once again at large, inhibited by safe browsing but at least back in action. Passing Oxfam Books in Chiswick the other day, we saw a notice in the window: "Re-opening midday July 9."

And so we were there. It is a compact shop with a mixed stock of generally good quality. On previous perambulations, we have left with treasures but, as diligent readers know, we do not go in search of treasure; rather an appealing book in decent condition at a reasonable price.

On this occasion, we came away with a tight orange Penguin (price, 99p) of William Faulkner's novel *Intruder in the Dust*, published in 1948, the year before he was awarded the Nobel Prize for literature. Should anyone care to know, we consider Faulkner the greatest American novelist of the twentieth century, a provincial chronicler of universal scope. Yet it must be next to impossible to teach books such as *Intruder in the Dust* and *Absalom, Absalom!* in American literature departments today, policed as they are by linguistic censors and peopled by the shocked, the appalled, and the offended.

As it happens, we have other editions of this novel, as of much of Faulkner's oeuvre, and it was with heartening recognition that we read again its ominous opening sentence as we left the shop with our Penguin:

> It was just noon that Sunday morning when the sheriff reached the jail with Lucas Beauchamp though the whole town (the whole county too for that matter) had known since the night before that Lucas had killed a white man.

The kernel of the story of *Intruder in the Dust,* and the moral about to be unfolded, is contained in those few words. The "whole town" knew that Lucas, a Negro—to use the politest word on the lips of the ill-intentioned gathering crowd—was guilty. No due process, no witness, no confession. Mob justice will do for Lucas.

They didn't have Twitter mobs in 1948, and the outcomes for contemporary victims are less drastic than they look like being for Lucas Beauchamp. But serious enough none the less. *Intruder in the Dust* was made into a film in 1949. The director of a modern remake might go in for a bit of imaginative casting and put Woody Allen in the Lucas role. The mob at the jailhouse would be made up of workers at Hachette, who walked out when they learnt that their company planned to publish Allen's book, *Apropos of Nothing,* though he has never been found guilty of any crime. Actors who have righteously pledged never to work with him again will be given supporting roles. But no, please, not Colin Firth as the sheriff.

July 24

We have spent half a lifetime trying to avoid yielding to phrases such as "The world has gone mad," but defeat looms. A friend has sent us this communication from the MacDowell Colony in New Hampshire, founded in 1907 by the composer Edward MacDowell and his wife Marian as a refuge for artistic types in search of peace and quiet. Old boys and girls include James Baldwin, Leonard Bernstein, Alice Walker, and Thornton Wilder. Perhaps someone is having a joke at our expense?

> We have some overdue and exciting news: The MacDowell Board of Directors voted unanimously on June 30, 2020, to adopt an official name change, dropping the word "colony" so that we simply are known as *MacDowell.* This move was prompted by a petition signed by all members of the staff.
>
> As many of you know, MacDowell has long been work-

ing toward a more inclusive and accessible artist residency program, and removing the word "colony" from our name is just one step among other deeper commitments to come.

Be well and stay tuned for more exciting news from us in the days to come!

Yes, it must be a joke. There can be no other explanation. The excited signatories—members of the MacDowell (Colony)'s Board of Directors—may be unaware that someone is making them look ridiculous. In any case, be careful not to get drunk in the Colony Room in Soho again, in case you end up oppressing someone. You won't be doing so anyway: it closed years ago, though not because of its imperial links.

August 7

There is something inevitably cheering in the arrival of *About Larkin*, the journal of the Philip Larkin Society. A typical issue might offer a scribbled-over typescript, an interview with a "Larkin muse," one of his lively drawings taken from a letter to his mother or a friend, news of Larkin walks—the last, one imagines, bringing a frown to the poet's brow in the hereafter, but giving abundant pleasure to Society members.

Only the most ascetic reader of Larkin's work could fail to be charmed by the "Twenty-fifth Anniversary commemorative volume," edited by its outgoing editor, James Booth, in cooperation with the new arrival, Kyra Piperides Jaques. It consists of 200 pages selected from the foregoing forty-nine issues. The striking thing is how strongly the mass of material appears to reflect the inner life of Larkin himself, even in its more inconsequential items. Ann Thwaite's memoir "Having Larkin to Stay" recalls his account of lunch at Buckingham Palace, during which the Queen's cousin, Princess Alexandra, "fired questions at him":

Q. What sort of poems do you write?
A. Gloomy.

Q. Why are they gloomy?
A. Because I'm a gloomy sort of person.
Q. Why are you a gloomy sort of person?

In response, he sent her a copy of *High Windows,* "but it was never acknowledged . . . or so he said." A further encounter with power occurred in 1982, when Larkin was invited to a dinner hosted by the historian Hugh Thomas, in honor of Margaret Thatcher. In a rake through the Thatcher papers, Janet Brennan found Thomas's briefing notes for Mrs Thatcher on the guests. They included "A. Alvarez (Poet. Some works of criticism and general brooding, eg. on suicide); Anthony Powell (Conservative, surely); Isaiah Berlin (No need to explain)." Also invited were Tom Stoppard, Mario Vargas Llosa, and V. S. Naipaul. In her thank you letter to the Thomases, the Prime Minister said she "enjoyed every minute" and hoped the other guests did, too. Considerately, she added: "I was a little worried that Philip Larkin was so silent." Ms. Brennan thinks that Larkin's apparent detachment might be explained by his deafness.

Mr. Booth relates his efforts to secure an interview with Monica Jones, the best-known of Larkin's women. She put him off, but eventually he succeeded. In answer to a question about her own work, she revealed that she had thought of writing a book on Crabbe.

Q. Did Philip like Crabbe?

A. I've no idea. He wasn't interested in anything much except modern. And he was more interested in himself than in anything else.

Booth tells her that another of the poet's women, Maeve Brennan, had said "that Philip was very interested in her Catholicism." Jones: "Well Maeve would say so."

In the first issue of *About Larkin* (April 1996), Maeve Brennan interviewed a third lady friend, Winifred Dawson, and the talk embraced yet another, Ruth Bowman. The frankness and warmth with which the two women speak about themselves, about Ruth and about Larkin, is heartening. The intricacy of the web is suggested by the fact that Larkin wrote a love poem to Winifred in 1954, on the day of her marriage to another man ("Where can I turn except away, knowing / Myself outdistanced . . ."). She found out about it only thirty-four years later. Winifred was a presence in other poems, including "Maiden Name." The anniversary issue would be worth it for this conversation alone.

Among much else in a bountiful collection is a facsimile of "Larkin's last attempt at a serious poem." It was called "Letters to my Mind" and the pages show that it ran to forty lines. Here are five of them:

Are you still on my side?
Several times an hour,
Lately, you scald
With miniatures painfully,
Perfectly recalled . . .

August 21 & 28

It gave readers a thrill in the bad old days to come into possession of a banned book. *Ulysses*, for example, which must have baffled many in search of titillation, or *Tropic of Cancer* or *Lady Chatterley's Lover*. The books would be smuggled from France, in appetizing Obelisk or Olympia editions, or else purchased from a select shop in Soho.

Books are rarely banned now; rather, they—or their authors—run the risk of being "canceled." In far-off times, a publisher or editor would be praised for trying to publish Joyce or Nabokov. Now, an editor is in danger of being sacked for publishing something that doesn't fit someone else's definition of "appropriate."

Last month, the editor of *Poetry* magazine, Don Share, resigned after publishing a poem deemed to be racist. "Scholls Ferry Road" by Michael Dickman appeared in the issue of July/ August 2020. When a Twitter user claimed to be traumatized at the sight of it, Mr. Share and his employers, the Poetry Foundation, parted company (see above, July 10).

People admire someone who stands by their judgment, and are apt to despise one who doesn't. Like transgressors in the Soviet Union under Stalin, Mr. Share begged his superiors to disgrace him. In what someone called "an abject act of self-mortification," he confessed to a crime which, in the view of most people, he hadn't committed. "I accept sole responsibility for publishing the poem, and apologize unreservedly for doing so. My poor judgment demonstrates that *Poetry* has much work to do in considering how poems center certain voices at the expense of others, and the impact this has upon our readers."

The July/August issue of *Poetry* is now hard to find. The contents of the issue are online, with one exception. The infamous "Scholls Ferry Road," the website declares, "will not be published online or added to the archive." How about a printed copy of the magazine? "This issue is sold out." Don't you believe it. It's been canceled. The Poetry Foundation declares itself "committed to a vigorous presence for poetry in our culture," yet no longer supports the freedom of the imagination.

Luckily, our copy was posted in the US before the Share show trial, and has just arrived. Not quite a banned book, but at least a canceled poem. What's it like? "Scholls Ferry Road" occupies thirty pages, though several contain only a single line. The poem represents the scattered thoughts of the speaker's grandmother, an elderly woman on the verge of dementia, mediated through the words of the speaker. It is drama, in short, impressionistic and imaginative. On the fourteenth page of text, the speaker says of the grandmother: "'Negress' was another word she liked to use." She is observed in the act of a passive racist gesture:

> On the bus she dropped her purse
> I was with her
> A nice Negress handed it back

The usage here is mimetic, if not ironic. The next line is a long one: "She put out her hand to receive it the whole time looking out of the window never said a word."

Mr. Share went willingly to the guillotine for *this*? America's most illustrious poetry journal was shaken to its foundations for *this*? Eager as we are to have a canceled publication in our hands, it seems hardly worth it. A simple parallel occurs to us. The TV series *Mad Men*, set mainly in the 1960s and illustrating changing mores over the course of its numerous episodes, contains disobliging remarks about women, Jews, African Americans, and others. No one, not even the dimmest wit at the Poetry Foundation, believes that they are the views of the script writer, the director, the actor or anyone else. It's drama. "Scholls Ferry Road" is dramatic verse. The words in the television serial are aimed at discerning adults. It's quite a comment on contemporary literary intelligence that the same approach cannot be taken to the contents of *Poetry*.

September 4

Writers Who Are More or Less Forgotten. There has been some understandable confusion over this rubric. More or less forgotten does not mean unjustly overlooked. To be more or less forgotten, a writer has to have been once seriously taken note of. John Galsworthy, winner of the Nobel Prize in 1932, is one example; Françoise Sagan is another (see above, August 7, 2019; February 14, 2020).

The sheen emitted by the name Alain Robbe-Grillet has faded in English-speaking countries. Yet he was once an unignorable figure for any self-respecting reader of post-war avant-garde literature. The hard man of the *nouveau roman* was a stern aesthetician whose novels were measured to certain specifications. Linear narrative and character psychology were banished. Barely any scope existed for character development, and they tended to be identified by initials: A... in *La Jalousie* (1959),

JR in *Projet pour une révolution à New York* (1970). In Alain Resnais's mesmerizing film *L'Année dernière à Marienbad,* of which Robbe-Grillet is the author of the script—a celluloid relation of *La Jalousie*—the main characters are A, X, and M. His novels were dubious even about membership of the genre. Wasn't the novel supposed to be dead?

Robbe-Grillet (1922–2008) was nevertheless among the leading French writers of the post-existentialist epoch. By 1960 he had written four novels and was being published in Britain, where a certain francophilia persisted among cultured types as a counterweight to the Amis and Larkinite "I like it here" anti-Europeanness. Robbe-Grillet's theoretical manual, *Pour un Nouveau Roman,* came out in French in 1963, in English two years later.

Authors who attempted a British version—Giles Gordon, Alan Burns, B. S. Johnson—were dubbed "the enemy of the good read." But it was new, it was anti-parochial, it was fashionable. With Nathalie Sarraute, Marguerite Duras, and Samuel Beckett, Robbe-Grillet was picked up by Grove Press in New York and John Calder in London.

Robbe-Grillet's intelligent face, peering challengingly from a Calder Jupiter Books edition of *Jealousy* (translated by Richard Howard), prompted these musings. We rescued him from a book barrow in Charing Cross Road. All Jupiter Books are attractive objects, and this one invites us to open the novel again, to see what magic remains of the last French literary movement to captivate the world. PsychoBabel of Didcot, Oxfordshire, have an identical copy on offer at £70. From the barrow, ours set us back a pound.

September 18

After more than twenty years of perambulation around the second-hand bookshops of London, Edinburgh, and places beyond, of wise-man maxim-making, of laying down the literary law in *The TLS Reviewer's Handbook,* of staring in disbelief at styles of English that are incomprehensible to everyone but academic cultists, of administering our own book prizes, we are giving up the ghost. You can add to that list the habit of exploring the derivation of phrases such as "giving up the ghost." And of brushing up our O Levels in Cornish, Jèrriais, Manx, Breton, Gaelic, Latin, Esperanto, and other lesser-used languages of Britain and Europe. Who knew what rewards a Poor School education could bring?

We take the opportunity of thanking those who have answered the call to contribute to one or other of our series. Remember "Poems into films"? The first telephone call in fiction? There was the search for technological firsts in literature (train, bicycle, automobile) and pop songs with classical reference ("Fools Rush In" and "Roll Over Beethoven" being two). Fiction and metaphysics started out by looking at novels in which the protagonist is writing a book of the same title as the one you are reading, although the two bear scant relation to one another. *The Tremor of Forgery* by Patricia Highsmith and Alexander Trocchi's *Cain's Book* are examples. Learned readers helped to keep it all going.

An apologetic hand is extended to those who wrote or rang up to request copies of the sundry Basement Labyrinth publications. They included successive editions of *Wise Man Say* (don't miss the gorgeous Harry and Meghan edition, "by appointment," with gold-leaf lettering on the spine), the *Dictionary of Received Phrases*, for which the late John Ashbery was co-editor, and the *Reviewer's Handbook* mentioned above. The *Handbook* was based on a belief that good writing strives to adhere to the three Es: elegance, eloquence, and entertainment. The last means, essentially, "don't be boring." Readers who inquired about purchasing the *Handbook* accepted with good grace the cruel reality that such publications belong to another realm—a Basement Labyrinth realm, let's say, though no less real for that.

The prizes, never again to be awarded, include the Incomprehensibility Prize; the Most Unoriginal Title Prize; the All the Prizes Prize, for authors who have won every prize going, not to be confused with the All Must Have Prizes Prize, for authors who have never won any. Among the most coveted was the Jean-Paul Sartre Prize for Prize Refusal, which set a fashion among self-respecting authors for turning down awards. When the judging panel tried to give us the All Must Have Prizes Prize, we loftily proclaimed ourselves above the literary circus—only to be landed with a Sartre Prize for Prize Refusal.

Did we poke fun at pomposity, hypocrisy, and plain stupidity? Yes, but we never suggested that someone should be submitted to a form of show trial and removed from a post—such as the editor of *Poetry* (Chicago)—for committing a fault that merely goes against current trends. Being briefly mocked ought to be sufficient chastisement, bringing with it the right to respond in kind, as some mockees rightly did to us. The most dramatic change in the literary atmosphere during our stewardship is this: from the 1920s through to the *Lady Chatterley* trial in 1960 and beyond, it was the legal and political authorities who tried to ban books and restrict the freedom of the imagination. Radicals and rebels fought against the very act of banning. Prohibitions on speech and publication now arrive from the identity-conscious children of those same radicals, leaving it to the law to protect what were once taken for granted as freedoms of expression.

The interns who have worked tirelessly in the Basement Labyrinth, year after year, will pause for a moment to praise not only the readers who have contributed—"will The *TLS* in Literature / Art / Film and Television never end?" you must have asked (it will now)—but all who took the time simply to read the column. Where its attitudes were wrong-headed, we take responsibility.

On second thoughts, why should we shoulder all the blame? Whereas many colleagues helped consistently in the weekly production of NB, one of them occasionally proved a hindrance. Transparency is another buzz word. So why not expose him? Get thee behind me (us?), James Campbell.

Acknowledgments

My principal debt is to *The Times Literary Supplement,* which carried NB by J.C. from March 1997 until September 2020. I am grateful to the editors who oversaw the paper during that time, and over the wider period that I worked there: Jeremy Treglown, Ferdinand Mount, Peter Stothard, and Stig Abell. The first three have read and made improving comments on the introduction to this book, as have Vera Chalidze, Robert Messenger, and Maren Meinhardt.

Heartfelt thanks are also due to others, including those erstwhile colleagues and present friends, Lindsay Duguid, David Horspool, Alan Jenkins, Toby Lichtig, Catharine Morris, Rupert Shortt, Adrian Tahourdin, and Anna Vaux, all of whom at one time or another read the proofs of NB before the page went to press. They corrected errors of fact, spelling, punctuation, chronology, history, tone, and more besides. The late Mick Imlah and Adolf Wood, much-missed office comrades, did so, too. All were apt to make blue-pencil suggestions, as Bruce Richmond was to do to T. S. Eliot—and, to adapt Eliot on Richmond, I had to admit (mostly) that he or she was right. Help of a different but no less valuable kind over the years has come from Maureen Allen and Eleanor Stokes. At Paul Dry Books, I could not wish for greater patience and better assistance than that provided by Julia Sippel and Mara Brandsdorfer.

Index

James Campbell's books include *Invisible Country: A Journey through Scotland*, *Talking at the Gates: A Life of James Baldwin*, *This Is the Beat Generation*, and, most recently, *Just Go Down to the Road* (Paul Dry Books, 2022). He lives in London.